Nothing Has Been Done Before

Alternate Takes: Critical Responses to Popular Music is a series that aims to examine popular music from critical perspectives that challenge the accepted ways of thinking about popular music in areas such as popular music history, popular music analysis, the music industry, and the popular music canon. The series ultimately aims to have readers listen to—and think about—popular music in new ways.

Series Editors: Matt Brennan and Simon Frith

Editorial Board: Daphne Brooks, Oliver Wang, Susan Fast, Ann Powers, Tracey Thorn, Eric Weisbard, Sarah Hill, Marcus O'Dair

Other Volumes in the Series:
When Genres Collide by Matt Brennan

Nothing Has Been Done Before

Seeking the New in 21st-Century American Popular Music

Robert Loss

Bloomsbury Academic
An imprint of Bloomsbury Publishing Inc

B L O O M S B U R Y
NEW YORK · LONDON · OXFORD · NEW DELHI · SYDNEY

Bloomsbury Academic
An imprint of Bloomsbury Publishing Inc

1385 Broadway	50 Bedford Square
New York	London
NY 10018	WC1B 3DP
USA	UK

www.bloomsbury.com

BLOOMSBURY and the Diana logo are trademarks of Bloomsbury Publishing Plc

First published 2017

© Robert Loss, 2017

All rights reserved. No part of this publication may be reproduced or transmitted in any form or by any means, electronic or mechanical, including photocopying, recording, or any information storage or retrieval system, without prior permission in writing from the publishers.

No responsibility for loss caused to any individual or organization acting on or refraining from action as a result of the material in this publication can be accepted by Bloomsbury or the author.

Library of Congress Cataloging-in-Publication Data
A catalog record for this book is available from the Library of Congress.

ISBN: HB: 978-1-5013-2203-7
PB: 978-1-5013-2202-0
ePub: 978-1-5013-2204-4
ePDF: 978-1-5013-2201-3

Series: Alternate Takes: Critical Responses to Popular Music

Cover design by James Brown
Cover image © James Brown

Typeset by Integra Software Services Pvt. Ltd.

To find out more about our authors and books visit www.bloomsbury.com Here you will find extracts, author interviews, details of forthcoming events and the option to sign up for our newsletters.

Contents

Prologue: Nothing Has Been Done Before 1

Part One The Past in the Present 15

1. Revivals Are Revisions: New Millennial Folk Music Rolls the Dice 17
2. "*Love and Theft*": Transgression and the Cultural Archive 31
3. The Problem of Knowing Too Much: Meta-Rock and the Anxiety of Influence 53
4. Sounds Before Our Time: Replicating the Old to Make the New 67

Part Two The American Wow 83

5. Spectaglam! Katy Perry and the American Wow 85
6. The New Digital Empire: Consumerism, Technology, and the New 105
7. We Can Flux: Prince Queers Democracy and the New 119
8. Kanye's Night at the Museum: The Iconoclast Goes to Work 137
9. Power Up: Persona and Anonymity Trouble the American Wow 145

Part Three Shouting at the Hard of Hearing 159

10 On the Good Side: Antiwar Music in the 2000s 161

11 Shouting at the Hard of Hearing: Springsteen Finds a New Audience 181

12 Living in the Interval: Political Hip-Hop, Rap, Revolution, and *To Pimp a Butterfly* 197

13 Bodies in the River: Tradition and "The Body Electric" 221

Epilogue: Nothing Has Been Done Before, Again 233

Notes 236
Bibliography and Select Discography 249
Acknowledgments 261
Index 263

Prologue: Nothing Has Been Done Before

Seventeen Years Before the New Millennium

It is August 3, 1983. A humid Wednesday night in Minneapolis. Let's say you're pushed up against the stage at First Avenue where a certain, already legendary musician is about to play a benefit for the Minnesota Dance Theatre. Let's say you crane your neck enough to see a sheet of paper near the center stage microphone base and an array of guitar pedals: the almighty set list. Hallelujah! You're a major fan—you shelled out twenty-five bucks for the ticket—but some of these titles you don't recognize. In full: "Let's Go Crazy," "When You Were Mine," the Joni Mitchell song "A Case of You," "Computer Blue," "Delirious," "Electric Intercourse," "Automatic," "I Would Die 4 U," "Baby I'm a Star," "Little Red Corvette," "Purple Rain," and "D.M.S.R." One song from *Dirty Mind*, four from *1999*, and six songs you've never heard of. They must be new. There's a new guitarist, too. Wendy something. You hear the band's being called the Revolution. The woman with the windswept hair standing next to you says there's a recording truck parked out front. The lights go out. Your chest lurches. A church organ whirls to life in the dark, holding the same elegiac note as a projection screen runs through various computer-drawn portraits of the local hero. It hasn't been long since the end of his *1999* tour. He's been all over the world. What's he seen? What has he heard? What are these new songs? The organ note is still holding, vibrating as a white-hot floodlight from the back of the stage ruptures the darkness, and Prince is there, at the mic.

Let's say that for a split second, you decide to check your expectations. But then he says those first words to "Let's Go Crazy," and nothing will ever be the same.

Today, when I hear the music Prince and the Revolution made that night in Minneapolis and hear what became of it on the album released the following June, *Purple Rain*, I can convince myself that Prince was the living embodiment of musical newness. Listen to his work in the 1980s, from *Dirty Mind* through *Lovesexy* in 1988. Listen to their B-sides and outtakes. Listen to *The Black Album*, which was finally released in 1994. Most of all, watch and listen to him perform live. Doesn't it sound like he and the musicians who play with him, from Wendy Melvoin to Sheila E., are capable of anything? Prince melted down nearly every sound and style in popular music's recent history and fused them into his own. "Computer Blue" takes a little of *The Man Machine*-era Kraftwerk and adds new wave's buzzing synths, the smack of Linn drum machines, dance pop's urgency, a touch of punk rock, and the wet precision of funk. As the song begins to detour, there's a burst of Hendrix's bluesy guitar flair with one wah-wah note. The song turns left into an extended bridge wherein Prince's guitar solo has this Southern rock bravado, especially at its high point, but it's also composed, stately, a love letter. *All in a single song.* There was a gleeful, reckless quality to Prince's musical ultra-fusion. Live, it became a carnival, a celebration of music itself, and an argument that nothing has been done before.

Everything Is New, Nothing Is New—Parmenides Spreads His Roots—Nothing Has Been Done Before—History, a Box, and an Art Critic

Thirty years later, using the word "new" to describe popular music has become commonplace and ambiguous, even meaningless. A much-anticipated new record, hot new artist, new genre, or new sound: as objective as these descriptions may seem, they're not innocuous. "New" always has a value, implying progress, the future, being contemporary, change, and originality, to name a few. It's also a lot more exciting than the alternatives. My local radio station CD102.5 has a bumper that says it all: "Experience new music first, experience more music now." How boring that would sound as, "Experience old, derivative music yet again."

At the same time, in the final decades of the twentieth century, we became more cynical about the new as we became more cynical about popular culture and the marketplace. The music critic Nick Tosches' declared in 1984 that "[t]he grand illusion of newness is popular culture's greatest sucker's-racket. …. To begin to see that there really is nothing new under the lucky old sun is to begin to understand the nature of popular culture and the business of fame."[1] At a formal level, postmodern music emphasizes remixing, recycling, and appropriation: rap's use of samples, punk's revision of early rock 'n' roll, grunge's blend of punk and arena rock, contemporary country music's blend of tradition and pop. Listen to Alabama Shakes' "Hold On" and you hear Motown. Listen to Beach House and you hear an evocation (to put it kindly) of Cocteau Twins and Slowdive. Popular music today seems drunk on the past. The music critic Simon Reynolds wrote an entire book about this, *Retromania*, in which he describes the music of the 2000s as "flat" and possessing a "deficit of newness."[2] A desert plain on which there is nothing new under the sun.

The question of popular music's newness is influenced by a long history of philosophical debate about the new, reaching back to the ancient Greek philosopher Parmenides and his axiom, from his lone work, *On Nature*, that "nothing comes from nothing." Since being is complete, he argued, there can be no such thing as the new.[3] From Aristotle to country music critic Grady Smith, who in a 2013 video mashup showed how similar the year's top country songs were—trucks, girls, beer, yuks[4]—we have long acknowledged that ritual and repetition are pleasing. They signal enjoyment. We take comfort in them. (Recently, during the 2016 election campaign, I played Protomartyr's *The Agent Intellect* every day for about a month.) But sameness multiplied over days, weeks, and years becomes claustrophobic, from the omnipresent single in every advertisement—I'm looking at you, "Turn Down For What"—to that creeping sense we need some new music in our playlists, as if *we* have become stagnant. At the same time, we're keenly aware of all the groundbreaking, original, fresh new music that has preceded us, whether it's the advent of rock 'n' roll or that night in Minneapolis in 1983. The cultural importance of these events weighs on us; originality seems a thing of the past. "The future no longer seems to promise anything fundamentally new," writes the philosopher Boris Groys in *On the New*; "instead, we imagine endless variations on what already exists."[5]

Is there such a thing today as popular music that's meaningfully new? If so, how do we define it, and what does it mean for us in the twenty-first century?

Music has the power to remind us that this moment, right now, is unique from the previous moment, that the next moment will be unique from both, and so on. Because we rarely perceive life this way, the first task of music is to force us to remember. It has to break the monotony of daily life with what amounts to an aesthetic trauma, pleasurable but severe, sometimes bewildering, somehow lasting. It has to make us hear the truth: nothing has been done before.

Performances occur in time, over time, and accumulate into history. And history is crucial to understanding why, in fact, nothing has been done before. This seems like a paradox. Wouldn't ignoring history more easily make everything seem new? Without comparisons to the past, though, we're unable to see significant differences in the present. This is what Arthur Danto meant when he wrote, in his book *After the End of Art*, "There really is, in history, no such thing as having done something before"[6]—the sentence from which I've shaped this book's title. An aesthetic philosopher and art critic, Danto was talking about the artwork that haunted him his entire career, Andy Warhol's *Brillo Box*, a hand-crafted replica of a box of laundry soap. Danto asked how we can distinguish between the transformation of the ordinary in the pop art of *Brillo Box* and in Marcel Duchamp's ready-mades, which appeared roughly fifty years prior. "That there is an outward resemblance between Duchamp and pop is one of the things it is the achievement of pop to help us see through," wrote Danto. "Situating pop in its deep cultural moment helps show us how different its causes were than those that drove Duchamp half a century earlier."[7]

Formally the works seem similar, but their ideologies and historical contexts were actually the inverse of one another.

If we stand outside of history—we really can't, but if we try to—forms and styles will naturally seem more similar than different, which means that recent work will seem derivative. This comes up in *Retromania*, which uses the kind of cloistered art history perspective Danto criticizes, but for Reynolds, Duchamp is neo-garage rocker Billy Childish and Andy Warhol is the White Stripes and there is no fundamental difference. If you're playing what's formally considered garage rock, then you're always just repeating the past no matter when or where you happen to play it. But when and where do matter, so long as music is more than sonic information.

Thinking historically is more than understanding the past; it's what allows an artist to shape the present and the future. When the musician recognizes where she is in time, she recognizes that history is also *what may yet happen.* In *The History of Rock 'n' Roll in Ten Songs*, cultural historian and music critic Greil Marcus argues that a subjective understanding of music from the past can lead to new artistic expressions which realize the possibilities that have lain dormant in that music. Marcus understands that all ambitious artists, driven by the necessities of creation and assertion, working by intuition and formal affinities, are magpies for whom history is filled with shiny objects—hints and mysteries, scraps of sound and structure, a chord progression here, a lyric fragment there—around which their own singular expressions can be constructed. They can fret about what's been done before, but sooner or later, if they're makers, they have to make. Recognizing one's relationship with history—even intuitively, vaguely, despondently—is the only way a musician can take control of history and actually act on it, perhaps to the extent that she can make us believe she has spontaneously generated *the* original rock 'n' roll song, "regardless," as Marcus writes, "of any rumors that something vaguely similar might have happened before."[8]

Thus, the new begins as choice in the field of time and history. The new *happens*. We normally think of it as material or form: a new sound, beat, or genre. But really, "new" ought to be a verb.

The Case for Performance—Drinking Glass—Unfinishing—Action

Before we can truly dig into the miasmic guts of how and why music is perceived as new or not-new, we should ask what music *is*. My answer is performance: singing, or playing music with an instrument, be it a saxophone, two blocks of wood, or a turntable.

Not everyone will agree with me. In *Rhythm and Noise: An Aesthetics of Rock*, Theodore Gracyk argues that rock 'n' roll has been treated by philosophers too much like classical music, resulting in a massive underestimation of the importance of the recording itself. Prior to the advent of sound recording, there was a simpler distinction between the score and its performance, a distinction thrown out of whack by wax cylinders, vinyl records, magnetic tape cassettes, digital compact discs, and MP3s. Since we primarily listen to musical recordings, and since music is created and recorded for those mediums, Gracyk argues that in rock 'n' roll, and by extension, nearly all popular music today, recordings are "the standard end-products and signifiers in rock music. …"[9] This has the benefit of being true to common experience. Nearly all of the music I discuss in these pages I've heard by way of a recording, not live. The argument especially makes sense once it's massaged a bit, as Stephen Davies does by making a distinction between "works for live performance" and "works for studio performance," plus a special category for works "conveyed directly, unadulterated by performance," mashups like Danger Mouse's *The Grey Album*, which mixed Jay-Z's *The Black Album* with the Beatles' *White Album*.[10]

But each of these works, even Davies' special category, contains performances. Though we engage with a performance through the vessel of a recording, that's not the same as saying we engage primarily with the vessel. That would be like saying: when I drink a glass of water, I am drinking glass. If the tap water is poisoned, I'm going to get sick whether I drink it out of a plastic cup, a chipped glass that cuts my lip, or straight from the faucet. Ultimately, every recording contains at least one performance. We listen for performances. We argue about performances. We practice by performing so that our performance in front of an audience will be as good as it can be. Live performance has a unique power tied but not limited to recordings.

The consequences of performance for the new are important, so let me break down my case in detail:

1. Performance is the being of music. It is the nexus of music, the source of it being what it is. Any performance brings together a number of chosen variables such as rhythm, words, various instrumental sounds, and the sound of a space, and, for a time, binds them into a singular unit. Performance does not require a literal audience; otherwise, a performance in a recording studio would not be a performance. A performance is a moment of heightened awareness, perhaps collaborative, which energizes musical elements that would otherwise be inert.

2. We usually compose songs so they'll be performed. The process of composition is typical but optional. Improvisation is composition through the act of performance.

3. A song, or composition, is usually performed, and often that performance is recorded, maybe a number of times, maybe once. The performance might happen in a professional recording studio or some other setting—a basement, a porch, a field, a concert—but without the performance, that space would not be recorded. Eventually, those involved choose a *definitive recording*. There might be a few alternate takes, which are either considered trash or gems. (Down the road, either can line the pockets of the record companies with gold.) The definitive recording is released to the public usually with the artists' consent, which is what makes it definitive: it's a sanctioned release.

4. The song and the recording have one thing in common: performance. Without performance, a song is unactivated as art. The performance creates the song. Even the process of composing a song requires a performance of it. Without performance, there is nothing for a recording to record. The performance creates the recording.

5. *Each performance is a singular instance in time.* Each instance might have no importance whatsoever, but each is a historical happening. If music is performance, then music is a historical instance.

6. Here's where things get tricky. In nearly every recording, the performance we hear contains overdubs in which performers play their parts at separate times. It's also likely that the recorded performance has been manipulated, engineered so that, for instance, the guitar pans right to left. It's also been mastered to meet various artistic and/or commercial expectations. The debatable question is to what extent the disjoint of time and the manipulation after its occurrence morphs a performance into something less unified, something that feels more like a construction. But even when a recording primarily consists of elements put together in a way we don't usually consider to be performance, as in EDM, the artifice of the recording is intended to nonetheless create the illusion of a singular instance. In his book *Performing Rites*, Simon Frith writes about such records:

> I listen … in the full knowledge that what I hear is something that never existed, that never could exist, as a 'performance,' something happening in a single time and space; nevertheless, it is now happening, in a single time and space: it is thus a performance and I hear it as one, imagine the performers performing even when this just means a deejay mixing a track, an engineer pulling knobs.[11]

And isn't a deejay's mixing of a track a kind of performance? Even *The Grey Album* contains performative choices made by Danger Mouse on top of the choices made by Jay-Z and the Beatles. Isn't the engineer's manipulation a kind of performance? We don't think of it this way, but we should. Overdubbed performances are still performances. On a fundamental level, each overdub, tweak of compression levels, and standardizing of the volume across the tracks is an action performed within a singular but collective instance (the "session"). Frith also gets at the importance of how the listener hears the recording, which requires imagination. All art requires a suspension of disbelief which fills in the logical gaps, even when, on closer examination, they're not really gaps.

7. No instance of performance is ever exactly the same, but live performances tend to have the most variability: slight variations in elements like tempo, dropped or changed lyrics, certain instrumental parts deleted because the band can't afford a horn section on tour. Even for prerecorded music, there's a tremendous difference between performing or hearing it privately (i.e., in a studio or through headphones) and experiencing it publicly. The chosen variables of a song—words, rhythm, tempo, melody, the instruments used, et cetera—*do not cease being variables once the performed song is recorded*. Musicians may avoid variance, but for those who face the prospect of playing the same song hundreds of times, variance is a godsend if not just an instinctive way of doing things. Late in his career, Prince slowed "Let's Go Crazy" into a hard rock stomp.

8. Each instance is unique because it happens at a concrete, distinct moment in time. This is crucial. Performance puts the song and even the definitive recording into motion *by putting them into the context of time.* Performance happens in historical time, which draws attention to the "in time" quality of what can seem, in the case of popular recordings, timeless. History is a randomizer in the spectrum of chance a song already contains. World events can destabilize or at least threaten to destabilize what seemed stable but never really was stable in the first place. Not every performance will feel "up in the air," but it always *might*. It always has the potential to be new.

9. This variability is a source of significant difference, a source of newness; it is only activated through performance. While the definitive recording seems to create a singular object, corralling the variables through performance into a thing, the song still contains multiples. We might say, then, that a song is a singular multiple. When we listen to the recording of Prince's "Purple Rain," we hear a singular performance that creates multiple possibilities. Isn't this why amateurs like you and me cover songs? Why we say, in fact, "This would've been better if it was faster." This is because the quality of variability is *built into* a song's unified but always temporary wholeness. There's even more variability because of the potential for more performances. Even the definitive recording suggests this potential because, in our culture, live performances are expected.

By 1985, fans *expected* to hear "Purple Rain" played in concert. If Prince didn't, there would've been riots.

10. For all of these reasons, each performance (instance) of an existing song which has been released as a definitive recording is always the *unfinishing* of that recording, its performance, and even the song itself. Every performed instance rewrites the song to some degree, no matter how small. If the differences are significant aesthetically, the degree of unfinishing might be considerable. The instance exposes the fact that the definitive recorded version was just a version and may call into question the power of the "original." Prince's version of "A Case of You" unfinished it into a soul ballad; his slowed-down grinding version of "Let's Go Crazy" unfinished it into a hard rock song.

11. A performance is a collection of miniscule and grand choices which can be thought of as actions. We experience these actions as a unit, so for me, "performance" and "action" mark the same phenomenon. Just as everyday actions might create unintended reactions, the variability within a performance also creates a sense of uncertainty, an irresolution of meaning, since it exists in the field of time and history.

12. Performance can't be untangled completely from the recording process, its duplication into a product, or the commodification of music, but if we treat the *object* created by performative actions as the essential source of meaning, then the generative power of performance wanes. We forget the power of music as an art form. Undoubtedly, my perspective stems from the fact that I've been playing music since I was in the fourth grade. When I sat in front of the drum set made of rubber practice pads in my teacher's studio, I wasn't thinking at all about recording, but I was thinking about performing for him and for myself. What's more, while I wanted to get the rudiments correct, I was also entranced by the newness of the sounds and rhythms I could create—their potential.

This book, then, retrieves from the clutches of objectification the significance of performance and its ability to create potential and newness.[12] The search for newness is always tied to what precedes it, i.e. the marks left on history by previous musicians. (In fact, I can still picture the marks made on those practice pads by the drumsticks played by those who came before me.) But only through performance do we work our way through these private and cultural memories to new possibilities. They may not be radically new. They may be small formal innovations, reclamations of a lost promise, the carving out of a new phase of one's career, or arguments for localized political change. But the big fish every musician chases is the newness that is total and overwhelming, one that creates artistic and social earthquakes, ruptures the fabric of normalcy, and creates an entirely new range of possibilities. This is what the French philosopher Alain Badiou calls the event.

A Howitzer at a Tea Party—Music and the Event—Impossible Possibilities

Imagine a music festival. Let's give it an artsy name: Sphere. At Sphere, we find six stages, and at each you'll watch and listen to a different lineup. You'll try to catch as much as you can, but this is a three-day festival and somebody has good weed in the campgrounds, which is where you are when a man storms by, shouting, "That Prince set was an *event*!" And, only because I'm writing you, you think, "An event in Badiou's sense of the word?"

Bringing the philosopher Alain Badiou, his concept of the event, and his mixture of ontology, set theory, historicity, and existentialism into this discussion about music and aesthetics is like bringing a howitzer to a tea party. And I have to admit: I'm not sure I know how to operate the howitzer. But a friend and colleague of mine who studied with Badiou at the European Graduate School said the students' motto was that cheery line from Beckett: "Fail better." So here we may fail, but we will fail better. That should be the definition of thinking and, at the very least, criticism. (And we'll leave out the set theory.)

Let's go back to the music festival. In Badiou's terminology, Sphere and everything that surrounds it—the politics of the time, the art trends, the people—is the *situation*. Within that situation are many sites, i.e. very specific locations. There are six stages at the Sphere festival; each stage is a site.[13] Each is represented with a giant banner bearing a name and probably a corporate logo. Badiou would say these are normal parts of the situation, the kind of thing you'd expect at a festival, otherwise it wouldn't be a festival. The performances that happen on these stages are also normal. However—and this is where my extended metaphor gets weird—imagine a patch of grass, a small field off to the side that is most definitely not a stage. Suddenly Prince is playing there. Everyone runs over to listen. Now this space *is* a stage. The act of performance makes an empty ordinary space into a stage. In a 2016 interview, Bruce Springsteen described how this happens from the performer's perspective. "You're there to manifest something," he said.

> Before you go in, it's an empty space. It's an empty building. So the audience is going to come, and you're gonna show up, and together you're going to manifest something that's very, very real, that's very tangible, but you're gonna pull it out of thin air. It wasn't there before you showed up. It didn't exist. It's *real* magic, you know?[14]

At Sphere, we'll call this magical stage created by Prince the Grass Skirt Stage. This, roughly, is the equivalent of what Badiou calls an *evental site*.[15] The space was there all along, but no one considered it a stage. However, it really only becomes an evental site if we can call Prince's performance an *event*. Without an event, there is no evental site. "It is not because the site exists in the situation that there is an event," writes Badiou; rather, an evental site is a kind of invisible potential that we can't see until the event happens.[16] Now, all of a sudden, the event belongs to a situation; it is "the arrival amidst the visible of the invisible," or the inaudible amid the audible.[17]

On any stage, during any performance, the event is a constant potential. Most shows will probably go as planned: we'll enjoy ourselves, have a few drinks, applaud, and have an ordinary good time. But because we don't know what will happen, each performative site has the potential to radically unsettle things, to completely upend the norms, and to turn even an actual ordinary stage into the site of something extraordinary—into an event. Hundreds of other performers, including Prince, had played on the First Avenue stage before that night when he and the Revolution debuted most of *Purple Rain*. Unlike those other performances, the show on August 3, 1983 transformed what was possible for the entire historical situation for music because of the ultra-fusion in Prince's music. There were other reasons, other transformations, too, which I'll get to in a later chapter, but the crucial point here is that his performance turned the impossible into limitless possibilities. If a performance does this, it's an event. It *is* the new.

Badiou's concept of the event is not for small formal innovations, novelties, or a personal sense of the new; neither is it confined to a change in social values. Instead, a radical newness comes into the world and fundamentally changes what is possible. Period. One of his frequent examples of the event is the French Revolution. That's the scale we're talking about. The new possibilities of an event are infinite; they create what Badiou calls an *evental sphere*. Musical genres are a bold example of this. The advent of jazz generated an entire musical language, an infinite number of musical forms. It also created new possibilities for how people might live—for instance, how African-Americans might make and hear and move to music that claimed a right to the true freedom promised in the nation's founding documents, music that expressed sorrow and demanded joy, and music that proved them to be incredible technicians of sound, masterful lyricists, arrangers, soloists, businesspeople, citizens, and architects of not just American culture but America itself.[18]

In music, performance creates the new. Everything that comes after performance is valuable, but it's secondary. The potential described by "nothing has been done before" means that every performance has the possibility of becoming an event. Most won't, but they all might. What's more, the musical event intrudes on the normal order of things only because of the action of a performance *in a historical situation*.[19] As the translator of *Being and Event*, Oliver Feltham, puts it, "For Badiou, it is the structure of historical situations alone that provides a possible location for an event. ...."[20] If we think of music only as an object, construction, or product, then performance-in-time ceases to be important, which means that not one but two crucial components of the event are lost.

In the following pages, I listen to a festival of musicians who in one way or another have been seeking the new in the twenty-first century. Performers, genres, and nationalities not mentioned in these pages are not excluded, as if by some critical magic, from chasing or achieving newness. By the same token, the musicians who are included here don't have a monopoly on the new. I've come by them honestly over time, and in some cases, over the course of decades. This book presents a constellation of ideas and possibilities, an interdisciplinary dialogue between thinkers and musicians who rarely meet in print, and a consideration of our historical moment. In the end, I'm following a hunch that although the event may be the pinnacle of the new, there exists a range of newness that is valuable and necessary to our lives, and that if we change the way we think about music, we might begin to hear it differently.

Part One

The Past in the Present

1

Revivals Are Revisions: New Millennial Folk Music Rolls the Dice

Was That It?

The wind picks up, but that could just be a coincidence. Cars are stopping in the middle of the road. The time approaches. And there you stand, ready for the end of the world. The End of All Time. That promised moment of release and revelation, the end of all worry, and the unveiling of something new. All sorts of two-bit preachers and secular prophets have foretold The End. Even a few artists. But their visions never came true. Yours will. You just know it. And what then? Something great or, at least, something different. The people around you hold their breath. They mutter. A man is weeping. The clouds gather into a dark quilt. You check your watch. The moment is here. You tilt back your head and spread your arms.

And then the moment has passed.

You look around with the same bewildered eyes as everyone else. The questioning turns angry. *Was that it?* The sky is now just overcast. The people curse, pack up, and head home with their unanswered questions.

You go home, too. You get stoned and try to sleep. The still air presses against your eardrums.

What now?

That's the moment *Time (The Revelator)* begins: four strums of two notes a half step apart and played on an acoustic guitar, the music suspended, dissonant, waiting to be resolved.

The Land of Tomorrow—Down from the Mountain

"We were all futurists," Douglas Rushkoff says in *Present Shock* about the years leading up to December 31, 1999, "energized by new technologies, new theories, new business models, and new approaches that promised not just more of the same, but something different."[1] Well, we weren't all futurists. Optimism about the new millennium clashed with Y2K panic, an anxiety based on the inability of our incredible new technology to handle the clocks changing. If some were looking forward to something new, others were terrified of it. And then the clocks ticked over and nothing changed: no apocalypse, no planes falling from the sky, but also no flying cars, no space travel for everyone, no utopian Land of Tomorrow. "The anticlimax of the millennium," Rushkoff calls it. "People stopped thinking about where things were going, and started to consider where things were."[2] In his estimation, futurism ceded to "presentism": a blinding focus on the immediate moment made possible by digital technology, specifically the internet. "Everything is live, real time, and always-on," says Rushkoff; "[i]t's not a mere speeding up" but "more of a diminishment of anything that isn't happening now—and the onslaught of everything that supposedly is."[3] As the present moment distracts us, he argues, we've ceased being interested in traditional narratives, including historical narratives.

Well, not all of us were presentists either. In music, a certain revivalist spirit marked the first two years of the millennium. In July 2001 alone, the White Stripes released *White Blood Cells* and the Strokes released their debut album *Is This It*, cementing the garage rock revival that had been developing for years in the Stripes' hometown of Detroit. Meanwhile, everywhere you turned, you could still hear the old-time folk soundtrack to the Coen Brothers' film

O Brother, Where Art Thou?, released in December 2000. Featuring Welch on "Didn't Leave Nobody But the Baby" and "I'll Fly Away," the album occasioned a tour and subsequent concert album, *Down from the Mountain*. By March 2002, it'd sold 4.2 million copies.[4] Marked also by a growing neo-soul movement and an alt-country scene highly attuned to a classic country sound mixed with rock, the beginning of the twenty-first century seemed hell-bent for leather to revive the past and relive the old. Maybe it was the residue of that millennial anxiety, a grasp for something familiar. Or maybe it was the result of being let down by the new that didn't happen.

Unprecedented Relations—Lost in American Time—Painting a Boarded-Up Window

Anticlimax is what I hear in those four lazy and dissonant strums that begin "Revelator," the first song on *Time (The Revelator)*. Recorded by Welch and Rawlings in April 2001 and released that July, *Time (The Revelator)* drifts along, a hazy American daydream of disappointment. Listening to it, I'm always reminded of that shot near the end of the Rolling Stones documentary *Gimme Shelter* when the exhausted hippies are staggering down a hillside in the night, scrambling their way home or just away from the violence of their communion. But *Time (the Revelator)* sounds more traumatized by what *didn't* happen—the lack of revelation, the lack of any direction. With a stillness behind every song that is the complete opposite of presentism's frenetic pace, Welch and Rawlings take their sweet time, certain there's nowhere to go anymore. On "Revelator," Welch greets us in a voice so laconic, so sleepy, and stoned, we might miss the wink and the warning of its first lines: "Darling, remember when you come to me/I'm the pretender, and not what I'm supposed to be." They're a jab at her critics, the people who couldn't get over the jarring disconnect between the anachronistic "Dust Bowl" sound (a lazy journalistic trope if ever there was one) of her first two albums and the fact that she'd been raised in California by adoptive parents who wrote music for television.[5] Those two lines also hint at the pensive questioning of the album, the way it interrogates what's authentic and what's inauthentic without anxiety or urgency. "April the 14th Part I" is lost in time, moving from the Titanic to a "five-band bill, two-dollar" rock show where exhausted musicians are doomed to a life of wandering and poverty—and despite that, Welch wishes she was rocking out. After a dissertation on the way the internet will affect musicians in "Everything Is Free," a song that now seems like soothsaying, Welch and Rawlings close the album with "I Dream a Highway," which just starts, as if the mics pick up a performance that began a few moments, or years, before. A friend of mine once told me, "It's the only song I can think of that actually *slows down*." Almost fifteen minutes long and composed of imagistic shards from American history, "I Dream a Highway" is an Odyssean plainsong of loneliness and longing. "I dream a highway back to you," Welch ends each verse, but back to whom? To what? There's only forward.

That said, *Time (the Revelator)* finds Welch and Rawlings standing on the highway, taking stock of where they are, and looking to the past for some sense. They stitch the album together with the country's official history and its abandoned ephemera: forgotten railroad lines and catastrophes, the assassination of the Great Emancipator, the sinking of the Titanic, the death of folk hero John Henry, the rise and fall of Elvis Presley. Quite literally, the songs are constructed from pieces of other songs that existed before them, from the old-time folk and country trope of the topical song—Blind Willie Johnson's "God Moves on the Water" or Woody Guthrie's "Dust Storm Disaster," both of which you hear in "April the 14th Part I" and "Ruination Day"—to subtle allusions embedded in the lyrics. "Revelator" references Johnson's "John the Revelator," Taj Mahal's "She Caught the Katy (And Left Me a Mule to Ride)," and maybe even L.L. Cool J's "Goin' Back to Cali." Somehow, the album suggests, all of this is connected. The singer *wants* them to be connected, or feels intuitively that they are. The plainness of Welch's singing flattens these disparate pieces of history into one story while Rawlings' sometimes ominous, sometimes ecstatic guitar dances around her voice.

The stitching together of the previously done, the previously made, into "new relations, new arrangements" is exactly what Michael North calls "recombination" in *Novelty: A History of the New*.[6] Recombination is a concept mainly concerned with materials and forms; in music: lyrics, melodic styles, rhythms, song structures, and genres. (It's also a frequent critical shorthand: band A = band B + band C.) Recombination is usually described as a postmodern strategy—remixing and repurposing—but it goes back much further than that. Blues singers were remixing lyrics as the genre formed. The evolution of common songs through oral culture, the folk process, is centuries old. African-American slave songs combined African and European melodies, biblical texts, and coded lyrical images to pass along news and other messages (see the great "Steal Away"). What's changed is our attitude toward recombination. Modernists, being fairly intense, believed it was a serious, significant innovation. If we're card-carrying postmodernists, though, we see it as play; it emphasizes the present day and the performative moment more than any sense of newness.

Recombination may result in *some* kind of new, writes North, but "only if unprecedented relations between existing elements can be considered truly new entities."[7] That he writes this in the conditional tense gives away that the newness of recombination can be ambiguous. What qualifies as unprecedented?

Time (the Revelator) obviously recombines fragments of American history and music, sometimes very subtly, as in "Dear Someone," a gorgeous cowboy ballad that nudges up against a Cole Porter tune, and sometimes blatantly, as in "Elvis Presley Blues." Lyrically, the album stirs together allusions to American tragedies, but what they mean is ambiguous at best. Lincoln's assassination, the sinking of the Titanic, and the Black Sunday dust storm in 1935 all happened on April 14—okay, but what of it? What feels unprecedented is precisely this lack of clarity. We often expect the new to illuminate the past, present, or future, but here the recombination of the American past resists anything so clear as a statement. Instead, *Time (the Revelator)* is a mood, a series of intuitions that connect pieces of American history into an uneasy sense of desire and doom potent enough to make it seem like Elvis' ambition sunk the Titanic. Even the more contemporary references, like the potential L.L. Cool J shout-out that I can't un-hear or the country all-stars name-dropped in "I Dream a Highway," take their place in this story of great deeds and great ruin, an epic in the traditional sense of the word: a narrative poem told by a nation about its past in order to understand itself. As best as it can, anyway.

If the past is a story, has it come to an end? Not here. One thing not taken into account by North is the significance of when a recombination happens. What makes *Time (the Revelator)* so powerful, so singular, and so new is what it says about America circa 2001: the continuing saga of an ambitious but disappointed country afraid that its greatest deeds might be in the past. We yearn even for those great calamities since they were at least important. Whether they mean to or not, every American artist tells his or her version of the American story—whether it's framed that way explicitly or implicitly, it's inevitable—and on *Time (the Revelator)*, Welch and Rawlings sound like they're pouncing on this, picking their way through a new millennial America that was promised flying cars but instead got *Bush v. Gore*. The nation is wrecked, populated by wandering musicians, trembling drunks, ghosts of the past, distant lovers, and distant dreams. The size of America, its overwhelming scope, which once held so much promise, is now bewildering and gray. The minimalism of Welch and Rawlings' vocals, acoustic guitars, and banjo, and the austerity of the folk, blues, and country structures of their songs combine to create a landscape as stark as an abandoned town, like the kind my wife and I pass through on our way to her grandparents' farm in Northwest Ohio. At one corner, there used to be a general store, and then, in 2010, someone painted on its boarded-up window: Goooooone. In all of this empty space, there's plenty of room for us to blow through like the wind. Having lost our past and our present, we have lost ourselves. Thus, the newness in *Time (the Revelator)* that should be impossible because it's made so much from the musical past emerges because of the relationship between that past and this present. It becomes a revelation, but a revelation of a deeply felt uncertainty.

As an artist, though, Welch had never sounded more confident. Or ambitious. Without rejecting the old-time folk music which had so clearly influenced the original songs of her first two albums—her debut was titled *Revival*—Welch nonetheless parted ways with the rigidity that a blind-faith allegiance to genre and tradition can bring out in those who perform old-time music. She did this by claiming the tradition for herself. "Time (the Revelator) is explicitly a folk album," wrote Grant Alden in the magazine *No Depression*, "provided one understands folk music to be a continuum, not an archive," which means it can evolve, which in turn means it can be personal.⁸ This is how a work built so much from the American past can be more than a history lesson. If Welch had always felt her music was personal and not merely a re-creation of the past, she began arguing her case more fiercely after *Time* (*the Revelator*). "This album reflects Nashville, April, 2001," she said in December of that year. "It's what was going on in my life at that time. It might not seem that way, but I don't care. Of course the songs are personal because I wrote them. It's a funny misconception that people have, and it almost makes me too angry to address it."⁹ The newness of the past in the present depends on this intense subjective vision, and such a vision is at odds with the more typical way we expect to see the old resurface: a revival, which today serves the function of the epic by re-creating a supposedly authentic national past.

Revivals Are Revisions—O Brother!—You Get to Sing the Depressing Songs

A revival is the most obvious musical example of the other historical model of innovation defined in *Novelty*, "recurrence."¹⁰ Like the rising and setting of the sun, recurrence is a renewal that's often seen as cyclical, dependable, natural, and for some, the evidence of a divine hand. Recurrence "promise[s] the return in all its pristine glory of some original newness," writes North, adding that such returns tend to be sudden and total.¹¹ For instance, the sudden dominance of the *O Brother, Where Art Thou?* soundtrack. Like other music revivals, *O Brother* and the new millennial folk revival it stimulated implied the return of something good, some "original newness" worth saving from the remainder bin of history.

The trick with the music from *O Brother* is that it works differently in the film than it does on its own. The Coen Brothers' romp isn't particularly interested in a revival; it's a send-up of our cultural memory of the Depression-era South, particularly Southern white culture. Its convict heroes wear convict costumes, John Goodman is a traveling Bible salesman who's every bit the shyster you'd expect him to be, and then there's the infamous scene in which the Ku Klux

Klan stomps around a field of burning crosses looking like a marching band and sounding like the flying monkeys from *The Wizard of Oz*. Only one thing escapes the Coens' skewering: the music. Nearly always, it shines with a pristine, beatific glow, as if it's the only uncorrupted aspect of this silly but mean world. By itself, the music on the *O Brother* soundtrack could use some sinnin'. Despite the album's few somber tunes, notably "Po' Lazarus," John Hartford's fiddle version of "I Am a Man of Constant Sorrow," and Ralph Stanley's petrifying a capella "O Death," the soundtrack is mainly a chipper Smithsonian tour through American history. It recombines nothing; it only purifies. Committed and unified, it edifies an already official version of the country's history for the sake of a new mass culture that's forgotten to remember the newness of its own past. But why *should* we remember? The best answer here is that our musical past possesses an essential value that should make us feel good today, make us feel at ease.

Weak revivals flatter themselves. They assume the uniqueness of the present without bothering to define it, show it, or fight for it. At the same time, they bind themselves to the past as if today is the same as yesterday. Usually, this is why they end up sounding too faithful. Reproductions, homages. Countless contemporary folk recordings sound this way: Gillian Welch on her first albums; Iron & Wine on *Our Endless Numbered Days* and The Milk Carton Kids on *The Ash and Clay*, both effortlessly recalling Simon and Garfunkel pastoralism (more Garfunkel than Simon); the fine Dave Alvin records *Blackjack David* and *Public Domain*, entertaining and affectionate and too precise despite Alvin's gruff voice.

While revivalists often claim to simply recreate the past, returning a certain style or spirit to our contemporary moment, it's never as simple as that. "Popular music is nothing if not dialogic," writes American Studies scholar George Lipsitz, "the product of an ongoing historical conversation in which no one has the first or last word."[12] A concept established by the Russian philosopher Mikhail Bakhtin in the early twentieth century, the dialogic is simply what it sounds like: a dialogue between texts. For Bakhtin, though, all language is dialogic, and so the conversation between works and their predecessors never ceases. What's more, the dialogue changes the preceding texts. *Time (The Revelator)* turns its American texts into vapor, but the performances on *O Brother, Where Art Thou?*, as in many revivals, seem to leave the history of their songs untouched. The meaning of Stanley's "O Death" isn't that different from "O Death" as performed by Kate Mann on her 2012 album *Rattlesnake on the Road*. (Camper Van Beethoven's 1988 version, on the other hand, is a damn party.)

Since a revival is inherently and explicitly dialogic, however, these choices will always entail a revision of the past. A revival selects and rejects certain historical particulars, e.g., specific musicians and their works, as it lays claim to a resuscitated historical essence. The question of newness really comes down to what Lipsitz describes as "the ingenuity of artists interested in fashioning icons of opposition."[13] The film *O Brother, Where Art Thou?* fashions such iconic oppositions: music is holy, people are not. (Even the convicts become holy when they sing.) But the soundtrack, the music alone, is just holy. To the extent that there are opposing icons, they're troubling ... as in, guess who only gets to sing the sad songs? Just three of the soundtrack's cuts are performed by Black musicians—Chris Thomas King, who portrays a blues musician named Tommy Johnson in the film, plays "Hard Time Killing Floor Blues"; legendary gospel group the Fairfield Four sings "Lonesome Valley" (and play gravediggers); and, in a 1959 recording, prisoner James Carter and his fellow inmates sing "Po' Lazarus"—and you'll notice that these are among the most somber, despairing, and stoically spiritual performances on the album. There are no Black string bands, jazz combos, blues rags, or lightning-fast gospel songs. There are no Black women at all. The old-time past presented by the album reinforces a familiar understanding of history—white people get to perform in diverse ways and Black men are limited to moaning—and brings that ideology into the present-day revival.

Mallarmé Rolls the Dice: The Interpretative Intervention

The results of recombination and recurrence will remain a fundamental question of the new in music. Almost always they work together. As a language, music is inherently recombinatory. As culture, it's prone to recurrence. While each might seem dwarfed by Badiou's theory of the event and its unlimited possibilities, consider this: rap, founded on the recombination of preexisting music, radically changed what could be said in music and American culture; as a recurrence, it reclaimed the original and too often obscured newness of Black music and the revolutionary potential of civil rights. In less than ten years, rap proved that recombination and recurrence can contribute to an event if they create new possibilities.

Badiou argues that the event can't be known or named as it occurs. He doesn't mean we can't intuit or recognize that something new is happening, just that we can't really say we know for sure, or that we understand the significance of this new situation being introduced. The event is all about uncertain beginnings. Only later, after the event, is it "given to us to bet," writes Badiou in a reading of Mallarmé's poem, "A Cast of Dice."[14] What's needed is an "interpretative intervention," an assertion that names the event in the past: *There: that was new*. Naming it is the beginning of an effort to force it to matter. This is the bet, the roll of the dice. Maybe the gamble loses, maybe it wins, but it is never a disinterested game of chance. The interpretative intervention claims a revelation about the past: a rupture that created new possibilities which can be realized in the present.

Every revival in music is a form of interpretative intervention. *O Brother, Where Art Thou?* points back to the American past of old-time folk, country, and blues and argues for its original newness. In its way, *Time (the Revelator)* does the same but far more ambiguously, which is why it felt like the more interesting, alienated stepchild of the film's soundtrack and not really a revival. As a form of recurrence, the revival may lean on that sense of natural cycles, a kind of inevitability which will not seem very new. The effect is very different, though, when a revival truly feels like an intervention.

The Fiddle—They Taught "Dixie" to Dan Emmett—New Traditions

A fiddle's sinewy tune works its way from the mid-nineteenth century into the present, gliding through tall grass and barb wire, around cottonwood branches, across wooden fences, through any American city, any town, swaying, rubbing against signs that read COLOREDS ONLY, crossing through Memphis on April 4, 1968, crossing through sad days and jubilant days, through Los Angeles in 1991 and Chicago in November 2008, until it's caught and played by Rhiannon Giddens of the Carolina Chocolate Drops in their song "Snowden's Jig (Genuine Negro Jig)." Ten years after the new millennial folk revival, the fiddle's melody renders a verdict on it: *"Incomplete."*

On their 2010 album *Genuine Negro Jig*, the Carolina Chocolate Drops play deeply historical music based on the tradition of Black string band music: Dom Flemons on four-string banjo, jug, guitar, and the bones, a skinny castanet-like instrument popularized on the minstrel circuit, Justin Robinson on fiddle and hand/foot percussion, and Rhiannon Giddens on five-string banjo and fiddle. Hers is the most arresting voice, but they all sing. As a group, they choose on their own terms what from the tradition to keep, what to leave out, what to rearrange, and, in the case of their cover of Blu Cantrell's swinging 2001 hit "Hit 'Em Up Style (Oops!)," what to re-imagine completely. (Their version is a succinct example of recombination; Cantrell's version itself remixes jazz and R&B.) The album intervenes on the folk revival of the 2000s in order to retrieve a more honest history, a short- and long-term dialogism that reclaims the importance of Black string band music, its technicality, its exuberance, its diversity, and what it has to say about America then and now.

The North Carolina-based trio put that discussion onto the stage; their live shows were raucous and casual, their performances intense, their instruction subtle, their motivations personal before they were polemic. "We don't want to be the end of the dialogue, we want to be the beginning," Rhiannon Giddens said in 2012, and as an example, she offered the history of the banjo, a crucial component in Black string band music though it's often assumed to be exclusively a white, bluegrass instrument.[15]

> Just saying Black people were the only people playing the banjo for the first hundred years of its existence—that's a huge statement, you know? It's a fact, and that makes a lot of other questions come into being: "What does that mean? What came next? How can I find out more about this?" Which is what we want.

The history of Black string bands in America has been little more than a whisper despite their fundamental influence on folk, country, bluegrass, and the blues, and every genre those have informed and formed since. "It's about American history," Giddens said, "and so much that's been covered up and not talked about: the whole idea of the Great Migration, Blacks living in the country, the formation of roots music." In other words, how newness came into being.

From the empty space marked out by the foot stomps and handclaps that begin "Snowden's Jig (Genuine Negro Jig)," the fiddle's melody rises like smoke, playful, sorrowful, and resilient. There are no vocals, no words spoken except in the sounds. Flemons' bones chatter like teeth. The melody sways through its first eight bars, starts climbing and descending, up the ladder, down the ladder, pauses, and then goes through it all again, telling its story.

Near Mount Vernon, Ohio, northeast of Columbus, there's a gravestone for the African-American brothers Ben and Lew Snowden. Underneath their names is an engraving: THEY TAUGHT "DIXIE" TO DAN EMMETT. Who is this? In the mid-nineteenth century, Daniel Emmett more or less invents the minstrel show, changing its format from a series of individual performers into an entire group of white performers in blackface. So happens, he's from Mount Vernon. In fact, his family's property adjoins the Snowdens'. During a trip back home sometime in the mid-1850s, Emmett hears a tune from across the yard. It is being played or sung not by the young Snowden brothers but by their mother, Ellen, who along with her husband Thomas is a freed slave from Maryland. The Snowdens are professional musicians too; their family band plays a variety of tunes for white and Black audiences around Central Ohio, including songs made popular by minstrels. Emmett, meanwhile, relies on Black-anchored authenticity and pop originality for his success, like any minstrel. He's also a goshawk for new material. This tune he hears, maybe even the words—they're alluring.

Daniel Emmett debuted "I Wish I Was in the Land of Dixie" in New York City in 1859, and according to most official history, he wrote it. In their book *Way Up North in Dixie*, Howard L. Sacks and Judith Rose Sacks argue that he most likely learned "Dixie" from Ellen Snowden. Though they admit there is no evidential "smoking gun," the Sacks make a convincing case with their re-reading of the song's lyrics as if written from Ellen Snowden's perspective, either as "a document of black experience in the hostile North" or "a protest by way of parody," i.e. a signification in the tradition of African-American slave songs and spirituals in which crossing the River Jordan might be code for escaping across the Ohio River into freedom.[16] It's not hard to imagine why Emmett would have kept the source of "Dixie" to himself, or why the Snowdens would have felt unable to protest. One detail sticks with me, though. Found in the Snowden household after Ben and Lew's deaths were a posthumous article about Emmett and a portrait of him; in both, the public record declares him the author of "Dixie." Why did the Snowden brothers keep these items? Anger? Fascination? Pride?

It's very possible that the traditional tune known as "Genuine Negro Jig" was also written by the Snowdens and learned from them by Daniel Emmett, to whom it's usually attributed. Covering the song, parenthesizing its "original" title, and inserting a new title, the Carolina Chocolate Drops intervene on tradition. That, really, has been their entire project. Revivals generally name a past event, but the Drops show how a revival can be new when it also names an unrecognized or forgotten event—in this case, the variety of innovations of African-American folk music—and renews its importance today. The fiddle of "Snowden's Jig (Genuine Negro Jig)" winds through history, reasserting itself, grabbing us by our contemporary, spazzed-out, presentist ears and whispering *There: that was new*. The song also demonstrates the limits of our presentist culture in which we assume everything is at our fingertips. "[I]t's not that hard to find the original recordings of the old black string bands, so why re-create them?" wrote one reviewer of *Genuine Negro Jig*, adding that "this is the 21st century, after all, and the whole history of recorded music is readily available."[17] This is record-reviewer perspective, a wad of subtle self-flattery. Casual listeners won't even know what the original music is unless someone's playing it now. You couldn't even hear Black string band music in *O Brother, Where Art Thou?* except for the slightest echo in John Hartford's version of "I Am a Man of Constant Sorrow."

On *Genuine Negro Jig*, the Carolina Chocolate Drops revised the official versions of folk revivalism, and in doing so, created the possibility of a new tradition. That phrase might seem antithetical to the new, but only if (and perhaps inevitably when) the tradition itself stops being interested in a new understanding of the relationship between the present and the past. There is no new tradition in the music of O Brother, Where Art Thou?, only a surge in the importance of a familiar tradition at a time when the country wanted to reaffirm its past. And then there's *Time (the Revelator)*, groping its way forward, rolling the dice, too singular to dismantle a tradition or inspire a new one—though who can say. It's possible that its time has not yet come.

2

"Love and Theft":
Transgression and the Cultural Archive

There is the old and the new, and you have to connect with them both. The old goes out and the new comes in, but there is no sharp borderline. The old is still happening while the new enters the scene, sometimes unnoticed. The new is overlapping at the same time the old is weakening its hold. It goes on and on like that. Forever through the centuries. Sooner or later, before you know it, everything is new, and what happened to the old? It's like a magician's trick, but you have to keep connecting with it.
—BOB DYLAN[1]

Strange Things Happening Every Day

The first time I listen to Bob Dylan's *"Love and Theft,"* I am sitting in my truck on September 12, 2001. My arm hangs out the window, a cigarette pinched between my fingers. Seeking a familiar voice, maybe even looking for some wisdom, I tried to buy Dylan's new album the day before, but the store was closed by the time I got off work. Even today, the parking lot is all but empty. I crank the volume. "Tweedle Dum and Tweedle Dee" busts out from the shadows it's been hiding in, a jalopy trailing sparks and leaking oil with two reckless and powerful idiots riding up front. They've got dangerous grins. They carry "two big bags of dead man's bones."

As the songs flow by, I'm stunned by what I hear. From the stoic "Mississippi" and the cavorting "Summer Days" to the herk-and-jerk "Cry a While" and the closer "Sugar Baby," the album is an outpouring of American historical events and figures, especially musicians: Robert Johnson, Clarence Ashley, Big Joe Turner, and Dock Boggs. Like Welch's album released a few months prior, *"Love and Theft"* epitomizes the contemporary view that to make the new in a culture in which everything seems to have been done, the artist has to recombine preexisting materials in a new surprising way, but unlike *Time (the Revelator)*, Dylan's album stitches at a flick-of-the-wrist pace. There's nothing ponderous or uncertain about it. On "Tweedle Dee and Tweedle Dum" alone Dylan tosses out lyrical references like a blackjack dealer: the RCA Victor dog Nipper ("His master's voice is calling me"); the land of Cain's exile, Nod; Tennessee Williams' *A Streetcar Named Desire*; Johnson's "Love in Vain"; Mardi Gras ("Throw me something, mister, please!"); and with the line, "Your presence is obnoxious to me," the mid-1800s minstrel sketch *Box and Cox: In One Act*. (Not that I catch that one right away.)

"Love and Theft" is a bewildering and somehow, on this day, comforting remix of American culture. Funny, too. On "Floater (Too Much to Ask)" I imagine Dylan doing a little soft-shoe across a creaky wooden stage. These songs, they're filled with strange and terrible events, but they sound ordinary. Like Sister Rosetta Tharpe's song: "Strange Things Happening Every Day." Today they make all the sense there is to make.

"Love and Theft" sounded new then, and still does, for many reasons. Like *Time (the Revelator)*, it pulls off what seems like an impossible trick: weaving the new out of the old. Although it's not soused in echo like *Time Out of Mind*, Dylan's excellent previous album, "Love and Theft" is nonetheless drenched in old sounds: cakewalk rhythms, jazz chords, weeping fiddles, Augie Meyers' Vox organ, and slide guitar. It also seemed new, or at least contemporary, for what it happened to say about America: a nation coming apart in the face of the threat of constant disaster. "High water risin'," Dylan sings on "High Water (for Charley Patton)," "Risin' night and day/All the gold and silver are being stolen away." In nearly every song, the narrator schemes as the weather turns sour—fog, thunder, dark clouds, a flood or two—and society turns anarchistic, every man, woman, and child for themselves. This was the alternate story that sunk in during the weeks and months after the terrorist attacks of September 11. Without knowing what context his album would suddenly find itself in when it was released, Dylan had imagined the new United States we were living in, an America shocked, confused, and weighed down by a sense of doom and catastrophe, a nation in which a horrible violence would become an occasion for those in power to get more of it by selling fear, silencing complexity, and cultivating even more confusion.

Remarkable as that was, the newness of *"Love and Theft"* is also inextricably tied to what had become of Dylan's career at the millennial turn and where it would go in the following years. Like a lot of people, I wondered in the days leading up to the album's release if it would be a clunker, and if 1997's *Time Out of Mind* had been a one-off success like (but far better than) 1989's *Oh Mercy*. Instead, *"Love and Theft"* established a new consistency of quality in late-era Dylan, though it's a more vivid and diverse album than the ones that have followed. But the striking difference is Dylan's persona: the stoic and almost beaten guy on *Time Out of Mind* has become a confident, leering, and nimble hustler who at the end of every song is sneaking out a window. And then, in 2003, Dylan really became a wanted man. With the cries of "Dylan's back!" ringing out for the umpteenth time in his career, he was accused of being a plagiarist. The story broke in that bastion of music criticism, the *Wall Street Journal*: Dylan had swiped a handful of phrases from the Japanese physician and novelist Junichi Saga's *Confessions of a Yakuza* and put them into *"Love and Theft"* on the sly.

Binding all of this together, particularly Dylan's new persona and the charges of plagiarism, is an ingredient that's often necessary for the new: transgression. By refusing to become a greatest hits act, he denied the expectations of a rock 'n' roll narrative wherein the old fade away or burn out and cease to matter as generators of newness. Instead, he reinvented himself as a lusty old man still capable of turning a few heads. By using repurposed materials in a way some who don't understand art call plagiarism, Dylan challenged still-potent myths about his own aura of authenticity and Americans' cultural knowledge about their own nation. *"Love and Theft"* makes the old new by transgressing against social and cultural laws, and it has a blast along the way.

The Cultural Archive and the Profane Realm— Astronaut Food—The Newport Event/"My Hands Are on Fire"—Authorized Rebel

More than any other living musician, Dylan has carried with him the burden of what the philosopher Boris Groys in his book *On the New* calls the "cultural archive": a culture's official valorized story about itself, its tradition, a "materialized cultural memory ... in the keeping of various institutions that are [as] hierarchically structured" as that culture's values.[2] Since Groys focuses on visual art, his version of the archive centers on museums, galleries, and libraries, but it can certainly include government institutions, the media, the market, and nonprofit organizations like the, *ahem,* Nobel Prize Foundation. "The basic principle governing the construction of the cultural archives is that they necessarily integrate the new and ignore the derivative," writes Groys, but as much as they shift and adapt to the new, the archives nonetheless always seek order, always organize a viewpoint centered around particular shared values.[3] The Rock and Roll Hall of Fame and Museum comes to mind, eh? Who's in and who's not, what history gets told and what history is marginalized: Green Day is in, Warren Zevon is not; rock 'n' roll as youth emancipation is in, rock 'n' roll as corruption and payola is ... well, it's *mentioned*. Although a friend of mine calls it the Rock Hall and Mausoleum (a lot of us do), such an archive exists to confirm and celebrate values that were, at one point in time, new.

For nearly his entire career, Dylan has been uncomfortably tied to this cultural archive—hell, he has *been* this cultural archive—precisely because of the newness he created: The Voice of a Generation, the iconic Rebel Against the System, the Restless Genius. You could see the discomfort on his heavy-cheeked face as he accepted a Lifetime Achievement award from Jack Nicholson at the 1991 Grammys just after playing "Masters of War." From the late 1970s through most of the 1990s, Dylan seemed to be caving under the weight of his own artistic influence; occasionally he would scamper out and cut a brilliant song, even a damn good album like *Infidels*, but often it seemed like he'd given up. As he would later write in his memoir *Chronicles* of the place he'd found himself in the late 1980s, "I had too long been freeze frozen in the secular temple of a museum," as if he was a mummy, or a package of astronaut food kept for posterity.[4]

To worm his way out from under this weight, Dylan seemed to know that his best recourse was to find his place in what Groys calls the "profane realm," which is simply "all the things that are not included in the archives."[5] If the archive is official culture, the profane realm is the ordinariness, the repetitiveness, and the derivativeness of everyday life. The term "profane" only means the things that have been rejected or not yet been consecrated by the cultural archive and its memory; they are unneeded, insignificant, and in many ways, unseen. Or unheard. In Groys' theory, there are no alternatives to the cultural archive or the profane realm. Works exist in either or both, but not neither. Writes Groys, "Things in the profane realm are not deliberately conserved; unless they are saved from destruction by chance, they eventually disappear."[6]

Even though Dylan often found himself on the verge of disappearing culturally, he was trailed by the shadow of his archival self. Thus, to be new, he had to set up shop in the profane realm, regroup, and return. Why? According to Groys, "[t]he source of the new is … the valorizing comparison between cultural values and things in the profane realm"—a confrontation he calls the "cultural economy of exchange."[7] When this exchange occurs across the "boundary" between the two realms, a cultural value is reappraised or reconsidered, and then it's either accepted into the cultural archive or thrown back into the profane realm like garbage.[8] If the value's accepted, a different value is rejected. (Groys does actually talk about garbage.) But for any of this to happen, the archives and their traditions must take notice of the profane.

Cue Dylan, circa 1965–1966. The deep irony of Dylan's existence in, embodiment of, and struggle with the rock 'n' roll cultural archive today is that it's built very much *on him*—on the massive, revolutionary, and still awe-inspiring year-plus in which he changed what popular music could be, essentially by launching his assault on the cultural archive that was folk music. He was just one man, but he seemed like a mob. By early 1965, Dylan had already been drifting away from his role as a socially concerned, authentic folk singer; he'd introduced new elements from the realm of the profane, like writing his own songs and pushing his lyricism into a more ambiguous and personal language. With the release of *Bringing It All Back Home* in March 1965, however, he challenged the folk establishment with music that it heard as literally profane: commercial, loud, sardonic, and seemingly unconcerned with social issues. In other words, rock 'n' roll. From there, the war escalated quickly. The release of "Like a Rolling Stone" on July 20, 1965. His electric set at the Newport Folk Festival on July 25. The release of *Highway 61 Revisited* in August. The subsequent tours backed by the Hawks, soon to become the Band, through the United States and Europe during which he was heckled and booed for selling out by playing pop music. Then, of course, the infamous showdown at Manchester Free Trade Hall in England on May 17, 1966, when one fan shouted "Judas!" and Dylan responded, "I don't believe you. You're a liar," then turned to the Hawks and growled, "Play fuckin' loud!" And lo, they did. And that is how Bob Dylan burned this particular cultural archive to the ground like Queen Boudica did to London in 61 AD, when she left behind a layer of ash thick enough to be discovered millennia later by archeologists.[9]

Too dramatic? Yes, it was; that's why history broke. There is no doubt in my mind that Dylan's year-long, self-destructive, aesthetic bloodbath was an unqualified event in the sense that Badiou means it. Dylan entirely, irrevocably changed what was possible for the situation. Not just the situation for music, but the entire historical situation. The flashpoint, the event of the event, was that summer night at Newport. You can tell because people have been reinterpreting it ever since. Recent custom, especially since the turn of the millennium, has been to undercut the newness of this event by blaming the boos, as Pete Seeger would later claim, on the loud volume and/or the crappy quality of the sound. ("As if good or even halfway decent sound quality in rock and roll shows was at that time something anyone would be familiar with," Greil Marcus would say in 2015.)[10] Other explanations have been mushed into a gravy of historical ambiguity and dismissals that anything radically new happened. For example, Elijah Wald argues in *Dylan Goes Electric!* that the booing has been exaggerated, that "the central conflict" of Newport "was timeless," and that the 1965 showdown was "not the death of an old dream and the birth of a new, but the clash of two very old dreams," a Pete Seeger-embodied communalism and a Dylan-embodied "libertarian ideal of the free individual."[11] Wald claims that Newport and the folk revival were irrevocably changed, but that Dylan remained—somehow—unchanged.

If you want to know what happened, watch and listen to Murray Lerner's documentary, *The Other Side of the Mirror*. Here we go: backed by the Paul Butterfield Band with Al Kooper on organ—an assemblage of musicians pulled together the day before—Dylan performs three brand-new electric rock 'n' roll songs. After the first, "Maggie's Farm," a storm of booing blasts the stage. After the second line of "Like a Rolling Stone," Dylan flashes a look to his left, maybe offstage, or maybe to Barry Goldberg who was playing Al Kooper's organ part because Kooper was playing bass. Anyway, I know that look; every musician knows that look. It means, "Are we getting out of this gig alive?" As the band finishes the song, another wave of booing descends from the shocked folkie audience. The band presses on through "Phantom Engineer," later retitled "It Takes a Lot to Laugh, It Takes a Train to Cry," and then they bail. They've only rehearsed these three songs (barely). Peter Yarrow looks afraid for his life as he promises Dylan will come out for another tune. He does: "It's All Over Now, Baby Blue," a perfect kiss-my-ass song, and to conclude, "Mr. Tambourine Man," which that spring had been a pop hit for the Byrds. And then he's gone.

After the final half of the night's lineup concluded (yes, somebody had to follow that maelstrom), there was an after-party. The folksinger Maria Muldar asked Dylan if he would like to dance. He responded, "I'd dance with you Maria, but my hands are on fire."[12] (An unchanged man said this.) Weeks after Newport, a dejected Seeger wrote that Dylan's performance was "some of the most destructive music this side of hell."[13] Jim Rooney, stage manager at Newport, wrote, "Hope had been replaced by despair, selflessness by arrogance, harmony by insistent cacophony."[14] Paul Nelson in *Sing Out* wrote that it was "a sad parting of the ways for many, including myself. I choose Dylan. I choose art."[15]

My hands are on fire. This side of hell. Hope replaced by despair. I choose art. Are these the words of people reacting to music because the sound quality was shitty?

No, this was an ideological break, a rupture of sound and belief in what was possible and what counted as good. But you know what's funny? I don't think Dylan meant to burn down the folk revival at Newport. Instead, he offered a reconciliation between the folk movement's belief in tradition, authenticity, and community, and pop's spontaneity, imagination, and individualism: that *there didn't need to be a reconciliation.* Electric pop music, rock 'n' roll, could be artistically significant, socially concerned, even political, and still be on the radio and still make you shake your ass. Dylan lobbied no arguments against folk music. If you wanted dulcimers and autoharps, then you could go right ahead. "Today there is no longer any pale of history," Danto writes in *After the End of Art*, describing the ideology of the Warhol-led pop art scene. "Everything is permitted."[16] That's what Dylan was saying onstage at Newport at roughly the same time as Warhol, essentially introducing the audience to the anything goes of postmodernism. This is something of what historian Benjamin Filene means, I think, when he writes that instead of rejecting folk music, Dylan "seemed to embrace *everything* as a potential influence"[17]—and as a potential outcome. New words, sounds, voices, postures, attitudes, and, as Danto says of pop, a more liberated and enjoyable way that people might live their lives: these were the unlimited possibilities created by Dylan's event.[18]

Dylan knew he was transgressing, but knew he was offering more, not less, possibility. "I did this very crazy thing," he would say later in 1965. "I didn't know what was going to happen, but they certainly booed, I'll tell you that."[19]

Badiou never suggests an event can't be *sensed* as it occurs; we just don't know exactly what it means yet, what newness it will create. This is because events happen on the boundary between the profane realm of everyday life and the cultural institution, a boundary characterized by turbulence and destabilized hierarchies. At the time, no one knows exactly what's going on except that decisions need to be made, sides need to be taken, opinions need to be voiced. Groys calls this the cultural exchange; more individualist, Badiou calls this the interpretative intervention. The arguing that went on after Newport '65 was precisely this, an exchange of interpretations, a naming of the event's value, a declaration about what values had shifted. It didn't take long. Folk music as it was? Done. I mean this in the way Danto means "the end of art": the end of a need to live out a certain story or narrative or myth or ideology in art. Folk music itself didn't end, but certain values that it represented, especially the authenticity of tradition, were rejected back into the profane. Other values, like the alliance of music and protest, were no longer its province alone.

The event cannot originate in institutions, but the hashing out of what it means usually is settled by the cultural archive. For Groys, there is no other way; innovation is an exchange over the boundary between the archive and the profane, but the archive alone determines what's new because it alone has the power to determine what lasts. Naming, the function of the interpretative intervention, has to be agreed upon to some extent. So maybe it's possible that the archive claims and interprets an event, this source of newness, and absorbs it through a complex cultural economy of exchange which valorizes a transgression, and that's how you end up with not only late-night TV cash-ins—"Remember the Sixties?"—but also an institutionally authorized rebel: Bob Dylan. It's how you end up with the most profane moment in the history of American popular folk music becoming the most sacred event in the history of rock 'n' roll.

On the Trail of the Buffalo—Terminals—Becoming

And *that* is what Dylan as an artist has been fighting against ever since: the sacralization of his greatest transgression. *Freeze-frozen in a secular temple*, a.k.a. the Rock and Roll Hall of Fame and Museum. (It sure looks like a secular temple.) The entire emotion of his wandering journey, his attempts to get away from the archive, is captured so precisely in *Chronicles* that it hurts. He's watching a jazz combo playing in a bar in San Rafael, California. The singer's style enlightens Dylan, who thinks to himself, "I used to do this thing."[20] What a brutal sentence. The event and its demand for new possibilities have tracked him just as much as the musicians he's inspired. As he tells the story in *Chronicles*—a hash of fiction and nonfiction, myth and history, all of it true—he finds the transformation he needs soon after that night in California on a stage in Locarno, Switzerland: "Now the energy was coming from a hundred different angles, completely unpredictable ones. ... If I ever wanted a different purpose, I had one. It was like I'd become a new performer, an unknown one in the true sense of the word."[21] In other words, he'd become an ordinary musician in the profane realm. The music theory lesson which follows having to do with the power of two, well, it might all be bullshit, really, but exaggerated or not, its truth is that a musician might find his way back to the core elements of music—its rhythms, noises, intuitions, variations—in order to find his way forward to something new.

The journey from there to *"Love and Theft"* is, as Jack Nicholson said of Dylan, a riot. At those 1991 Grammys, as the Gulf War played out on television, he completely unfinished "Masters of War," ripping it up with his crack touring band who were dressed like they'd just held up a bank in Chicago in 1934. He was already a couple years into what he offhandedly called the Never-Ending Tour, a ceaseless string of more than a hundred shows per year, every year, during which he experimented nightly on his own songs like a scientist. Nightly, he would also run through a few commonplace folk, blues, country, and early rock 'n' roll songs that had once been his language. Now they belonged to no one and he was trying to get them back. Reflecting on the bootleg *Golden Vanity* and its collection of folk ballads Dylan performed live 1988–1992, Greil Marcus writes how "these songs appear ... not as culture at all, but as some sort of contradiction, anomaly, or disruption, coming out of nowhere: speech without context, a foreign language"[22]—which sounds like the beginning of an event. Nothing sounds as foreign as Dylan's performance of "Eileen Aroon" in Englewood, Colorado, in June 1988: here he is at his own personal apogee, "scattered far" like one of the chieftains in the song, sounding utterly alone as beside him G.E. Smith adds a few licks and redundant strums.

In the vast black cave before him—Dylan must hear it all—voices chatter, whistle, scream, and laugh.

Haunted by the long shadow of his own event, Dylan's immersion into archaic-sounding blues idioms and modal folk ballads allowed him to disremember it. *You think I was a big deal? How about "Trail of the Buffalo"?* I caught Dylan's act in Akron, Ohio around this time, and maybe it was during "Trail of the Buffalo," a.k.a. "The Hills of Mexico," that he appeared so withdrawn it was clear he was playing for himself most of all, trying to figure something out. But while intervening on his own event, these performances also continued the same argument he'd made in 1965–1966 that "everything is possible," which includes the possibility of constant, significant renewal. "You have to realize you're constantly in a state of becoming," Dylan would say years later in the documentary *No Direction Home*, and though he never explained when he realized this truth, I think he's intuited it his whole life.[23]

Those ancient folk ballads and American blues songs formed the basis for *Good As I Been to You* (1992) and *World Gone Wrong* (1993), spare and foundational recordings on this journey back that featured just Dylan, his guitar, and his harmonica. They're also the spine of the rollicking, loose Supper Club shows from 1993, two nights with two sets each, Dylan accompanied by a full and mainly acoustic band; the shows were meant to be used for MTV's *Unplugged* but they were ditched, naturally, because Dylan still had a habit of ditching his best work. Four years later, *Time Out of Mind*. Here's an album so unified in mood and philosophy that it sounds like a decree. Even though they were recorded in January 1997, five months before Dylan's brush with death from a life-threatening heart condition called pericarditis, songs like "Love Sick" and "Cold Irons Bound" and "Highlands" collectively sound like an operation performed by the artist on his own spirit. Dylan was fifty-six but he sounded twenty years older.

That all of this happened while Dylan was essentially living on the road cannot be stressed enough. Touring relentlessly, he found audiences who were neutral enough that he could experiment on them. The shows became ordinary, the job of the troubadour, not spectacles of nostalgia—and if they were spectacles of nostalgia (undoubtedly, for some, they were), then that gave him just the right amount of resistance to work against. Like I said, this was the profane realm, the ordinary and everyday environment far removed from the archive.

But musical performance is not exactly ordinary, either; its heightened attention to the moment is not how we normally go about our lives, even for a musician. The intensity of a ninety-minute set is really unlike anything else. Also, Dylan was still Dylan, and even if he had receded into the profane realm, in that realm he was still Bob Dylan. It makes sense, then, that the stage is a place where the profane and the cultural archive meet—a terminal. Like the airport, train, or bus terminal, the performative space of the terminal is an in-between site where values are exchanged, where directions change, where destination is desired but never guaranteed. Performers pass through just like their audiences. The terminal is more volatile than the cultural archives, but more orderly and more intense than everyday life in the profane realm. This is essentially what Groys means by the boundary, but a terminal strikes me as a more specific way to name the empty space described by Springsteen, a space where something tangible is manifested, where everything is in a state of flux, and then it all recedes and the space becomes empty again, like an airport in the middle of the night.

Dylan had to get back on the road and play in those terminals in order to put himself in a position where he had something to prove, which is the position of musicians in the profane realm. Nothing else puts you in a state of flux and ordinary living as traveling long stretches of highway. Even three hours on I-70 through the flatlands of western Ohio and eastern Indiana are enough to remind you that, no matter how much trouble you've caused in the past, a lot of people don't care.

Song and Dance Man—Wrinkly Reprobates Tip Their Caps—Negative Adaptation

So there was Bob Dylan on the cover of *"Love and Theft"*: thin, almost gaunt, haunted but self-possessed, looking younger than sixty, and looking, frankly, like *he* didn't care about his past, either. He was just a working musician now.

In the songs on *"Love and Theft"* Dylan sings as if his slippery phrasing is the most ordinary thing in the world. He had become what he wanted to be from the beginning, what he had prophesized in a December 1965 interview:

> REPORTER: Do you think of yourself primarily as a singer or a poet?
> DYLAN: Oh, I think of myself more as a song and dance man, y'know.
> *Laughter.*
> REPORTER: Why?
> DYLAN: Oh, I don't think we have enough time to really go into that.[24]

As a song and dance man with a hefty dash of the old bluesman thrown in, he sounded like he'd rediscovered the kid in him, too, the Chaplin, the rascal. There was an urgent and lusty quality in Dylan's voice, lyrics, and music. *"Love and Theft"* is his bawdiest, funniest, and most profane album since *Highway 61 Revisited*. There are classic blues double entendres, like "I'm short on gas, my motor's starting to stall," from "Summer Days." There are wild images, including the exhortation "Jump into the wagon, love/Throw your panties overboard!" in the middle of the disaster in "High Water (for Charley Patton)." There are flagrant absurdities, like the woman in "Honest With Me" who has "a face like a teddy bear." (A compliment? A put-down?) The writer Nadine Gordimer once observed that "the violent upsurge of sexual desire in the face of old age is the opposition of man to his own creation, death."[25] The wrinkly reprobates in Dylan's songs tip their caps to Death. Skipping town, living on the roads of the profane realm, performing in the terminals, and often wearing white Nudie suits and looking more Hank Williams Sr. than any of Hank's offspring, Dylan claimed the characteristics of those places—mobility, change, adventure, but also inconsequence, imagination, sex, and humor. All of which we associate with youth.

This was not the role the cultural archive had written for him: the elder-statesman-sort-of-a-savior hero who was always profound and socially concerned. The stoic, lonely resistance to death in *Time Out of Mind* absolutely fit the role expected of an older Dylan. That album is about enduring the sensation of being lost, of fading away and out of cultural memory; it would have been a fitting end to Dylan's career in the eyes of some, I bet, and at the time it sounded to me like a slow stop, a graceful acceptance. With gleeful indignation, and with Dylan playing the old man who would go down swinging in more ways than one, *"Love and Theft"* hurls eggs at the institutions of the cultural archives and speeds away. But even that he took a step further. By weaving together old forms, old language, old music, he complicated what a song and dance man could be: serious, corny, ambiguous, blunt, horny, spry, entertaining, and prophetic. There is nothing socially uplifting on *"Love and Theft,"* nothing redemptive or political in the ways that were expected of him. The album sounds new because it voices dissent. He dares to enjoy himself, to turn the resistance to death into exuberance and outright defiance. So many performances on *"Love and Theft"* are swift, agile, like the chugging "Summer Days" or the fleet-footed "Floater (Too Much to Ask)" or the switch-offs between an ambling rhythm and a jittery two-step in "Cry a While." This is dancing music, made better with a partner. Dylan's transgression at age sixty was, to some extent, simply enjoying himself.

His transformation into the song and dance man was successful enough that, by 2002, the consecrated story of his past could be lampooned by his stage manager Al Santos' spoken introduction to every show, more or less as follows:

> Ladies and gentlemen, please welcome the poet laureate of rock 'n' roll. The voice of the promise of the '60s counterculture. The guy who forced folk into bed with rock. Who donned makeup in the '70s and disappeared into a haze of substance abuse. Who emerged to find Jesus. Who was written off as a has-been by the end of the '80s, and who suddenly shifted gears releasing some of the strongest music of his career beginning in the late '90s. Ladies and gentlemen, Columbia recording artist: Bob Dylan![26]

This parody, based on a live review in the *Buffalo News*, is accurate without being true. That was the point of using it. Those things happened, but Dylan now had the verve to go past them, or at least try to go past them each night onstage and make the story seem as ridiculous as it sounds. In its place was the potential that any night could be new since it was a different night, a different stage in a different town. "The new ... is always possible again," Groys writes in *On the New*, "since the boundary with respect to which it is defined is new again every time—independently of the innovations that preceded it."[27]

Dylan's revision and expansion of the song-and-dance-man role is what Groys calls a "negative adaptation" of the cultural tradition. The artist's work connects to some element of the tradition, i.e. the song and dance man, then flips it, makes it profane, i.e. a horny old man. If it's good enough, this act forces the approval of what was formerly considered worthless. For Groys, negative adaptation *is* innovation, and he might as well be talking about *"Love and Theft"* when he writes:

> Innovation accordingly means a strategy that links a positive to a negative continuation of the tradition in such a way as to formulate both the continuity and the break with the greatest possible clarity and intensity. The work of art thus becomes, for a moment, the locus in which hierarchical differences disappear, traditional value oppositions lose their validity, and the power of time—in the guise of a contrast between the valuable past and valueless present and future—is overcome. This gives rise to the experience of being outside time, of ecstatic delight over a realized utopia, of freedom and magic omnipotence, which accompanies the successful, that is, radically innovative cultural act.[28]

The clear and intense break was Dylan's revaluation of rock 'n' roll's orientation toward youth on *"Love and Theft"* and in the live shows which followed. He dared people to believe that an aging musician could create wild music worth talking about, music that was neither timeless nor a nostalgic lesson in universalities that the young folks had better sit down and learn, but instead, music that was rowdy, performances that were urgent for the performer himself, not as history, but as life being lived. The continuity, then, was this new tradition Dylan created, the possibility that any artist over fifty, sixty, and seventy could keep moving, keep changing, and keep becoming.

That said, while *"Love and Theft"* thrives, it isn't an event. At best it's an event for music and absolutely an event for Dylan's career, which matters a great deal. Even if Dylan recalibrated the expectations and allowances for what older musician could do within certain audiences and communities, for other audiences he continued to be a gravel-voiced old man playing outdated music. For many of my college students, he's a novelty, a wild raccoon someone let onto the stage of the American spectacle. But even if *"Love and Theft"* isn't an event, it is potential enacted, an embodiment of the possibility of the new. That's the gamble in the eyes of the man on the album's cover. It is an argument for art—*I choose art*—and art's transgressive powers of invention. A person whose back is against a wall might hear in *"Love and Theft"* a voice saying with a wink, *You have to get creative. There is no jam you can't wiggle out of with enough grease.* If you're unhappy with who you are, be someone else.

Make it up.

The Archive Strikes Back—A Trial Begins—Strangers Trespass—Objects of Fear

Ever since the 2003 exposé of Dylan's so-called plagiarism, I've always taken a perverse pleasure in his most vociferous critics' shock and disdain. My pleasure comes from Dylan coercing people, mainly those within the cultural archives (including myself), into confronting and explaining what we think art, including popular music, should be. His transgressions—and they are transgressions, though not plagiarisms—forced easy and usually wrong assumptions about artistic honesty, authenticity, authorship, and history out into the open.

Here's what happened. Although he'd been crafting creative adaptations for years—there are countless examples, including "Blowin' in the Wind," which uses the melody of the spiritual "No More Auction Block"—Dylan apparently went too far by lifting phrases from Junichi Saga's novel *Confessions of a Yakuza*. Saga didn't seem too bothered, saying, "Please say hello to Bob Dylan for me because I am very flattered and very happy to hear this news," and asking only that our lyrical yakuza add a note to further pressings of the album.[29] (He didn't.) The floodgates opened. It was discovered that, among other things, Dylan had appropriated a famous line from *The Great Gatsby* on "Summer Days," which may be about the novel. Whole song structures are lifted: "Sugar Baby" is built on the 1928 weeper "The Lonesome Road," and "Floater (Too Much to Ask)" borrows and speeds up the not-exactly-original melody of "Snuggled On Your Shoulder." (If only Dylan had used that title!) Most of these are buried fragments of American culture that no one today would immediately recognize; no one seemed to miss them much, except maybe Dylan. It was the density and breadth of his recombinations that seemed to offend his detractors, but their breathless responses revealed, too, that they felt betrayed. As early as 1967, the rock critic Ellen Willis wrote, "Many people hate Bob Dylan because they hate being fooled."[30] Well, he'd fooled them again. Dylan's stature in 2003 and the success of *"Love and Theft"* fueled this sense of betrayal, no doubt, and it only got worse after more research discovered that the critically acclaimed 2006 album *Modern Times* contained more thievery of musicians as diverse as Memphis Minnie, Bing Crosby, and the Stanley Brothers. New Mexico deejay Scott Warmuth identified lines that had been lifted from the Civil War-era poet Henry Timrod, after which we all pretended to know who that was.[31]

Dylan was a marked man. Some critics defended him, like the *New York Times*' Jon Pareles, who wrote that Dylan had always created "information collages," which is a mechanical way of putting it.[32] Others struck a more moderate tone. There was a rich, almost melancholic sense of confusion in an op-ed by folksinger Suzanne Vega in which she struggled to come to terms with Dylan's larceny. Claiming that it wasn't part of the folk process (it is), she wondered if the bard possessed a "photographic memory" and more or less couldn't help himself. Finally she settled on his public persona: "He's never pretended to be an academic, or even a nice guy. He is more likely to present himself as, well, a thief. Renegade, outlaw, artist. That's why we are passionate about him."[33] The idea that he might not actually be what he presents himself to be, especially when he writes songs, doesn't come up.

The combination of Dylan's savior glow and his signification of Rock's transformation into Real Art via the events of 1965–1966 have fueled both sides of the debate. Alexander T. Deley in *Dissident Voice* claims Dylan's methods "reduced him in stature" (good one) since "[i]ntellectual and artistic honesty remain some of the most important features within a free society," as if, by plagiarizing, Dylan had weakened democracy around the world.[34] Like Deley, scholar Edward Cook accuses Dylan of being "lazy," as though weaving together quotations from disparate centuries and cultures into a four-minute song, as Dylan does on *Modern Times*' "Nettie Moore," is a piece of cake.[35] Their indignant passion is matched by Warmuth's spiritual passion. Using digital search engines like Google Books to uncover the appropriations and semi-fictions in *Chronicles*—hello, Sun Pie!—Warmuth has set out on a quest to discover, in his words, Dylan's "Da Vinci Code," as if it might unveil secrets equal in stature to some hidden truth about the life of Jesus Christ. "He tells you plenty about himself on the surface," Warmuth said in a 2014 interview, "but what's going on beneath the surface is even more fascinating."[36] The positive Warmuth and the negative Deley are both chasing the same white whale, the essence of Bob Dylan, as if that's what art is supposed to do. And yet, in all of this criticism and pursuit, very few ask *why* Dylan might have transgressed and what he might have intended to say.

Look, it's there in the title: *"Love and Theft."* If you push a little, every song on the album is a trap door that drops you into an American past filled with racism and stolen identities. Placing the album title in quotation marks, Dylan made obvious his debt to Eric Lott's book, *Love and Theft: Blackface Minstrelsy and the American Working Class*. As historian Sean Wilentz and others have pointed out, Dylan was continuing the long-standing folk and minstrel tradition of lifting song structures and lyrics from older works, a process put to use by Dan Emmett when he wrote or appropriated or stole "Dixie." For better and worse, a bit of thievery was always the method of the minstrel, a method used to entertain, to keep a crowd, and to make a buck. For Wilentz, Dylan is a postmodern magpie who "steals what he loves and loves what he steals."[37] Dylan uses a traditional method to expose tradition, specifically the American tradition, to acknowledge the complexity of the forbidden, secret adoration of Black American culture by whites, an adoration that was corrupted by a racialized need for power into blackface minstrelsy.

This relationship between power, race, and music isn't relegated to the distant past, either. You can hear it in any song from *"Love and Theft"* really, but take just one example: "Tweedle Dee and Tweedle Dum." As the jalopy swerves down the road, the circular intro riff and the chugging rhythm and the syncopated guitar part in the verses are all undoubtedly lifted directly from "Uncle John's Bongos," a 1961 single by the country duo Johnny and Jack perhaps best known for their 1954 version of "Goodnight Sweetheart, Goodnight"—which was an R&B number written by Calvin Carter and James "Pookie" Hudson and first performed by Hudson's doo-wop group the Spaniels in the same year. Warmuth argues that "Tweedle Dee and Tweedle Dum" bears a serious debt to 1960s folk revivalists the New Lost City Ramblers, which is true, but ending the story there whitewashes the history Dylan weaves into his album.[38] If you're going to tell American history truthfully, you've got to acknowledge the constant transgressive innovation within it, a constant dialogue between Black *and* white, love *and* theft. Throughout history, someone always has been trespassing, listening in on music they weren't supposed to hear, loving what they steal and stealing what they love.

This is the tradition of artistic theft, and it's Dylan's game. In a contentious and fun 2012 interview for *Rolling Stone*, after Mikal Gilmore pushes Dylan on the subject of mortality in his newest album at the time, *Tempest*, Dylan refers him to folk songs like "Frankie and Johnny" and "Delia," then snarls that he "can name you a hundred songs where everything ends in tragedy. It's called tradition, and that's what I deal in. Traditional, with a capital T—

> Maybe people have to have a simplistic way of identifying something, if they can't grasp it properly—use some term that they think they can understand, like mortality. Oh, like, 'These songs must be about mortality. I mean, Dylan, isn't he an old guy? He must be thinking about that.' You know what I say to that horseshit? I say these idiots don't know what they're talking about. Go find somebody else to pick on.[39]

This is the opposite of Welch's claims about *Time (The Revelator)* being personal. Where some might assume autobiography, and for whatever personal connections he must have to the songs, Dylan works from American cultural tradition so that the songs will reflect back onto and implicate the listener. (In a previous interview with Gilmore, Dylan responded to a similar question about mortality regarding *Time Out of Mind* by saying, "I didn't see any one critic say: 'It deals with *my* mortality'—you know, his *own*."[40] Touché.) So while Dylan's recombination of old materials says something about the past, its emphasis is really on the present. And not just Dylan's present: ours. If artistic theft in the service of newness *is* our national tradition, then we are implicated in the thievery. We always have been, we just don't like to admit it. We don't like to admit there's a profane element within what is valorized by the cultural archive, or that we put it there. Dylan's transgression attempts to force the recognition of what has been deemed by the archives as profane, even though it's always been part of that archive's claimed tradition. What's more, it forces us to ask if those intimate and complex relations between race and music are still going on, and if perhaps we take them for granted.

In the entirety of the discussion of Dylan's so-called plagiarism or not-plagiarism, no one has asked if we, as a culture, have done anything wrong. If we might be a bit misguided, even ignorant. If we are the problem. If, perhaps, we haven't come so far from the romantic ideal of the lone individual of exceeding merit or genius as we like to think. Our focus has been entirely on Dylan. To my knowledge, no one has pinned down Larry Campbell or Charlie Sexton, the two guitarists who played on "Tweedle Dee and Tweedle Dum," and asked which one of them agreed to play the riff from "Uncle John's Bongos" note-for-note. No one has petitioned Columbia Records. Furthermore, no one has asked if perhaps we should have immediately recognized Dylan's recombined materials since they're all supposed to be part of our great American cultural heritage which, like that one reviewer said of Black string band music, is at the tips of our fingers thanks to the internet. Right? But if Dylan had given us a pop quiz, we'd flunked. What you hear mixed among the objections and cries of plagiarism is embarrassment and resentment. I'm no different: the quote from *The Great Gatsby* wasn't obvious to me the first handful of times I heard "Summer Days," and that's a little embarrassing. But how strange it would be to hold Dylan accountable for what I've forgotten.

For many, Dylan's so-called plagiarism remains his trial, confirming that many of us still believe, or in bad faith insist upon, the notion of the authentic artist as one who comes up with his work from nothing, or from divine inspiration.

But what if it's our trial, and what if Dylan meant for it to be?

The oldness of Dylan's methods is not as important as the historical situation in which he used them and the revaluation he forced by making us hear ghosts and see ourselves in them. Dylan's recombinations reveal our suspicions of the artist and of art—that in seducing us, tricking us, they might get ahead of us, destabilize us, prove our values to be wrongheaded, expose that our own cultural tradition has become unknown to us, unrecognized: profane.

Art's profanity stokes its power. I consider Dylan's actions to be violations of cultural laws; I believe Dylan willfully transgressed; that's what artists do. The purposeful act of transgression is a triumph of the artist's freedom over cultural permission, especially when the transgression sounds so damn good. In *On the New*, Groys writes that "[t]he new is a new object of fear, a new danger, a new valorized, dangerous profane."[41] *"Love and Theft"* and Dylan's transgressions became, in their way, new objects of fear. The fear that we and our country are not so simple or innocent as we think. The fear that we don't really know ourselves. The fear that the truly new, the greatest innovation, must always be a transgression.

Tap into that and you just might win yourself a Nobel Prize for Literature.

3

The Problem of Knowing Too Much: Meta-Rock and the Anxiety of Influence

A Reviled Species Emerges—
The Meadowlands—Meta-Rock

Q: How many indie bands does it take to screw in a light bulb?
A: *Never mind, you've probably never heard of them.*

Sometimes I let myself think that the hipster was conjured by the Wrens on their 2003 album, *The Meadowlands*, in a single lyric from "Everyone Chooses Sides": "I'm the best seventeen-year-old ever." As if they spoke the words and magically there appeared a bearded guy in a striped tank top and skinny jeans in front of a food truck. He might have emerged all at once from the song, his brain from its crunchy opening chords, his heart from the martial drumbeat, his eyes opening with the first strike of a glockenspiel. But that's unfair to the Wrens and *The Meadowlands*, which is gut-wrenchingly honest about getting divorced, going nowhere, being broke, and being a band—specifically, a band that gained some ground with its 1996 record *Secaucus* and then floundered for years in a dispute with its record label and the search for a new label.

The Meadowlands is an example of how, by admitting to the self-consciousness and anxiety of being musicians in a belated musical culture, a band might work through the trap of "it's all been done before" into something new by way of a strategy called meta-rock: rock 'n' roll about rock 'n' roll.[1] In the most general sense, meta-rock's history is the history of the genre itself, dating back to songs like Chuck Berry's "Rock and Roll Music" and "Johnny B. Goode," Elvis Presley's "Jailhouse Rock," and Danny and the Juniors' "Rock and Roll Is Here to Stay." First-wave meta-rock proclaimed the genre's importance and longevity. By the 1970s, a second wave of meta-rock consisted of songs like Grand Funk Railroad's "American Band" and Bob Seger's "Old Time Rock 'n' Roll," tunes that surfed on a resurgence of rock 'n' roll nostalgia. So along comes the 1990s and another revival of meta-rock, but this was ironic to the point of being parody. Bands like Archers of Loaf, Pavement, and Sebadoh (especially their hysterical "Gimme Indie Rock") inverted the typical egotism of meta-rock with self-critique, self-loathing, and absurdity in order to overcome the weight of the past: the cultural, mythical, generational, corporatized, mediated, visualized, and value-soaked history of rock 'n' roll culture. It was as if by owning up to their latecomer status, they could more honestly try to make something of their own, maybe even something new.

Like their immediate predecessors and peers, the Wrens answered the sopping wet weight of rock culture's history on *The Meadowlands* with a ton of cynicism. On "This Boy Is Exhausted," the band goes from "triple guessing" every song to the brief release and promise of "once in a while ... play[ing] a show that makes it worthwhile." "Hopeless" could be a salty letter to an ex, or to the band's former label. But the summit of their self-interrogation is that verse in "Everyone Chooses Sides" where Charles Bissell's vocals sneer back at him in the mirror. Broke, approaching 40, he's nonetheless got the hip judiciousness and cool lifestyle of an advanced teenager. The most scathing moment is actually the line, "We're losing sand, a Wrens-ditch battle plan," the band equating itself with desperation and futility. But the music! It's desperate, sure, but it's not at all futile. With guitars so distorted they sound deep-fried, a glockenspiel flittering around, and a pulsating electro-riff under the beat, "Everyone Chooses Sides" keeps raising its stakes into the chorus, evaporates into a breakdown centered on falsetto vocals, then veers back into noise and what sounds like fifteen different guitars. Rock 'n' roll isn't dead here, even if, nearly at the end of the album, the band sounds like it's tying the rope to hang itself with. And then the song cuts off, kicking away the stepladder.

Usually, third-wave meta-rock of the 1990s had a cleverness that let the singer and the band off their own hook—see: most of Pavement's 1994 *Crooked Rain, Crooked Rain*, songs like "Range Life" and "Cut Your Hair"—but *The Meadowlands* is self-anointed American apostasy, the aged hipster searching for courage and coming up empty in a broken-down New Jersey wasteland that stands in for all of America. In fact, *The Meadowlands* can convince you that American rock 'n' roll is nothing more than a fraudulent myth, a place where men never mature, where they fail at relationships and wallow in depression and poverty. But by God, they're in bands!

A Poet Misreads—The Past Looms above Us—The Triumphant Failure of the New

Meta-rock is a way to work the problem of the past and what the literary critic Harold Bloom in 1973 called "the anxiety of influence." In his book of the same name, Bloom essentially argued that not only is anxiety creative and a way toward the new, it's the only way. His thesis is deceptively simple, easily dramatized. Say an ambitious younger poet reads the work of a well-known precursor, or a young songwriter listens to Bob Dylan. Although the young musician experiences a sense of belatedness or inferiority due to the precursor's culturally celebrated talent, she is willful and imaginative, and because of this, when she reads the lyrics to "Desolation Row," to some extent she *misreads* it. This is good. This is what Bloom calls the *clinamen*, or the "swerve," a term adopted from the Roman philosopher Lucretius' theory that atoms fall in a straight line but sometimes slightly change direction, and, *voila*, newness comes into the world. The young songwriter's misreading is a slight yet artistically significant misinterpretation in which her creative mind reads, or hears, what it likes. If our young poet is a "strong" poet, her strong misreading "clear[s] imaginative space" for herself as an artist.[2] A "really strong poet … can only read [herself]," writes Bloom.[3] You might say she steals what she loves and loves what she steals.

The anxiety of influence has not been banished, though. In fact, the anxiety only begins now, with her misreading and the crucible it creates; now she must make something from it, something new. A wannabe sits around and talks about the great songs he's going to write. The real artist begins by ripping off Dylan or Gillian Welch or the Wrens if that's what it takes—she gets to work. She must, because the implication of Bloom's theory is clear: unless the poet overcomes this *agon* (conflict), she will never create the new. Our young songwriter then uses what Bloom calls six "revisionary ratios." Each is a kind of misreading put to use: in *tessera*, for example, the poet puts together the left-behind fragments of her predecessor but turns them into something different, while *kenosis* humbles the old *and* the young poet, clears the board, and allows for something new.[4]

Bloom's archetypically masculine contest still has something wonderfully liberating within it: the best art, *new* art, comes from an initial failure. Not from getting it right, but from getting it wrong. And this is the method of the greats! For every poet, argues Bloom, the inevitable gaps of understanding create the possibility of the new in the shadow of the revered. "A poem is not an overcoming of anxiety," writes Bloom, "but is that anxiety." The crucial thing is that "poetic influence need not make poets less original; as often it makes them more original, though not necessarily better."[5]

Meta-rock in the 1990s responded to an anxiety of influence, but while individual influences and specific musicians appeared from song to song—"Gimme Indie Rock" lists the Velvet Underground and Pussy Galore, among others—generally this meta-rock reacted to the entire influence of rock 'n' roll culture and history. For Bloom, Shakespeare looms over us all; for those who came of age after punk, take your pick: the Beatles, Dylan, Janis, Jimi, the Velvet Underground, Patti Smith, the Sex Pistols. And that's a pretty short list. The massive culture of popular music had already become institutionalized, filmed, box-setted, and written about voluminously in the popular press, the niche rock press, and even in academic circles. No surprise, musicians who grew up in the 1980s keenly felt the burden of rock's *achievement*. Third-wave meta-rock answered this anxiety first by admitting that when you stacked Woodstock '69 (e.g., The Who) against Woodstock '94 (e.g., Porno for Pyros), the 1990s came up short. But it was also deeply suspicious of the glorified and commodified past. Even grunge, which musically tapped into the pleasure and ambition of 1970s arena rock, grounded itself with punk cynicism. Pearl Jam's "Spin the Black Circle" may have been a thrashing ode to vinyl records, but it also sounded like it was about shooting smack. The utter negation of meaning combined with rage-filled music gave us another meta-rock shard you may have heard of, "Smells Like Teen Spirit," in which Kurt Cobain turns boredom and inarticulacy into pure sound. As the group of twentysomethings in the song find that their confidence, talents, and togetherness keep caving in, Nirvana's music pummels you (especially in live recordings). This tension between despair and propulsive energy doesn't mark all meta-rock, only that which edged toward being new.

Archers of Loaf's meta-rock aesthetic balanced the witty snark of Pavement with a burly hybrid of punk muscle and angular post-punk guitar. Like their North Carolina neighbors Superchunk, the band sometimes went full bastard on the volume, painting a fearsome noise thick as tar. The physicality and endorphins counteracted all the self-obsession and worrying in lead singer Eric Bachmann's weary voice and the chirps, whimpers, and shrieks Eric Johnson pulled out of his guitar, often at odd times and in quarter-note gaps, like he'd been hung out to dry. From their debut album *Icky Mettle* (1993) to 1995's full-length *Vee Vee*, and to a lesser extent on the following year's *All the Nation's Airports*, Archers told sharp but ambiguous stories about life in the local music scene and the underground nation of sound guys, college-radio hits, guests lists for two-dollar shows, indie-rock sexism (see "Plumbline"), and battles over authenticity, as on "Slow Worm" when Bachmann sings, "And everybody's tired of the noise that you make/And everybody's tired of the voice you're faking." Their most concentrated blast of meta-rock is *Archers of Loaf Vs. The Greatest of All Time*, a five-song EP about indie-rock circa 1994, a guitar-detonating battle between the crooked world of shady A&R reps and the hope for a shred of musical integrity.

For some, meta-rock signaled the end of the new, an expression of 1990s indie's "solipsistic and clichéd" character, as Michael Azerrad put it, a "tactical retreat" that possessed a "suffocating insularity," all of which are arguably traits of meta-rock.[6] In *Retromania*, Simon Reynolds writes, "Drifting off into its own self-referential universe, record-collection rock"—basically a more nuanced, sound-based meta-rock—"made music into something separated off from real life," which is true only if making music and listening to it is not real life.[7] I hear stoicism in meta-rock, a kind of grudging defeatism met with the stubbornness of continuing on even if the music isn't by some standards new. So often we think of the new as a triumph; in Bloom's theory, it's a victory over the old. Meta-rock as practiced by Archers of Loaf, Pavement, and the Wrens doesn't have victories. Robert Christgau once wrote of *All the Nation's Airports*, Archers' penultimate studio album, that "basically what it gives off is intelligence, as a given you live with rather than a goal you achieve."[8] A reaction to knowing too much, meta-rock around the millennial turn assumed the same thing about the limitations of newness, but in flashes, and historically, this is what made it new.

Tracked by Hipsters in the 2000s—Boy Songs— Freed by Self-Condemnation

Reynolds briefly mentions Bloom's theory in *Retromania*, but argues that "from the mid-1980s onwards, gradually but with increasing momentum," musicians' desire for originality "changed into an impulse to create something very much heard before, and moreover to do it immaculately, accurate in every last detail …."[9] This bewildering claim either ignores or discounts bands like the Pixies, R.E.M., Dinosaur Jr., Sonic Youth, Archers of Loaf, and, for God's sake, Bikini Kill. (And what about hip-hop?) Like me, Reynolds sees the anxiety of influence as a parallel to an increasing awareness of music, but Reynolds argues this knowledge has led to the end of anxiety, the end of artists trying to be original. Hands are thrown up in the air. *To hell with it, we're derivative.*

Reynolds implies that the disappearance of the anxiety of influence has led to more "weak" artists, i.e. "weak" poets, but for that to be true, the anxiety has to have disappeared. And indeed, Reynolds argues that in a post-postmodern world wherein we don't even cite our sources, "[c]oncepts like the anxiety of influence or the pathos of belatedness … are irrelevant."[10] In this version of the story, we have defeated influence, or influence has defeated us. In any case, there is no *agon*, no anxiety, just a lot of playful, nerdy remixing of the past. Bloom's argument is that this aesthetic Oedipal struggle has existed since the Renaissance. Did postmodernism sweep it away in the matter of, what, thirty years? Or have the nuances of the situation simply changed?

Rock music in the twenty-first century doesn't support the claim that the anxiety of influence is extinct. The Wrens' *The Meadowlands* is one example. Turn to another: Listen to the radio static that may be a guitar, the train rumbling that turns out to be drums, the total cacophony that swells and evaporates into the precise, Nintendo-bounce synth riff that carries "Losing My Edge," LCD Soundsystem's 2002 single, on its journey into anxious absurdity. "The kids are coming up from behind," says front man James Murphy over a multilayered cake of 1980s beats, crisp, cutoff, with manufactured echo. As the song unspools into the singer's paranoia that he's losing his status to all these damn hipster kids who know so much thanks to the internet, the sonic homages pile up, reaching further back before working their way forward: 1970s German electronic music, Suicide's drones, hip-hop, rave. Even Murphy's voice, deadpan, tired, looking for its pride, sounds like an homage to Jonathan Richman. LCD Soundsystem's self-titled 2005 debut, with its mashup of punk and EDM, was a critique of taste, subculture, and influence, from "Daft Punk Is Playing at My House" to "Disco Infiltrator" to "Beat Connection," which describes one of those everyone-has-their-arms-crossed nights at the club or bar: "Nobody's getting any touch/Everybody thinks it means too much."

Meta-rock didn't magically disappear after the millennial turn, though its capacity to be new never was (and never is) a given. On the flipside of Murphy's explicit anxieties, and entering into the realm of awful music, you had bands like Fall Out Boy and Panic at the Disco admiring themselves and rock culture in the mirror on early albums like, respectively, *From Under the Cork Tree* (2005) and *Pretty. Odd.* (2008). Panic at the Disco rips off the Beatles and Queen on the bombastic (it has chimes) "We're So Starving," explaining their absence from the scene—did somebody ask them to?—by saying they've been off writing songs and, in the process, apparently, studying "A Day in the Life." At least the song never pretends to be anything more than ridiculous. Emo band Fall Out Boy, on the other hand, tries to pass itself off as emotional and damaged but also witty, what with the long titles and all: "I Slept With Someone In Fall Out Boy and All I Got Was This Stupid Song Written About Me." Well, it *is* a stupid song. Obnoxious too. I imagine she might have responded, "Really, keep the song. Please." These two songs epitomize the way the critique of self, music culture, and history that I've called meta-rock can dissolve into juvenile self-flattery, but their glibness cannot hide how thoroughly terrified of trying to be new they are in the face of the rock 'n' roll that's preceded them.

Meanwhile, the 2000s saw the return of many indie rock bands from the previous decade-and-a-half who'd called it quits: the Pixies, Dinosaur Jr., Pavement, Archers of Loaf, Guided By Voices, and a bit later, Afghan Whigs and Sleater-Kinney, among many others. You heard whispers and snorts—you always will—that some of these bands were better left to mothballs, that they just needed the money, and that all those solo projects must have been failures so they were falling back on what they knew. Regardless, each of these bands had to confront, to varying degrees, the anxiety of their own influence on what had become of indie rock in the new millennium. Bloom's theory is oriented toward young poets, which betrays a myth about the new that we often take for truth: that it emerges from the young. And these folks weren't young anymore. While bands like Archers didn't have to contend with a Bob Dylan-sized impact on the cultural archive, they did have to wager that something new could come of their return.

At the Cat's Cradle in Carrboro, North Carolina in August 2011, thirteen years after what seemed like their final show on the same stage, a reunited Archers of Loaf has to find, of all things, their incompetency. The danger of a rock band coming out of retirement isn't that they're rusty, but that they've become too assured in their skill and too comfortable with what they know. The encyclopedia from which they draw has only gotten bigger, and if there aren't any new songs to play, then the band is very much at risk of doing something that's already been done before. And if a band can't escape everything it already knows about rock 'n' roll and tap into that rebellious, standing-on-a-fault line feeling, how can its audience?

On their home turf, Archers has every reason to relax. And yet: "We never knew it could be this way," bassist Matt Gentling says, giving the audience a little of the hyperactive comedic persona he always played during live shows. "I've never done this before," he adds, laughing before drummer Mark Price counts off the tempo, guitarist Eric Johnson plays the clown-car lead, and the band careens into "Lowest Part Is Free." The band sounds like they truly have never done this before—not that they're incompetent, but that this moment is a first. Throughout the Cat's Cradle performances captured in the documentary *What Did You Expect?* and the live album *Curse of the Loaf*, the band searches for the newness of the moment, the visceral performance that will resolve their tug-of-war between knowing too much and being honest about what they know. Knowing too much has always been a risk in rock 'n' roll, something you negotiate with, since for many of us, its pleasure is not-thinking and not-knowing. The intelligence Christgau said Archers lived with was true to a point, but they also fought against it, mocking the minor strains of fussy cleverness in their music with self-deprecation—"TONIGHT BINGO WITH ARCHERS OF LOAF" reads a cheap marquee at the start of the "Harnessed in Slums" video—and full-throttle energy.

For the Loaf, the only way to resist the nostalgia of consumerism and the passivity of being a slacker, both symptoms of the anxiety of influence, was to write your own mythology and put yourself into it. Maybe no song captures this as well as one song from *Vee Vee*, one of their best: "Greatest of All Time." A winking elegy for rock's mythos and its ruthless underside, the song begins with the drowning of "the front man of the world's worst rock 'n' roll band" by a giddy, drunk, stoned audience taking pleasure in his suckage. The song flips: now everyone's mourning a rock hero "blasted from a plane," standing by their radios to hear this falling angel give one final, great performance. In 1995, he was Kurt Cobain, dead in April 1994 of a self-inflicted gunshot blast to the head; he was also Buddy Holly, killed in a 1959 airplane crash, and the members of Lynyrd Skynyrd killed the same way in 1977. Who is he in 2011? Archers of Loaf? Or do they get drowned in the river? Either way, the song says, rock 'n' roll is a brutal life. You either die a loser or a martyr, mocked or worshipped, but as Bachmann repeats the song's odd, seemingly out-of-place mantra, "The underground is overcrowded," you start to wonder if the moral is this: any dead musician's absence means more room for the rest of us.

That the song surges toward its end on Bachmann's sandpaper vocals and the band's sheer force, tightening and then released, freed by this dark-as-hell story—well, it's an example good as any of how meta-rock can work: fighting through everything that's already known and taking a leap anyway.

New Theories of Everything Prompted by Guided By Voices Appreciation Night

Columbus, Ohio, December 2009—With his guitar bag slung over his shoulder and his frizzy three-pronged beard hanging midway down his chest, my buddy Eric Nassau approached me in the Treehouse's tree room, where the bands would play in the city's first-ever Guided By Voices Appreciation Night. Eric would be the lone folkie troubadour. And yes, there actually was a tree in the middle of the room. A silver maple.

"Bob Pollard's sitting in the corner," Eric said, nodding toward the back corner.

"Oh shit." I glanced around the tree. "And you're going first?"

"Yeah."

"Time to nut up or shut up," said our friend Thom, and Eric went off for a whiskey.

There is no greater meta-rock event than a tribute show, i.e. a rock show celebrating the original newness, the source, the font, if you will, of rock. (Or any other music. Columbus leans rock.) There's also no more pressure-packed a confrontation with influence than when the honoree of that tribute is camped around a table in the shadows with his brother and Nate Farley. Will you kneel, or like one of Bloom's warrior-poets, will take your predecessor's sword and make it your own? There's a well-deserved tendency to see a tribute show as a regressive or sentimental throwback, a sacrifice to the gods of nostalgia and lost innocence, but a good tribute show wants to do more than recall the past. It wants to motivate new discoveries. Those could entail a performer or listener finding something unexpected in a certain song like "Back to the Lake" or "Watch Me Jumpstart"—itself a tribute to renewal—but more generally a tribute show is an opportunity for musicians to exercise their license to imagine and figure out how their influences might yield new directions for their own music. A tribute show might valorize the past but it can also seize the opportunity for a different future.

Eventually, Eric approached the mic like a sacrificial lamb. I would find out later that he'd gone over to Pollard's table:

ERIC: Hey, I'm Eric, I'm going to be butchering your songs pretty soon.

POLLARD: Cool.

The rest of their conversation concerned the oddity of a German choir singing "Goldheart Mountaintop Queen Directory" and the strictly nonmonetary bets Pollard was placing with his brother Jim about which song would be played first, Bob having wagered on "Unleashed! The Large-Hearted Boy." Informed of Eric's choice, "Big Chief Chinese Restaurant," Jim Pollard approved, partly because he cowrote it.

After the bizarreness of hearing Eric nail the song—"Introducing the amazing Rockethead! You know what the deal is, dude! Excuse me, Napoleon …!"—the anxiety dissolved. With the help of local singers Miss Molly and Sean Woosley, who would close the night with his band, Eric's set had the ragtag appeal of a lot of tribute shows. It didn't get everything exactly right, but that wasn't the point, especially at a Guided By Voices Appreciation Night.

Apparently, we were not the first GBV tribute show to be graced by Bob Pollard's presence; he visited a similar show in Cincinnati and even appeared onstage at Heedfest, the annual salty salute to all things Voices in Dayton. (During that event, you can take a bus tour of important Voices sites.) All of this makes perfect sense: it's laid-back cool, winkingly egotistical in the same manner as Pollard's stage persona. The karate kicks and microphone twirling only worked because Pollard seemed like your next-door neighbor cranking up the Marshall on a Saturday afternoon.

Guided By Voices had always sounded newborn, forward-leaning, and with Pollard's onstage charisma and commands, the music had a prophetic quality: a prediction of what must someday happen, a claim that searching for the new was a dire necessity. The band's music rarely meta-rocked in terms of its lyrics, but in the music you could absolutely hear the wide and weird expanse of rock's history and a desire to find the burrowed-away spirit of invention and assertion that you hear in so many early rock 'n' roll records and underground performances that were "proto" before anyone called them that. Part of that spirit, though, is the anxiety of stepping forward without any handrails or guidebooks, working from the profane realm without institutional support. Musicians see an empty stage, a mic, and they decide to get on both. That's the risk that makes the thrill. Early Guided By Voices albums sounded like they'd already battled with those anxieties and chased the thrill anyway. That's why songs like "Over the Neptune/Mesh-Gear Fox," "Echos Myron," "Motor Away," "Don't Stop Now" sound prophetic, as if Pollard has been to the future and is now reporting back from just up ahead, standing, as he does in the video for "Motor Away," on the roof of a clunker in a varsity jacket and white jeans.

If a tribute show echoes the cultural pressure about the past, the voice that says, *You can't possibly do anything new*, it can also be a staging ground from which to work through everything you know, including the nihilistic belief that your actions will be meaningless, and to instead take the leap of performing anyway. Art has always required a certain amount of winging it. In an essay about Ralph Waldo Emerson, Mitchell Meltzer writes that Emerson, seeking a new national literature, understood the need for "a claim of authority that would somehow override the sheer arbitrariness of the naked fact of simply setting out ...." Additionally, "Emerson continually preached that the way to begin in the new United States was by means of a self-assertion amounting almost to prophecy."[11] A century later, the Christian theologian and existentialist Paul Tillich argues, in *The Courage to Be*, "Courage is the power of life to affirm itself *in spite of* [its own] ambiguity, while the negation of life because of its negativity is an expression of cowardice."[12] The *in spite of* is a critically important acknowledgment of the truth of life's essential characteristics and its historical conditions, and a crucial element, religious or secular, in the search for the new despite the overwhelming DON'T presented by the past's remnants in the present. If Bloom's warrior-poet seems heroic, it's because she faces down the ambiguity that comes from the anxiety of influence. The choice to write and perform is an affirmation of life in spite of that anxiety.

As local bands like Spd Gvnr, Bookmobile, and the Woosley Band picked up Guided By Voices' songs, they picked up that prophetic quality, that *in spite of* quality, and tried it on for a while to see how it fit. A tribute show can be seen as a meta-rock confrontation with influence's power to negate. In other words, the music performed at a tribute show examines and asserts its own continued generative power, its possibilities, in response to every voice that demands impossible originality, fraudulent authenticity, and ultimately, when such standards become too daunting, encourages silence. The tribute show is dialogic. Bakhtin was convinced that past meanings were instable, and while this can cause problems of interpretation, it also means there's a constant, maybe inevitable, potential for renewal. He wrote, "Nothing is absolutely dead; every meaning will have its homecoming festival."[13] At the Treehouse, that meaning was the courage to be. Talk about dialogic—*did I mention Bob Pollard was sitting in the corner of his own tribute show?* Not every tribute show will have its honoree drinking a beer in the shadows, of course, but the locality of Guided by Voices Appreciation Night mattered; it meant something that Guided by Voices is an Ohio band, and Bob Pollard a native of Dayton, which is less than an hour from Columbus. This is the positive aspect of indie rock localism, the plus side to the sniping and claustrophobia you hear in the Wrens and Archers' lyrics. Pollard's presence ended up being ordinary, which made the night ordinary and stripped away all the barriers of anxiety.

All meta-rock, including tribute shows, has the potential to clear space for the artist to create the new through the misreading of predecessors and the retrieval of potential from the cultural archive that curates it. Meta-rock can return that potential to the profane realm of everyday life and everyday musicians, forcing what has been recognized to become unrecognized.

4

Sounds Before Our Time: Replicating the Old to Make the New

> What has been will be again,
> what has been done will be done again;
> there is nothing new under the sun.
> Is there anything of which one can say,
> "Look! This is something new?"
> It was here already, long ago;
> it was here before our time.
> —ECCLESIASTES 1: 9–10

Perfect Southern Rock Sound Forever—Greenberg Gets Entrenched—The Swerve

All it takes is a second or two and the guitars in the Drive-By Truckers' "Let There Be Rock" call to mind the influential bands Patterson Hood name-checks later in the song: 1970s Southern rock legends Lynyrd Skynyrd, Molly Hatchet, and .38 Special. Aside from a certain amount of clarity and bite, it's the same sound. Just as Bloom's strong poet reads herself in her predecessors, the Truckers on their 2001 album *Southern Rock Opera* hear themselves in

Southern rock's belief in the power of big guitars, big riffs, and big solos. The inherent muscle of a Les Paul plugged into a Marshall stack. The twang of a Strat. *Chunk-a-chunk* rhythms. Guitar effects? How many you got? Flange, chorus, about ten different levels of distortion. Shredding isn't a dirty word here, either. On "Let There Be Rock," Mike Cooley's solo darts off, curls, and gives way to a unison duet with Hood's guitar that owns the song and could have been played in 1976.

In *Retromania*, Simon Reynolds writes, "At a certain point, music seemed to become disconnected from History and to reflect inwards on itself, on its own accumulated history," which, combined with his claim about immaculate accuracy from the mid-1980s onward, would certainly seem to apply to the Truckers' *Southern Rock Opera*.[1] The great laugher here is that, while this immaculate accuracy is being framed as a postmodern ideal, it sounds a bit like the art critic Clement Greenberg's definition of Modernism. Greenberg despised the novelty of Warhol's pop art, partly because it reflected the times rather than the permanent essence—the tradition—of self-critique he saw in Abstract expressionism and all truly Modern art and thought. "The essence of Modernism lies, as I see it," he wrote in 1965, "in the use of the characteristic methods of a discipline to criticize the discipline itself—not in order to subvert it, but to entrench it more firmly in its area of competence."[2] As Danto points out, Greenberg's ethos is one of "purity," less in a cultural sense than in terms of art's ideal subject: itself.[3] Like plenty of other modernist critics, Greenberg's fear was that art would cede to the impurity of the commodified market.

If we think of a genre like Southern rock as a discipline, we might ask, What are the Drive-By Truckers criticizing? In the trio of great albums they made between 2001 and 2004—*Southern Rock Opera*, then *Decoration Day* and *The Dirty South*—the Truckers complicate what Southern rock and being from the South mean: its mythologies, realities, and traditions of masculine, hard-drinkin', family-centered good-ol'-boys living in a working-class pastoral landscape ravaged by drugs, poverty, and racism. On *Southern Rock Opera*, the band confronts all of this through sound as much as words, though the album's concept puts the sounds into context. Six years after Archers' exploding plane in "The Greatest of All Time," the Truckers juxtaposed the myths and history of Lynyrd Skynyrd with an invented but parallel story of a young man who rises from adolescent ashes to become a rock god himself ... until *his* plane crashes. In a 2015 essay about the Confederate flag and Southern tradition, Hood wrote that *Southern Rock Opera* "wrestled with how to be proud of where we came from while acknowledging and condemning the worst parts of our region's history."[4] The pride is voiced in the band's unashamed, pitch-perfect Southern rock sound and forms, especially those loose, lazily syncopated rhythm guitar parts saturated in echo on "Days of Graduation," which approaches Neil Young levels of Les Paul-in-a-haunted-cave sound. "Plastic Flowers on the Highway" stretches that reverb-drenched echoing into something more sensual and fated, which is where the acknowledgment and condemnation starts to creep in. The album stares hard into the ways that working-class stoicism transforms into blasts of self-destructive violence. Even on a song like "Let There Be Rock," the band doesn't buy into any romanticized notions of glory. You can hear the resistance in the singers' voices. If Hood's rasp sounds skeptical, Cooley's twang sounds like it hasn't been impressed by anything since the Carter Administration.

Drive-By Truckers might be criticizing Southern rock, but they're not out to subvert it, and I think they could give a fig about the genre's competence. The meta-rock of *Southern Rock Opera* is far more personal since the band is from Alabama and Georgia, and for that reason, its only anxiety of influence concerns Southern culture. Unlike Archers of Loaf, the Wrens, or LCD Soundsystem, the Drive-By Truckers are trying to hold onto a tradition by rewriting it, struggling to belong to it on their own terms. In this way, they're a lot more like the Carolina Chocolate Drops. The ambiguities created between the past and present are, for the Truckers, a source of pain and conflict that emerges from the place and culture they call home—and still *want* to call home. This, as the Drops demonstrate, is how musicians try to create new traditions. *Southern Rock Opera* epitomizes the negative adaptation that depends on the sonic replication of obvious influences;

by putting them to work for a new purpose—and by complicating those influences, as the band does on "Let There Be Rock" by citing Blue Öyster Cult, Ozzy Osbourne, and, of course, AC/DC—they might force the cultural archive to adjust its values.

The problem of "retro" music in regards to the new seems simple: it replicates old sounds. Undoubtedly, since 2000, there's been plenty of music that lyrically may not be meta-rock but self-consciously *sounds* like music that has come before it, what Reynolds calls "record collector rock": the garage-rock revival of the Strokes and the White Stripes, followed closely by a new New Wave, bands like Interpol and, overseas, Franz Ferdinand; the old-time revival of *O Brother, Where Art Thou?*, countered by the freak-folk movement, itself a mash-up of late 1960s psychedelic and British folk; neo-soul typified by D'Angelo and Lauryn Hill, the Motown-inspired Sharon Jones and the Dap Kings, Alabama Shakes, and Nathaniel Rateliff and the Night Sweats, who sound like a Sam and Dave cover band. Each of these bands can sound like Greenberg's "entrenchment"; in their adherence to various traditions, drawing the past into the present, they seem only to tighten the grip of what those traditions mean. And yet, writing them off as unconcerned with originality, history, or newness seems suspiciously condescending.

Sometimes I wonder if the source of concern with retro sound, the mourning and skepticism that is the basis of Reynolds' book, is not the anxiety of influence or belatedness, but an anxiety about the scale of newness. We might call this the anxiety of the swerve, which brings us back to Bloom's use of the word *clinamen* and the philosopher Lucretius. It was more than 2,000 years ago in his long poem *On the Nature of Things* that Lucretius developed the theories of Epicurus and named the swerve in his attempt to describe how an atom's course might budge. This movement, said Lucretius, couldn't be controlled, so sit back and enjoy. Take that, Parmenides? Not really. For Lucretius and other atomists, newness was unremarkable since, as Michael North puts it, "[c]hange in this world is explained by the fact that configurations are always falling apart and being reassembled, as things die and are born again ...."[5] Which sounds like recombination. And recurrence. In fact, it sounds like, well, the nature of things in time and history.

Atoms and their swerving do allow for some degree of free will, argued Lucretius, but the question of newness remained. What could possibly be the significance of a slight budge in the course of an atom ... or a poem, or a musical genre? Quite a bit, it turns out. In his book *The Swerve*, historian Stephen Greenblatt describes how *On the Nature of Things* disappeared into history until it was found by one Poggio Bracciolini in 1417. This seemingly minor discovery, a swerve like one of Lucretius' atoms, changed the course of human history by articulating the blend of science and beauty that was the Renaissance, which begat the modern era, which begat you and me. "There were no heroic gestures," writes Greenblatt, "no observers keenly recording the great event for posterity, no signs in heaven or on earth that everything had changed forever."[6] And yet, everything did change, forever.

So it's possible that sounds which purposefully and explicitly replicate or mimic old sounds from the past, like the Drive-By Truckers' guitars, are nonetheless swerving in a way that might lead to something new. The crucial element here is history, that span in which things fall apart and come back together. If we only listen for the "things," the material, that is, the sounds and styles of music, then naturally they'll seem more repetitive than unique. Hell, just about all music today is marked by traces of the past, from the immediately recognizable chirring of a Vox organ to the harsh clamor of an early 1980s synthesizer. For all of Reynolds' concern with time in *Retromania*, the irony is that his book is obsessed by form and genre, by material and discipline, without much accounting for historical or cultural context outside of music itself. Without those contexts, music in the new millennium seems very repetitive indeed. But history and culture are always in flux; Lucretius' falling apart-reassembling meets Bakhtin's dialogistic homecoming and Groys' shifting cultural boundaries. The question still remains a matter of scale, the event as opposed to the swerve, a revolution in the cultural archive as opposed to an editing of a tradition, but a replicating, derivative sound can still be new if it makes some argument about its current moment, or if it makes some distinction between the present and the past.

Where there is critique, there is difference; where there is difference, the new is possible.

Do You Like the Eighties? *Flashdance*-Style Fonts? The Ferrari Testarossa? Neon Violet? Technological Alienation? Have I Got Some Music for You!

Synthwave is a swerve. To what extent and in what direction: these are the questions posed by the demands of the new. A portmanteau of "synthesizer" and "new wave," the term in the 1980s described bands like Psyche and Depeche Mode: friendlier and less experimental than Cabaret Voltaire, but heavier than dreamy Tears for Fears-style synth-pop. And let's be honest: everything goes back to the German band Kraftwerk and their massively influential albums between 1975 and 1981. Anyway, synthwave today has competing factions. One draws a line back to those 1980s bands. Another writes love letters to the electronic music found in 1980s pop culture like John Carpenter's film scores (think *Escape from New York*, *The Fog*, *Halloween II*, *They Live*) and video game soundtracks such as the crude theme of *Spy Hunter*, an electronic "Peter Gunn." This latter offshoot has been called "outrun" or "retrowave," and it emerged with a vengeance in the late 2000s mainly thanks to French artists Kavinsky and College. The latter collaborated with Toronto band Electric Youth on the ruthlessly sweet "A Real Hero" for the soundtrack to *Drive*, a hit 2011 indie film that may have done more for contemporary synthwave than anything or anyone else.

In the United States, turn to Lazerhawk, a.k.a. Garrett Hays. On three albums—*Redline* (2010), *Visitors* (2012), and *Skull and Shark* (2013)—all of the synthwave hallmarks are there: gated electronic drums thumping out on the two and four with a few roto-tom fills thrown in as pulsating bass lines shoot through the gaps, usually on straight eighth notes or sixteenth notes, regular to the point of being ordained, a guttural clock-clock-clock-clock underneath a full range of synth melodies: brittle chimes, distorted blatts, *zzzh-zzzzzh*s, and the serrated blades of what might have once upon a time been a pipe organ. Lazerhawk's songs are never slower than mid-tempo. His is a grimier sound than 1980s synthwave, influenced by house music of the 1990s, thrusting forward heavier bass and drums. Side-chained compression hushes the levels now and then, but overall this is louder music than that which it celebrates (which is true of nearly all music made since the mid-2000s, when the compression/max-level wars heated up). *Redline* in particular is the epitome of cyber-thrills circa 1984, post-*Blade Runner*, pre-*Matrix*. Some real *Shadowrun* shit. (You will notice the prevalence of the word "run.") On "Distress Signal" you're cruising through Midtown Manhattan around midnight, you've had a few vodkas and a bump or two, a Russian model sits next to you—this is a *trés* hetero-masculine genre—and you've got crime on the brain; by "Pedal to the Metal," with its Vocoder vocals and buzzing bass melodies, everything's gone wrong: you're flying through red lights and the model's emptying a clip at the banana-yellow Lamborghini chasing you. I want to write "You smell the cordite and burning rubber," but there's no smell in this world. No taste. Every texture is metallic, polished, and sharp.

Speed, cars, masculinity, the city, heroism, glorious violence—is it too much to draw a line back to Futurism? (What's a tirade on the new without the ranting Futurists?) Don't think of the imagery of the Futurists, those Italian painters from 1909 to roughly 1914 whose glorification of war and violence would become associated with fascism. Instead, hear F.T. Marinetti's words at the start of it all: "We intend to exalt aggressive action, a feverish insomnia, the racer's stride, the mortal leap, the punch and the slap."[7] Earlier in *The Founding and Manifesto of Futurism*, he spins a tale of high-strung young people who catch the sound of machines—the bus is not good enough; they need cars—and drive recklessly into the night, abandoning old myths, old stories, finding "nothing to make us wish for death, unless the wish to be free at last from the weight of our courage!" Marinetti then crashes his car in a ditch. Delighted, delirious, he unleashes his manifesto. Imagining a future in which institutions are demolished, he sees, too, the young who will come to kill him and his friends, who are themselves still young. "Art ... can be nothing but violence, cruelty, and injustice," he declares ecstatically.

There is an undeniable violence and cruelty in synthwave though it's implicit, contained; your body doesn't sway to it, your head only rocks, nods, twitches. You can feel it in the vibration and propulsion of a central synthwave motif: the sports car. You won't hear any synthwave songs about riding the bus. The cover of *Redline* is a glowing speedometer, Miami Nights 1984's album *Turbulence* features a car on a *TRON*-like laser grid, and, hell, Kavinsky actually has a song called "Testarossa Autodrive." The car is individualist, not communal—most synthwave acts are single artists working under pseudonyms—routeless, free, running hot. But it's the only freedom in the synthwave world; everything else is as rigid as the almost militaristic sonic throughline of Lazerhawk's music. On *Visitors*, Hays turns to sci-fi themes, on *Skull and Shark*, homages to Carpenter, but through it all seethes an alienation not to be found in the Futurists, who were trying to fuse the city and the machine with war. In Lazerhawk's world, the machine is a computer, and the computer—logic, efficiency, compressor, modulator—is everything: the city, the state, the atmosphere. The Futurists have won.

"It's almost like the music of the Futurists wasn't possible until the 1970s and 1980s," VJ Vendetta, a local artist in Columbus, replies one night when I tell him my Futurist/synthwave theory.[8] He reminds me that electronic music was an enormous change, a technological leap, the computer replacing the instrument and changing the process of composition. "Electronic music is generally bizarre," he says. "It's a form of music entirely built on recorded sounds, reclaimed sounds, repeated and combo-ed up, distorted, done with sample packs, patches, loops. Composing music, typically, has meant building from the individual notes on up. Electronic music production is built from sets of sounds." Indeed, electronic music qualifies as an event, not only because of the new sonic language it made available—the blips, quirks, yawns, and *boooum-booooms*—but also because it changed the grammar of that language, how it could be composed, which in turn challenged traditional notions of authenticity and originality. As with other revivals, synthwave of the 2000s is an interpretative intervention that names, or renames, the event.

The synthwave aesthetic captures the intense emotions of the early 1980s centered on the rise of more personal and mobile technology under the specter of nuclear holocaust and global annihilation. The futurism described by Rushkoff bred optimism about the inevitability of progress, but also anxiety that we were moving too fast, too heedlessly. The heedlessness was part of the thrill, though. It always is, in music as much as anything else. "When new technologies are able to create new noises," says Vendetta, "there's a certain rush involved because we've literally never heard those sounds before." Synthwave in the 1980s replicated the rush of technological discovery, but also the rush to produce and reproduce the discovery before the thrill of the new was extinguished.

Twenty years later, the interpretative intervention of synthwave names that event but also adds an element of melancholy about the presentism which today makes such thrills disappear sooner. In a 2015 article, Dallas-based synthwave artist Mega Drive recalls, "That whole time in my life"—the 1980s—"was pretty magical, as everything was still new and big." Nostalgia, in its least manipulative and commercialized form, often mourns a past sense of newness, but synthwave calls back to a time when newness was already being assaulted by the accelerated pace of new computer technologies and a hurried pop culture: the dawn of presentism. "Many movies from that time feel like love letters to a vanishing present, with impermanence embedded in every scene," a synthwave fan says in the same article. "*Ferris Bueller's Day Off* made me miss my teenage years while I was still a teenager."[9]

With its retro bell chimes and sinister sheets of electro horns, Lazerhawk does sound like he mourns the ephemeral presentism of the 2000s. In this condition, drunk on distraction, assaulted by always changing cultural noise, we live in a constant now that should seem new but doesn't, precisely because a relentless new loses distinction, difference; it becomes a landscape viewed from a high-speed train. This is why, unlike the Futurists, the synthwave grip is desperate, not ecstatic. On the website of Rosso Corsa Records, home to Lazerhawk, you'll find that the label "specializes in Outrun Electro, Synthwave and Chillwave in dedication to the 1980s."[10] *Dedication*. Setting aside my snide little subtitle above, the nostalgia for and replication of the 1980s in Lazerhawk's music, as in so much synthwave, is stiffened by his artistic commitment to limitations. Hays has drawn a tight box around what sonic variables he might use; devoted to the relationship, Lazerhawk can't stray, can't take the lover of an acoustic guitar or an unprocessed vocal. Like the Drive-By Truckers, Lazerhawk has no anxiety of influence about the music that's come before him or its sounds; instead, influence inspires commitment and measures one's attempts to resist the frenetic impulses of an anxious society. Maybe that fuels the doomed heroic quality in the music, the image it conjures of a man, always alone, who must confront the decadence and pace of the present-future without being corrupted by it. His only way of being free, though, is to outrun these temptations, all the while hoping that the possibilities of the new that he felt in the past will find their homecoming in the future.

The Enemy of the New Is Not the Old

One. The dim back room of a narrow bar called Barbès. The audience is crammed around the five or six players who make up Bill Carney's Jug Addicts, a stellar jug band that proves in about twenty minutes that it can play anything. Including "Stardust." One of the band members, a stout woman wearing sunglasses, takes the lead vocals; with an elevated chin and an expressionless face, she sings like a more reserved Ethel Merman, her voice filled with bitterness and stoicism. On the band's jaunty beat, accompanied by a swooning violin, she transports us to a Berlin cabaret, to a show in which the singing of a song is the performer's hesitant gift to the audience. The singer, scraping a washboard, never holds a note too long. At the song's climax, she snaps off the final line nonchalantly. It feels like a perfect replication of the mood of a bygone era but somehow it's not at all nostalgic. Is it new? I'm not sure. But it is gripping.

Two and Three. Future Punx and Vulfpeck. Arguably, Future Punx and its 2015 album *This Is Post-Wave* are just as derivative as Lazerhawk, but songs like "Post Wave" and "I've Been Wrong Before" don't make any distinctions between past and present. Devo with heavier bass, essentially. If the Punx are just screwing around, that's fine, isn't it? I mean, in the grand scheme of things. Replication that comes wrapped in studious appropriation and the postmodern cliché of "play" isn't a crime. Future Punx aren't criminals, and neither are Vulfpeck despite their too-clever-by-half catalogue of 1970s funk and Steely Dan rip-offs, with some dog barks from a 1980s Casio keyboard thrown in for ironic measure. Give the band credit for scamming Spotify by releasing an album, *Sleepify*, which consisted of ten songs of silence—zip, nada, nothing—in order to fund their tour and let fans attends shows for free. They made $20,000 before the streaming service caught on.[11] You'll catch on to their actual music in about five seconds if you can get past titles like "Funky Duck" and "Walkies."

So what's the difference between these examples of the near-perfect duplication of old sounds and styles, neither of which bear an ounce of anxiety about their influences? Vulfpeck duplicates outré, cheesy sounds; theirs is a dream of crap, and it's the crap we already know and consider to be crap. Other bands, like Future Punx, copy what is already in the cultural archive, replicating past sounds and the remnants of those sounds that are once again popular today. Imagine a museum. You'll find the music of Vulfpeck and Future Punx somewhere on the main floors, above ground, even if they're shoved off into one of those side rooms without much lighting. Thus there can't be any negative adaptation or exchange of aesthetic value, really. It's like trading a dollar for a dollar. That night at Barbès, though, was like sneaking into the sub-sub-basement of the museum, into dusty store rooms where relics no longer considered interesting are kept in forgotten boxes. For a little while it felt like syrupy ol' "Stardust" was as archaic as a clay pot and vital enough to condemn the last sixty years of Western progress.

The old is not the enemy of the new. The old is merely out of fashion, that flimsiest version of not-new, clung to by so many. If you have to travel to the sub-sub-basements to get to it, then you have to be transported, like the singer in Barbès transported me. There's something to that metaphor. The sense of distance being traversed creates a feeling of dislocation, of oddness and difference, which is at least the potential for the new. Even though "Stardust" was a popular ballad once, and as such belongs to the cultural archives, the singer's voice and style brought it up from the basements that might as well be the realm of the profane. Her performance was not, I think, intended to be a rethinking or revaluing between the past and present, but regardless, it showed how just a certain quality of sound can transform the relationship between the two.

The challenge faced by Future Punx is the same one faced in the pop world by Taylor Swift's album *1989*. Just before its release in October 2014, the reformed pop country singer, songwriter, producer, and businesswoman claimed the album's title and obvious sonic references to 1980s synth-pop were more than a homage. "[The 1980s were] a very experimental time in pop music," Swift said. "There just seemed to be this energy about endless opportunities, endless possibilities, endless ways you could live your life."[12] Endless possibilities? 1989 was the year of Milli Vanilli's ascent. Nothing was more limited than "Girl You Know It's True." But if we're talking about the 1980s in general, then Swift's right, and she's chasing a similar energy that Lazerhawk chases in his music, the opening up of a musical pop language of synthetics, wall-to-wall reverb, and refined yet danceable energy albeit to tell familiar, intense stories of romance and tragedy in which the singer is always his or her own hero.

1989 is an excellent pop album, easily Swift's best album, filled with her sharpest songwriting, sharp hooks, and an energy which moves through Swift but isn't centered on her celebrity. It has four perfect pop songs—"Blank Space," "Style," "Out of the Woods," and "Shake It Off"—and, as many have noted, Swift spends much more time singing to and for other women than appealing to the male gaze. (Or ear. There's no good music-crit equivalent of that.) As she explained in many interviews, the break into full-on pop reflected a change in her life, a new maturity and confidence. The album was new for her, personally.

But as a work of art, it isn't new. I blast the hell out of "Shake It Off," though, and have never done that with a Nathaniel Rateliff and the Night Sweats song, which is another way of saying that it's sometimes better to be good than new.

From the perspective of newness, though, *1989* was already in trouble because its 1980s synth-pop sounds were common and valorized in 2014. There was no distance to be traveled, no trips to the sub-sub-basement of the cultural archive. That leaves us with the possibility that *1989*, though it sounds like a free, playful replication of its sonic influences, might rethink, revalue, or otherwise transform the relationship between the past and the present. But *1989* offers even less historical dialogue than Lazerhawk's *Redline*. Swift's sound replications celebrate the majestic plastique of 1980s synth-pop and affirm the promise of the original innovation; the techno-utopianism of the past is rekindled for today. The album's feminism honors and maybe revives the complex ways in which Madonna and the underrated Cyndi Lauper challenged the male gaze in pop, but I'm not sure it adds any complexity. (Or is any more challenging than Swift's contemporaries like Beyoncé or Lady Gaga.)

Instead, *1989* is the pop equivalent of Greenberg's modernist entrenchment. This doesn't mean it isn't any good. The truth is that such intensifications are often thrilling because they reach a supreme level of perfection and express the zenith of a genre, the quintessence of a mood. "Style" is such a song, right? That funky guitar opening, the ominous synthwave rhythm track pulsating in the background, an effortless chorus over a washing drone of fizzy synth strings, the backing vocals echoing with zero pretense of naturalness, Swift's squirrelish voice, pinched and punctuating. Because *1989* is such a pure expression, and popular, too, Swift may have refined our cultural memory of the 1980s, since, as Groys writes, "[c]ultural memory is the remembering of these [new] comparisons ...."[13] For Groys this remembering may lead to the new if there's some revaluation of the cultural memory itself—if a certain memory of the 1980s is replaced with a familiar but significantly different memory, which seems closer to what Lazerhawk is after. This isn't what *1989* accomplishes; neither, really, does Lazerhawk. They do, however, entrench the lasting effects of the new, or at least our cultural and historical sense of it. "[U]nless an innovation is subsequently replicated in some way," writes the scholar Leonard B. Meyer, "whether in another work by the same composer or in works by other composers, it is not *historically* significant."[14] Meyer argues that, in a perverse way, what's central to the new is that it becomes not-new: a deep-rooted cultural tradition.

The Enemy of the New Is Mediocrity, or, "Teacher Says, 'Every Time a Song Sucks, an Angel Loses Its Wings.'"

The past and its specters of old music cannot be erased from the present, just dodged. While it creates much hand-wringing, putting the past into music can create significant differences and highlight what's already true: that nothing has been done before *in history*. Even a replicating sound can prove why that's true so long as there's a reappraisal of the past's relationship to the present. Within this critique there can still be the warm reassurance of past ideals, as on Kamasi Washington's suitably titled jazz album *The Epic* from 2015, which reclaims the grandeur of African-American innovation throughout the twentieth century and reaffirms its importance today. The patently familiar music of any tradition—old-time, black metal, the torch song—may suddenly remind us of forgotten dreams, as on the Lowest Pair's haunting old-time album *The Sacred Heart Sessions*, or Agalloch's eviscerating black-metal pastoral *Ashes against the Grain*, or Isobel Campbell and Mark Lanegan's this-should-be-in-a-David-Lynch-film steamer "Come On Over (Turn Me On)" from their collaborative album *Sunday at Devil Dirt*.

One final question, then. If the old is not the opposite of the new, what is?

It seems useful to make a list of what lies underneath the aesthetic new in order to get to what is furthest from it.

1 The *neoteric*—The new without the rupturing force of the event; what Groys describes in the cultural economy of exchange (which occurs during an event, as well); Dylan on *"Love and Theft;"* successful meta-rock; the Truckers on *Southern Rock Opera*; a comparison of significant differences, though not necessarily the creation of new possibilities, by cultural and historical means in addition to musical form; not a term likely to catch on.

2 The *innovative*—A weaker neotericism, possessing a difference with little to no significance in terms of history or culture; maybe Lazerhawk's *Redline*, probably Swift's *1989*; often the language of business and technology, and not to be taken at face value.

3 The *novelty*—That which bursts to the surface of culture in the contemporary moment and subsides just as soon; purely a product of its time, the novelty will never be anything else; see also: *the novelty song*, which adds ridiculousness and hackneyism to this definition; the song knows this, exudes it from its every pore; in the 2000s, the ringtone fad-song "Crazy Frog," Rebecca Black's "Friday," Vulfpeck.

Finally, the only option left: the *mediocre*.

A friend of mine once told me his theory that rock 'n' roll died when 3 Doors Down had a hit single, "Kryptonite," with their debut album *The Better Life* in 2000. The problem, he said, wasn't that the song was horrible, but that it was horribly mediocre. There is, in art, a kind of living death, a zombie state, an enthusiastic day-to-day undead-ness which is mediocrity. Stagnation. The moribund. The opposite of the new is not the old, it is sameness, or anything that limits the generation of significant possibilities. Mediocrity is unavoidable and necessary; without it the new would be indistinguishable; it would not exist.

The mediocre song's influences are just as obvious as a neoteric or innovative replication, but the song is less committed or faithful to them. If a certain style is winning the day, particularly when that style itself has been deemed new, then mediocrity swoops in, arriving belatedly without anxiety, and tries to ride the coattails of that perceived change. For instance, Maroon 5. The band's 2002 debut *Songs About Jane* was a passable rip-off of late-1990s "alternative rock," even if "This Love" made ample use of the riff from Billy Joel's "Movin' Out"; 2007's *It Won't Be Soon Before Long* sounded like Adam Levine had been listening to emo and Outkast; by 2012's *Overexposed*, the band's transition to pop was complete, sealed by the *sssssszzzzzzZZZIT!* sample on "Payphone" that's in every pop song. 2014's *V* tried to catch the 1980s retro wave, including, on "It Was Always You," softcore-synthwave. It's not that Maroon 5—or Fall Out Boy and Panic at the Disco, whose works have a similar trajectory—are *way* behind the times. They're *just* behind, making the contemporary more popular but all the while marking its vanishing trace.

Mediocre music is redundant; often it sounds like it's not even making an effort to avoid redundancy. In terms of Badiou's theory of the event, the mediocre performance only confirms the present situation. As we shall see, Badiou would describe this as simply making visible what is already visible, making heard what is already heard, or making possible what is already possible. In Groys' cultural economy of exchange, the mediocre song is a dollar for a dollar.

Part Two

The American Wow

5

Spectaglam! Katy Perry and the American Wow

"Roar"

Look! A Pepsi logo formed by enormous glowing pebbles! A godly voice says, "The National Football League welcomes you to the Pepsi Super Bowl Halftime Show." Magically, the pebbles change color and part like the Red Sea—and here is Katy Perry, fierce and sleek as she rides onto the field atop a Transformers-ish lion that's all hard angles and reflections. Over an aboriginal drumbeat and synths, she sings/lip-synchs "Roar," her bouncy, inspirational pop hit about getting knocked down, getting back up, and reasserting yourself. With its swooping chorus, "Roar" is big enough to fill the stadium. Meanwhile, Perry's flame-licked costume looks like a rejected design from the chariot scene in *The Hunger Games*.

I am sitting on the couch with my fiancée, watching the Katy Perry Extravaganza on the television. We are eating, let's say, pretzels, and waiting to hear and see something new. We are skeptical. My gut reaction is a cheap kind of awe. The performance will surely be yet another ritual of American excess, glamour, and consumerism—but *what* a ritual!

The American Wow

Fifteen feet or so above the ground on her lion, Katy Perry is at this moment the epitome of the spectacle of hi-definition American pop music: the American Wow. A mixture of celebrity, bling, prestige, consumerism, technology worship, enthusiasm, youth, innocence, public authenticity, competition, and visual mediation, the American Wow is only one segment of American popular culture, but it's enormous: *American Idol* and its imitators, fashion, multinational corporations that own "independent" labels, awards shows, celebrity news, commercials that function as music videos, music videos that function as commercials, social media—oh yes, and the music itself. The American Wow is flexible in terms of genre, so long as the high end and low end are compressed and the volume is jacked. It leans toward R&B, dance pop, rap, and rock. Country and punk sometimes overlap. It is the world of Beyoncé, Maroon 5, Brittany, Kanye, Tim McGraw, Lady Gaga, and Green Day. The music doesn't have to be American, just imperial: crossover music. The mainstream. There is room for Mumford and Sons.

Tonight, though, it's Katy Perry's blend of dance pop and R&B. Tonight—February 1, 2015, Super Bowl XLIX—Perry is the American of good intentions, the decent person whose essential blamelessness is never doubted, who values a job done right, and who, in fact, excels at her job. She's precise without seeming too practiced; she's athletic and commanding; she is, above all, a professional. Over the next twelve-and-a-half minutes, Perry's performance will be watched by more people than will actually watch the game—and despite this, her reign on the throne of the American Wow will be brief.[1] That's just how it works in the pop spectacle. Someone else is always on the come-up. In fact, as "Roar" bounces by, Perry doesn't have a song on the Billboard Hot 100, which is topped by "Uptown Funk" and dominated by three Taylor Swift tracks from *1989*.[2]

And that, really, is the overlooked story of pop music in the new millennium: the fragile consistency of certain ideals within a transient, unstable culture. Pop music has always been defined by its pace and energy and valued for its constant sense of innovation. In 1972, the rock critic Ellen Willis described "the pop aesthetic," including the pop aesthetic at the heart of rock, as "a tradition whose first law is novelty."³ What a beautiful contradiction that is. Pop is a structure we've built to barely contain itself. The American Wow is a flurry of images and sounds, Douglas Rushkoff's presentism in action within pop culture. Today, the American Wow spins faster than it did in 1972, but its ideological urges are the same: order and freedom, the regulation of enduring and stabilizing social values and the offering of perpetual opportunity for any individual to say what they please. As a network of institutions, the American Wow promises to balance these urges. In fact, it's built on the idea that they can and should be balanced.

Which is order.

One Hundred Seconds

The one hundred seconds of "Roar" end with the Transformers lion awkwardly rearing up and Perry clenching a fist, which means we're not getting the cool glow-in-the-dark jump-rope routine she included at the end of "Roar" during her Prismatic tour. No time! Forward! Despite the breathless pace, like most American Wow music in the new millennium the Katy Perry Halftime Extravaganza will be devoid of spontaneity, offhandedness, or what the music journalist Paul Morley once called "the deviance and suddenness of *what pop really is*."⁴ Well, it isn't that anymore. Tightly choreographed, carefully designed, and meticulously rehearsed, live performance in the American Wow reclaims its musical theatre roots but updates them with a contemporary visual spectacle into a new fashion-musical theatre. Even on record, pop today sounds more like order than freedom. Britney Spears' smash 2000 hit "Oops! ... I Did It Again," OK Go's breakout "Here It Goes Again," "Good Feeling" by Flo Rida, Justin Timberlake's "Sexy Back," Rihanna's "Umbrella," and even Lorde's "Royals" all have a methodical, even fastidious quality to them. (For what it's worth, I love two of those songs.) Carly Rae Jepsen's teen anthem "Call Me Maybe," which is about taking a chance, is prudently constructed and performed. Institutional. Even oppressive. Proclaiming excitement, the American Wow often sounds like a representation of fun more than fun itself.

The old complaint about the American Wow is that it's just a bunch of commodified, market-tested, musical groupthink that takes no chances and can't possibly be new since commodification itself is a form of standardization. If something radically new does happen, the American Wow can always absorb it as a product and regain its equilibrium. On the other hand, the American Wow presents *everything* as new, as in "what's hot" or just over the horizon; when the music fails to convince, the Wow's visual elements can supply the needed sense of innovation. So as I watch Perry's show, I'm really asking myself if highly commodified art can create the new in our current situation. And since nearly all popular music is sold in some way, is the spectacle of the American Wow really any different?

Guy Debord Writes a Manifesto

You already understand Guy Debord's concept of the spectacle even if you've never heard of it. The spectacle is that all-encompassing, pleasurable but unnervingly frantic reality-as-TV-show that touches nearly all of us. In the first of the two-hundred-plus theses that make up his 1967 book *The Society of the Spectacle*, Debord writes, "In societies where modern conditions of production prevail, all of life presents itself as an immense accumulation of spectacles. Everything that was directly lived has moved away into a representation."[5] Despite that word, "representation," the spectacle is not an illusion, Debord stressed. It's a constructed reality, a way of living. Instead of a mere "collection of images," or any cultural products, really, including pop music, the spectacle is "a social relation among people, mediated by images."[6] Like Instagram. Aside from social media, there's no better example of the spectacle than the way the nation comes together around the Super Bowl, its commercials, and its halftime show: we comment on the ads, critique Perry's set on Twitter as it happens, tweet *at* Katy Perry while she's standing on a Transformer, and then recap the whole thing on the internet the next day. To the extent that Debord is right about the spectacle, the American Wow is one of its manifestations. The Wow isn't the center nor the entirety, which means, hey, let's not lay all the blame at the feet of pop music. Or Katy Perry. But the

American Wow does present itself as a social relation, a how-to guide that generates and normalizes certain cultural values like celebrity, enthusiasm, youth, and wealth: the spectacular glamour of the Spectaglam. There are no songs in the American Wow about being poor that don't end with the singer getting rich.

You might think that in 1967, Debord could have hardly imagined the full, hi-def brilliance of the spectacle in February 2015, but then you read this passage—

> The first phase of the domination of the economy over social life brought into the definition of all human realization the obvious degradation of *being* into *having*. The present phase of total occupation of social life by the accumulated results of the economy leads to a generalized sliding of *having* into *appearing*, from which all actual "having" must draw its immediate prestige and its ultimate function. At the same time all individual reality has become social reality directly dependent on social power and shaped by it.[7]

—and you think, well, maybe he was a prophet. Debord's primary target for criticism was capitalism. The first sentence in the quote above gives it away, since it revises the famous opening line in Marx's *Das Kapital*: "The wealth of those societies in which the capitalist mode of production prevails presents itself as an immense accumulation of commodities." In the Preface to *Spectacle*'s third French edition, written in 1992, two years before he killed himself, Debord says that "the current ideology of democracy" is "the dictatorial freedom of the Market, as tempered by the recognition of the rights of Homo Spectator."[8] In the past few decades, the spectacle and its market have excelled at speeding up, making easier, and making more public the slide from *having* into *appearing*. With credit, you can appear to own products you can't truly afford. Social media turns private identity into public performance. Using music streaming sites like YouTube, Spotify, Pandora, and Apple Music, we own access, not a physical copy of the record or album itself. Rushkoff notes that such sites are "constantly expiring resource[s] requiring ongoing replenishment," and so, "consumption becomes more like attending a performance."[9] In other words, the market has adopted the ephemeral excitement of the performing arts in which nothing is ever the same twice. The real outcome of the spectacle, Debord believed, is a never-satiated desire, the showbiz axiom *always leave 'em wanting more.*

"Dark Horse"

Still in the *Hunger Games* dress, Perry stalks into the center of a holographic chessboard as the show segues into "Dark Horse." One of Perry's most formally inventive songs, a fusion of jittery drill rhythms and a sidewinding melody, "Dark Horse" is superb except for Juicy J's lame feature and its fugly line about Jeffrey Dahmer. Even here at the Super Bowl, the performance breathes with allure, rising toward fulfillment and falling away unresolved. The verse slides into a section of music that hangs in the air, what at first sounds like a transition into the chorus. "So you wanna play with magic," Perry sings. "Boy, you should know what you're falling for." Oh, you think, this *is* the chorus. Pointing at the camera, she looks like a warrior goddess in an advertisement for a video game. It's as if she's being Photoshopped in real time. The song ascends again into the second half of the chorus, swelling with tension—and then it dissipates.

In the spectacle, we consume the commodified *idealized* versions of ourselves, which only proves the distance between the real self and the ideal self. That distance might be painful, but it's also what makes the build-up and release so delicious, what keeps us coming back for more—and what inspires a religious devotion. Because we're organized around the same accumulation of spectacles and commodities, Debord argues that the spectacle has become a contemporary sacred-secular church through which we can become our idealized selves.[10] But, as any pastor will tell you, you need to keep coming every Sunday. The result is an ongoing process of overcoming one's self-alienation. As Greil Marcus describes it in *Lipstick Traces*, Debord's spectacle transforms the ephemeral into the concrete and the concrete into a seductively advertised product that is precious because it's unattainable. "What was, once, yourself," writes Marcus, "[is] now presented as an unreachable but irresistibly alluring image of what, in this best of all possible worlds, you could be."[11]

At the Super Bowl, "Dark Horse" flies by before you can realize how this tantalizing unattainability is woven into the song's entire ideology. As a promise and a warning, "Dark Horse" dramatizes the listener's self-alienation, not the singer's. Though her love and sexuality may be idealized and commodified, Perry's persona is complete in itself. *You* are not.

Unrequited Love Becomes a Congealment

By engineering a thirst for the best possible version of yourself which you will never, never attain, the spectacle is a sinister model of contemporary innovation. That, for Debord, is what's wrong with it. Here Debord meets his precursor, the aesthetic philosopher Theodor Adorno, whose view of novelty can be read as a statement of unrequited love: "The new is the longing for the new, not the new itself: That is what everything new suffers from."[12] If, as Debord writes, the spectacle is "the omnipresent affirmation of a choice *already made*," it's also the celebration of our need to keep choosing, to keep purchasing, so that this time, maybe, just maybe, we'll finally catch the Roadrunner, kick the football Lucy is holding, or meet Godot.[13] *Fat chance*, says Debord. The potential for fulfillment is suppressed by the totality of the spectacle's commodification of desire. There is only *want*. This eternal craving overrides every kind of musical newness I've described so far. Recombination, the recurrence of revivals, meta-rock, the historicism of the swerve, and the event are never enough in the spectacle. The American Wow functions as a spectacular kind of cultural archive in which the profane is revalued and then presented back to us as our own idealized, redemptive ordinariness. (See in a bit: "Firework.") That the American Wow is an institution with traditions may seem counterintuitive until you consider the power of the Billboard charts, copyright laws, multinational media corporations, awards shows, and events like the Super Bowl. As Groys argues, such institutions exist to celebrate and protect the new. Debord is, surprise surprise, more pessimistic. "The struggle between tradition and innovation," he writes, "can be carried only through the permanent victory of innovation," which the American Wow confirms. But this innovation, says Debord, only ever becomes a congealment, a stifling of possibility and the stabilizing of dominant cultural values.[14] If he's right, then newness in the spectacle is just a mirage.

"Dark Horse"/"I Kissed a Girl"

The tail end of the "Dark Horse" not-a-chorus slides into the jock-rock rhythm of "I Kissed a Girl," and here, hello, is Lenny Kravitz, carrying forward the *Hunger Games* theme and for some reason singing the opening lines, immediately ruining what shred of girl-love empowerment might be left in the song. Let me run it down for you: woman's at a party, tries on another woman like clothes, honors the essential sensuality of women, and calls it a night. The instant Perry sings, in the chorus, "I hope my boyfriend don't mind it," the song loses all its guts. But then, it never had much to begin with. What matters here is the titillation of the idea for an uninitiated audience, the novelty of it. Like "Crazy Frog," "I Kissed a Girl" poses no threat. Even if it pretends otherwise, it's a song for men, a point made obvious when Perry drops to her knees and whips her ponytail around Kravtiz's crotch. There's a difference between the seduction, lack of resolution, and self-alienation in "Dark Horse" and the same qualities in "I Kissed a Girl." In the latter, we overhear an act of public intimacy as a spectator, a third party closer to being the boyfriend about whom is asked the song's only real question: *How is he going to react?* Answer: Why should we care? "Dark Horse," on the other hand, is entirely made of questions, primarily the question of "me" and "you," the singer and the listener. The singer is a woman taking action and being her own subject; the music, seductive but suspended, punctuated by finger snaps, is erotic instead of pornographic. The song is a democratic game of personae; the listener can take on Perry's role without the secondhand voyeurism of "I Kissed a Girl," take on the role of self-alienated suitor, or either role, or switch between roles. "I Kissed a Girl" never overcomes its commodified nature since its only content is a commodity, i.e. a *Girls Gone Wild* video, i.e. the same old cultural shit.

A Precious Subject

Fast forward a year and a half. I'm sitting with a colleague of mine, Matt Mitchem, a philosopher, in the NYU office of Boris Groys, another philosopher. The three of us are discussing narcissism. "We are more and more involved in the practice of self-presentation to the gaze of the other," Groys says measuredly in his considerable Eastern European accent.[15] Then he describes the mindset: "Let us not be interested in what we see, let us be interested in what other people see when they look at us. Because when we see, we are relaxed—and being relaxed is generally not good." Groys chuckles. "But when we are looked at, we are under pressure to be active." This would explain that feeling of work and discipline that stiffens so much pop music in the 2000s. It also reminds me of Rushkoff's presentism, in which we're constantly taking in the world just to see our own reflections. "The gaze of the other is such a pressure," says Groys. "It creates this kind of narcissistic anticipation of my own image, and this anticipation grows into production."

Our conversation wanders into art theory, then the French Revolution, and then what Mitchem calls "the self-satisfaction in the perception of being satisfying to somebody." And we're back to narcissism and the *choice* to make oneself into an object of desire.

"That's precisely what narcissists do," says Groys, "design themselves to be liked and admired. So you have this kind of self-objectification process that actually makes you, in your eyes, to be a 'precious object.'"

"And that explains pop music," I say.

Groys smiles. "Totally. So if something is based on this, it's pop music."

Thinking in terms of what Groys calls self-design, self-objectification, and precious objects strikes me as a more complex way of thinking about commodification in the American Wow. For one thing, the desire to be a precious object in the eyes of someone else usually precedes and kick-starts the process of turning oneself into a product. We are messy souls filled with contradictions that make it harder for large numbers of people to admire us; even a rare valuable stone is made rarer and more valuable by being refined, cut to shape, and polished. Musicians inherently present less of themselves than they actually are if only because of the limitations of performance, recording, and the music business. Most of them don't set out to become Barbie or Ken dolls, either. Even in—especially in—the American Wow, they know how the system works and, like most of us, think they can game it, or at least negotiate some middle ground between self-expression and standardization.

And you know who understands these negotiations quite well? Women. Female performers are acutely aware of the pressures of commodification, which, as I write that word, sounds like "modification" and "accommodation" combined—and that's the point, right? More than men, women who perform are expected to modify their behavior, their appearance, the sound of their voices, and the words they write to accommodate a popular audience that is assumed to be male or whose values are defined by men. The keenest example of this is when women sing about men, love, and sex and are met with accusations of being self-absorbed and obsessed, even though, (1) the American Wow *in its entirety is based on self-absorption and obsession*, and (2) as Taylor Swift put it, "No one says that about Ed Sheeran. No one says that about Bruno Mars. They're all writing songs about their exes, *their* current girlfriends, *their* love life, and no one raises a red flag ...."[16] Indeed, men in the American Wow groom themselves, manicure their personae, and present themselves to be liked and commodified just as much as women. What else is a boy band? What else is Justin Bieber? The lingering lie of the American Wow is that, regardless of how much they turn themselves into precious objects, male performers retain their power to be subjects, people who are capable of acting on their desires, while female performers somehow cannot. The truth is that every performance of popular music presents the singer as an object of desire in the sense that he, she, or they want to be admired, whether it's Bob Dylan or Katy Perry. It's a given. What more, then, is at work in a performance? Is it a capitulation to the gaze of the other, as in "I Kissed a Girl," or is there another layer (or three), as in "Dark Horse," in which the singer originates herself as a precious *subject* with the power to control the gaze and hearing of the audience, seizing on their own narcissism, which is the evidence of the spectacle.

"Teenage Dream"

After the *way* edgy minute or so of "I Kissed a Girl," the Katy Perry Spectacle abruptly shifts to harmless primary color beach balls, dancing sharks, and with a quick costume change, Perry dressed like a cheerleader to perform "Teenage Dream." (My fiancée and I are still eating pretzels.) Stretching her falsetto to sing the demur first line of the song—"You think I'm pretty without any make-up on"— Perry keeps her head tilted back, beaming, completely in control. She sings the line in the chorus about going all the way, but skips the second verse about a drunken motel escapade involving a fort made out of the bed sheets. Her dance moves are innocent, except for the one time she traces the side of her body with her palm. Unless you're offended by a woman flirting with a person in a beach ball costume.

Another charge leveled against the American Wow, especially its dance pop and R&B acts, is that it's for young people and *young people don't know good music from bad*, et cetera, which is a crap argument for many reasons. (Am I to believe that, conveniently, all of these critics had great taste when they were young and listening to Neil Diamond's "Cracklin' Rosie"?) Just about every ounce of the contemporary spectacle is built on and sells youth, which is another way that it sells newness. But you don't need to sell youth to the young. As Ellen Willis argues, pop is a tradition of novelty, but more specifically, it is a tradition of *eternal* novelty which at its deepest and most philosophical level becomes a "vision of a world in motion, a world not rendered insignificant but made more beautiful by its transience, its erotic energy, and its ceaseless change."[17] That's Stephen Greenblatt in *The Swerve* describing the Renaissance, but he could be describing Martha and the Vandellas' "Dancing in the Street," or the Raspberries' "I Wanna Be With You," Prince's near-manifesto "Pop Life," or Beyoncé's "Crazy in Love." These are songs that course with the potential of a youthful, constantly recharging, never-ending spring. The point, and what Perry's work has done so fluently since her 2008 album *One of the Boys*, is to shed the shackles of actual teenage life by having money and mobility while still being able to use its codes, behaviors, and ideals. (You can have a threesome and still build a fort out of bed sheets.) Perry's music projects a bubblegum quality into one's early twenties, or what the book industry calls the "new adult" market, and this new-adult quality then in turn becomes a vision of eternal youthfulness to be enjoyed by much older people. A 2014 study examined the listening habits of 13-year-olds and 64-year-olds via streaming services, and while there were some big differences, a clutch of contemporary pop stars landed in each listening group's Top 20, including Bruno Mars, Justin Timberlake, Rihanna, and Katy Perry.[18] While this is depressing news for 13-year-olds, it backs up the simple idea that the American Wow commodifies the sensation of the teenage dream for adults. This is the new of constant discovery, the ideal of always being on the verge while retaining your essential innocence, and in "Teenage Dream" that means a certain innocence about love, sex, and commitment.

"California Gurls"

None of that is particularly earth-shattering. What I find fascinating, though, is how much this eternal spring relies on a nostalgic repetition of what used to be new in order to commodify its *current* sense of newness. Witness: as Perry playfully hip-checks a beach ball, the Super Bowl set transitions into "California Gurls," another wet dream aimed at men ("we'll melt your popsicle") disguised as an ode to women based on how they look. Tonight, how they look is not California circa 2015 but a 1960s Coppertone advertisement in hi-def Technicolor. Joined by a phalanx of dancers in polka-dotted swimsuits circa the 1960s—not actually from the 1960s, mind you, just styled that way, sweetheart necklines and all—Perry works through a mix of retro dance moves like the Frug and the Swim. In the American Wow, these simple images amount to history. It's an *as if* history, a cultural dream (or a marketing scheme) about a place and a time, but mainly about certain ideals like youth and innocence staying the same while the world changes. Debord argued that the purpose of the spectacle "is to make history forgotten within culture."[19] However, if the American Wow seeks to balance a free sense of innovation with the order of enduring values, then *some* history is needed to make sure those values endure. The solution is nostalgia.

The problem with nostalgia isn't its interjection of the past into the present. As I've argued, using the old doesn't mean music can't be new. But nostalgia is an idealized and streamlined version of the old, the past, and history, particularly so in the American Wow since it aims to reach the biggest possible audience. Since the new, even in its least radical versions, is identified through comparisons to what preceded it, then the new depends on an understanding of historical context. Without history, we have no point of comparison. If nostalgia is substituted for history, ultimately it cannot match the complexity and disruptive possibilities offered by history. We're back to a cultural economy of exchange in which nothing is really exchanged: a dollar for a dollar. This truly is why the use of the nostalgic is so at odds with the new; it has nothing to do with "retro" styles necessarily, merely the poverty of history which those styles might express.

"Get Ur Freak On"—"Work It"—"Lose Control"

Left Shark! The reverberations of this person-in-a-shark-costume who was messing up the choreography with aplomb during "Teenage Dream" are still being felt across Twitter. Meanwhile, "California Gurls" is all fun and frothy and enormous and—and *bam*, here's Missy Elliott. The hook of "Get Ur Freak On" is so immediately recognizable that, unlike Kravitz, Elliott doesn't need an introduction. Stout, clad in what looks like a pit crew uniform, and refreshingly imperfect in comparison to Perry, Elliott is having a damn good time as she storms through "Work It," and Perry seems to genuinely enjoy being her hype woman until she runs offstage for another costume change, letting Elliott finish the miniset with "Lose Control."

Most critics will turn out to enjoy the surprise; a few will argue that Elliott upstaged Perry. Others will question why this relic was allowed to intrude on Perry's star turn. One perturbed columnist for *USA Today* will write, "Just when the Super Bowl halftime show threatened to be relevant to the current zeitgeist, Perry trots out a rapper whose last song to hit the charts was in 2008 and peaked at No. 95."[20] Elliott—who, in case you missed it, was just described as a horse—is "a fine rapper" but "probably unknown to a vast majority of the viewing audience," even though "Get Ur Freak On" and "Work It" are classic jams which, as many other reviewers point out, sound just as relevant today. But even among those positive reviews, there's a slight befuddlement about Elliott's appearance. After the show, some explanation will be supplied for the confused, including the young people on Twitter: since she contributed to a remix of Perry's "Last Friday Night (T.G.I.F.)," Elliott was invited by Perry as part of the pop star's ode to 1990s music on her Prismatic tour.[21] Otherwise, it's evidently something Perry just wanted to do.

It seems to me that, aiming for nostalgia, Perry injected some history into the show instead. We can tell because everyone, including myself, was a bit confused. Elliott's appearance presented a gap. Nostalgic images offer an immediate sense of the past: no gaps, no questions. (None will be raised about the "California Gurls" sequence.) The contemporary market and presentism itself offer explanations for other seemingly random gaps; no one asked why Kravitz was there, but he'd just been in *The Hunger Games* which I guess is relevant to the current zeitgeist. None of that was sufficient to explain why Elliott and her superb crew were breaking it down in the middle of Perry's set. It's telling that, to solve this mystery, people still went looking for a deeper sense of causation and that the response was a historical connection between Perry and Elliott as musicians. If history is crucial to understanding the new, Elliott's miniset is an example of how that process can begin. Instead of immediately suturing up any confusion, history creates gaps that encourage us to ask questions and make comparisons between the present and the past. As an aesthetic experience, the confusion can even be pleasurable and surprising. At the very least, it can make us pay attention.

The Limitations of Now

The kicker is that here, "history" amounts to the seven years since "Ching-a-Ling" and "Shake Your Pom Pom" charted, or, more realistically, the ten years since "Lose Control" went to #3 in 2005.[22] Pop life has always spun faster than ordinary life, but the presentist pace of the American Wow and American culture in the new millennium joins this spinning to a previously unimagined robustness of content. In *Present Shock*, Rushkoff makes the case that we essentially have become an attention-deficit society. "We tend to exist in a distracted present," he writes, "where forces on the periphery are magnified and those immediately before us are ignored."[23] (After Left Shark goes off-script during "Teenage Dream," I check Twitter to look for some zingers and only half-hear my fiancée ask how long this show is going to last.) Living in the moment, you'd think we would be more aware, or that everything would seem new, but "[n]ow" is fragile, "necessarily and essentially trivial."[24] It's like small talk at a party: if it's just a distraction, you can easily be distracted *from* it.

This state of constant interruption makes it tough to understand a story, especially a complex story that takes time to digest—like history. Rushkoff also makes the case, less convincingly, that traditional linear narratives have fallen by the wayside in the past twenty years, and in their place are games of connectivity, parodic patterns, and webs of meaning that have more to do with social context in the contemporary moment than they do with the traditional pleasures of a story or any complex sense of history.[25] Analyzing this breakdown of narrative through television shows and films, Rushkoff picks and chooses his examples, like *Lost* and *Pulp Fiction*, while ignoring the familiar formulas of sitcoms like *The Big Bang Theory* or the way reality television shows like *My 600-Pound Life* conform messy reality into more typical narrative arcs. Also, literature, theatre, film, and even comics have been testing antinarrative structures for more than a century. Still, to the extent that he's right, this pattern recognition means that we are often trying to determine what's new with only a sense of recent history, a near-past, and this is made only more difficult when we inundate ourselves with media and take no time to reflect on what we've just seen or heard. Since we desire the new, we become anxious. Fear not, though. The American Wow has us covered ….

Everything Is Possible

In *After the End of Art*, Arthur Danto argues that the postmodern era is marked by the aesthetic claim that "everything is permitted," a phrase that goes back to the philosophy of Nietzsche and the Russian novelist Fyodor

Dostoevsky's *The Brothers Karamazov*.[26] In their works, it meant the death of God and the end of our obedience to his rules. Danto uses it to describe an end to the aesthetic battles of the modernist era. Artists could do what they liked and the art audience could like what it liked. This sounds like the essence of the pop aesthetic—a promise of total freedom—and indeed, more consistently than any other arena of popular music today, the American Wow claims this as its truth. Since the turn of the millennium, largely thanks to presentism and technology, this aesthetic has only intensified into what Badiou has described as *everything is possible*.[27] It is, in many ways, the American Wow's response to the anxiety that nothing is new: the abundance of the now. Robust options. An engorged present. No limitations! There's so much out there, something must be new, right? New to you, at least.

For Badiou, this kind of "possible" is actually a limitation, even if it is, in a very weak sense, a kind of newness. It's really just a prescribed set of possibilities that, yes, with some work and imagination we can realize, i.e. bring into existence. What if we combine a Broadway showstopper with some grinding club music? Poof: "Firework." Fine. This is hard enough to do well. But these possibilities are defined and limited by the dominant culture of the day, like the American Wow, which means they aren't particularly new. For whatever formal innovation a new musical style might possess, it can hardly destabilize or disrupt if it already exists within a set paradigm of forms and values. Like Debord, Badiou thinks our government, corporations, media, and entertainment industries happily claim everything is possible, even if, in reality, they suppress what is possible by *not seeing it*—a perfectly insidious tactic in a visual culture—or *not hearing it*. In other words, we're told there's so much noise, there can't possibly be anything else to hear. "Everything is possible" sounds like saying "Nothing has been done before," but in the end, it's a more affirmative way of saying everything's been done before, that there is nothing new under the sun.

In Badiou's theory of the event, which is a theory of newness, the event intrudes on what we assume is possible. Like a plant growing out of a patch of barren irradiated dirt, the event grows out of a set of historical circumstances in which all rules, all customs, and all evidence deny the very possibility of its existence. Until it happens, it seems like an impossibility. Think back to the Sphere festival in the Prologue and the stage that materialized out of nowhere: it was just a patch of grass, an unused space, there but not there in a way that mattered until a performance happened. Now imagine that the patch of grass, the entire lawn, and the entire grounds of the festival are packed with people so tightly their feet suffocate the grass. There's no room for the plant to emerge or intrude because everyone and everything is present. This is the event in the American Wow: smothered and struggling to emerge. That is its challenge as an artistic culture: its own abundance of noise.

"Firework"

Here is Katy Perry, standing on some kind of skyhook device with two unlit stars at the top of it. The fever of Elliott's "Lose Control" has subsided into an inspirational moment: "Firework," the song that begins with that awkward "Do you ever feel like a plastic bag" line. The pace is slow, the song reconfigured as a ballad. I realize that Perry has gone through a social journey; she entered by herself on a lion, lined up her dance moves with rooks and knights, Lenny Kravitz, beach balls, sharks, California gurls, Missy Elliott, and now she's alone again.

As she finishes the verse, the skyhook lifts Perry into the air, the feat she used in "Birthday" on the Prismatic tour just before finishing the concert with "Firework" in a peacock dress. The stars and their conjoined tail light up, resembling the star in NBC's "The More You Know" campaign. (Twitter is taking notice.) The song's tempo hastens from ballad into dance number, bass drum thumping, synths lapping against a beach somewhere. Sparklers shoot out of the tails as Perry sings the chorus, still rising. Forty feet? Fifty? The contraption slowly glides over the field. The second verse kicks in with an offbeat guitar, a richer, looser sound than you'll hear on the studio recording. Meanwhile, fireworks! Spotlights! The longer Perry putters around, the more ridiculous it looks. The spectacle obscures the performance of the song and what it tries to say: *Don't give up. Show them who you really are.* It's a perfect example of how a song and its performer might work against themselves in the spectacle. Instead of being about the listener to whom the song is addressed—this happens in "Birthday," too, actually, after Perry pulls a fan onto the stage and seats her in a throne—"Firework" is about Perry and the spectacle surrounding her, the spectacle we all love. It says, *give up*. Let someone famous show you who *she* really is.

Is the Katy Perry Halftime Extravaglamacle new? No, but not for the reasons I expected. Those reasons have much less to do with the commercialized nature of this performance or any performance in the American Wow. In the end, the story of the American Wow is its innate, resilient, alluring appeal for social order. It accomplishes this by rewarding values as diverse as eternal novelty, prestige, nostalgia, presentism—a long, long list. Whatever its motivations, Perry's show capitulates to the American Wow's values; it represents and reproduces them.

After all the choreography of the set's first ten minutes, I wish Perry had just returned to the center of the field, sung the opening of "Firework," and that the stage had flooded with regular audience members dressed in whatever they came in. A raucous dance party, a celebration. As if to say, *Okay, we did all the spectacle, now let's just have a good time.* Even on the biggest stage of the year, even in this massive stadium, that small resistance would have been surprising enough to feel a little new.

Wolves in the House

As Debord describes it, the spectacle is a black hole. So is his book. At times, *The Society of the Spectacle* reads like a recombination of the 1949 film noir *The Third Man* and *The Matrix* from half a century later. Debord is fond of the phrase "agents of the spectacle," and is there any more noirish a statement than one of Debord's most famous: "In a world that really has been turned on its head, truth is a moment of falsehood."[28] There is an indisputable brilliance in Debord's prescient theories, but there is also an almost naïve absolutism, a totality that replicates the spectacle he's condemning. Its performers possess no individual agency, least of all the pop musicians who are "spectacular representations of living human beings, distilling the essence of the spectacle's banality into images of possible roles."[29] Every actor, every performer, is either a dupe or a con artist. Neither are they unique. If the spectacle is, as Debord argues, our contemporary church, it is one church, and there are no lesbian Unitarian Universalists, no Buddhists, no progressive Catholics, no Muslims in Texas, no atheists, no meaningful differences.

Like Debord, Badiou is convinced that the event is impossible within the spectacle. He writes, "Today, art can only be made from the starting point of that which, as far as Empire is concerned, doesn't exist."[30] Empire is his name (certainly not his alone) for the systems of global capitalism, roughly the equivalent of the spectacle and the American Wow—which means that, for him, true art cannot be made within the American Wow. In fact, he has a bad habit of entirely writing off popular music as being formally derivative of "serious" music.[31] While he believes that the artist can change the situation, he writes that "[i]t is better to do nothing than to contribute to the invention of formal ways of rendering visible that which Empire already recognizes as existent."[32] But this goes against Badiou's own emphasis on action, choice, and commitment. And if an event is an impossibility, doesn't that mean it can emerge in the impossible situation of the spectacle?

It is possible, instead, that an artist might render the already-recognized visible, but in doing so, stumble onto the invisible. It is possible that an artist might begin within the spectacle of the American Wow and decide to take the risk of declaring the impossible. The weakness of Empire and those that control it is hubris. The tragic flaw.

Whatever its ability to restrict, the American Wow must also account for the ebb and flow of taste, value, and, yes, real newness. Certain of its control, it must take the chance that certain performers and artists will be disorderly. (We are fascinated by Left Shark and intrigued or offended by Missy Elliott because they are out of order.) The American Wow plays out this drama, pitting canned vocals and lip-synching, tightly choreographed routines, fashion-runway posing, the fixedness of a performer's brand, the plotting of marketing plans, and the stiff, computer-articulated rhythms and plastic sheen of the music itself against its performers' willpower, chances, inventiveness, and their urges to seek a more radical new. They might strategize ways to turn the sounds, rhythms, conventions, and limitations of the American Wow against itself. They might find a way to ask questions which have no easy answers; to question, in fact, everything about the system in which pop music operates. Their music might demand new promises, ones that have nothing to do with money, prestige, youth, or even novelty itself. Instead of branding herself, a performer might seize the brand and aim its hot end at someone else for a change. A performer might inject history into the presentist stream through her art. She might reject the idea that because she presents herself to be seen and heard, she cannot be a subject. Like a wolf, she might sneak into the house and trash it so something new might take its place.

6

The New Digital Empire: Consumerism, Technology, and the New

Taking a Walk on Beef

In his impossibly clean studio apartment, some clean-cut Young Man from Anywhere takes a picture of a taco with his phone, presumably so everyone can know what a great taco he's eating. What follows is a montage of various young people holding a similar taco, the new Doritos Locos Taco as prepared for you by Taco Bell. "Taking tacos where no one thought they'd go," the 2012 ad promises. Well sign me up, then. Behind this absurd narcissism surges the jaunty synth riff from "Take a Walk," the lead track on Passion Pit's spotty but decent new album *Gossamer*. For the next few years, I'll never be able to hear this shiny, grinding bit of electro-pop without thinking of Taco Bell meat, and lots of it: canvas shoes trampling through a beach of grainy seasoned meat; mouths laughing and overflowing with beef mix; sidewalks, escalators, grassy fields, apartment hallways, and city park paths slathered in that addictive orange-brown mush as if spread by enormous butter knives.

Now, I know, *I know*: musicians have been licensing their songs to corporations for years, well before the new millennium. The days of Neil Young spitting out "This Note's for You" and grumbling that being endorsed by a corporation is "one of the first fucking lines that's ever been drawn" for rock musicians—well, those are the days that used to be, my friend.[1] There are so many songs in commercials that entire websites are now devoted to sorting things out for you.[2] And it's not just the so-called sellouts from the splashy-trashy American Wow. Bob Dylan skulked through a 2004 Victoria's Secret ad that used his song "Love Sick." It was so perverse I thought, well, who cares anymore? Still, there are some instances where the marriage of music and commerce can give you the creeps. In September 2016, LCD Soundsystem played the opening of a hip Manhattan bar-lounge owned by Pepsi. Said the company's press release, "The Kola House represents a new space for us to support our consumer-first approach to drive authenticity and innovation around our beverage offerings and ideals." Of course they used the word "artisanal."[3]

So how did it come to pass that Passion Pit crossed the line and licensed its song to Taco Bell? Before we throw all of these artists under the groovy love bus of 1960s idealism, we have to acknowledge that the historical situation has changed, and since music is a performance that happens in historical time, it can't be separated from the environment in which it occurs. We also have to admit that consumerism in and outside of the American Wow always intersects with technology. Even if my project is to retrieve the potential of performance, its volatility and possibility, I have to account for the massive shift in how music is distributed and heard thanks to the biggest sea change in the history of music technology since the invention of the eight-track cassette, a change that has also radically transformed how we perceive the aesthetic new.

O Techno-Utopia!—Values in, Values Out—Little Blue Orbs—Talking in Church

Somewhere I have this MP3 of Superchunk's "Detroit Has a Skyline," and it sounds like shit. Jon Wurster is beating the hell out of the drum kit, whipping the crash cymbals throughout the song into a wash of monumental noise—but here, in this little file, the cymbals sound like they're degrading the instant they're struck, even before they're struck: *xxxxkkkkkSSShhhkkxxxx*. On my original but now lost *Here's Where the Strings Come In* compact disc, the song probably contained about 40 megabytes of sonic information; the MP3 contains four. Still, I used to feed it into my iPod and play that through my car stereo, making do because I was broke; eventually the iPod broke, but who cares because now I can listen to a slightly better quality version on a subscription site I access on my phone.

The new digitalism is an amplification of two traditional pop culture values, accessibility and portability, and these values have always driven technological innovation. MP3s, smart phones, streaming services, and the internet all have their predecessors. The MP3: vinyl records/eight tracks/cassettes/CDs. Smart phones: boom boxes and the Walkman. Streaming services: the radio. The internet: the library. This history helps explain the difference between the new and "innovation," a term whose original Latin root is *novus*, or new, but whose meaning morphed in the mid-sixteenth century into *innovat*, meaning "renewed" or "altered." Not surprisingly, innovation is today most associated with that tender sweet spot where business and technology meet; its differences are functional, not aesthetic; it claims to improve on what already exists, including the values we hold dear. Art that is innovative usually has the same limited sense of newness. According to Google's Ngram database, which tracks word usage in Google Books, the frequency of "innovation" more than quadrupled between 1960 and 2008, perhaps reflecting our skepticism of the new.[4] Innovation still sounds sexy, though. It coos that familiar techno-utopian melody: *everything will be much better in the future.*

Digital technology and the internet are innovations that have changed nearly everything about how music is distributed, publicized, purchased (or otherwise acquired), and listened to—all in the name of core principles like mobility and portability, values that reveal our presentist urge. But in the economy of cultural exchange, when one value is accepted, another is rejected.

Since most listeners value accessibility and portability more than nice big cover art and high-end sound quality, the compact disc shrunk the canvas of the vinyl record sleeve and sharpened, chilled, and pumped up what tended to be the rounded, warmer, and quieter tones of vinyl. (The steady increase of vinyl sales in the 2010s suggests a revaluing on the subcultural level, since vinyl sales are still relatively meager overall.) In order to gobble up music faster, more cheaply, and more easily, we reject the importance of owning a physical artifact of the music. The MP3 at least promised equal fidelity by cancelling out useless signals that were taking up digital space.[5] Its physical space reduced almost to nil, the MP3 let you have more music, too, especially if it was freely downloaded. As an ideal, the MP3 reflected the same promise of unfettered democracy as the internet, but this ease of access has led to an economy of cultural abundance in which the musical performance has been devalued since it's plentiful, often free, and easily replaceable. No one gets angry about a few lost MP3s. (A few thousand is a different story.) The so-called democracy of the internet, meanwhile, reinforces presentism by intensifying the moment and reaching out in all directions without a sense of past or future. It's the ultimate form *and source* of recombination. While it's tempting to think of the internet as a cultural archive, it's too fluid, too global, too whole, and too fractured to be anything less than an infinite assembly of archives, like Borges' "Library of Babel" if it were run by multinational corporations, governments, fans, academics, click-baiting entrepreneurs, and white supremacists in addition to those manic librarian cults. Hooray for us.

The values promoted through the MP3 and the internet have devalued an artist's claim on the ownership of her work, even as high-profile court cases like *Eldred vs. Ashcroft* ended in victories for copyright holders.[6] This devaluation began as a resistance to onerous copyright laws and tight-fisted music labels, but its history reaches back decades to the rise of vinyl bootlegs like *LiveR Than You'll Ever Be* (The Rolling Stones) and the infamous 1969 Dylan boot *Great White Wonder*. The latter was released by two record industry insiders named Ken and "Dub," who told *Rolling Stone*, "We're just liberating the records and bringing them to all the people, not just the chosen few."[7] Today, we have liberated all of the records for all of the people. Talking Heads front man David Byrne skeptically notes in his book *How Music Works* that the genuine concept of "more free circulation and access to culture" is supposed to allow us "to build upon the work of our predecessors"—in other words, to at least encourage innovation if not create the new.[8] Thus the democratization of the internet and digital technology has been presented as a counterstrike against the same capitalist forces that limit innovation. Values in, values out, though. Intellectual property, musicians' rights, and remuneration—gettin' paid—seem to matter less to consumers. And really, if a work of art comes to me in such a pitiful, uniform manner as an MP3 that I download or stream, what is its claim to uniqueness and worth?

The story of music and technology is usually framed as this: new technology has created new values. But as scholar Mark Katz argues near the end of *Capturing Sound: How Technology Has Changed Music*, "Recording is not a mysterious force that compels the actions of its users," and I would extend that argument to all music-related technology. Instead, and despite the constant dynamic tension between the user and the machine, what we do with technology depends on our values.[9] In fact, the more I've thought about it, the more convinced I've become that the values we've held for half a century have engineered technology to give us what we want: accessibility and portability, but also participation and belonging. For instance, today there seems to be more equality between the audience and artist, the listener's new role resting somewhere between typical consumer, part-time publicist, and distributor. This perceived equality is really a collapsing of the distance between the fan and the artist, which is exactly what Ken and Dub were looking for in 1969. The difference today, though, is how thoroughly integrated and swift this is through the internet. We buy some downloads from Bandcamp, promote that band's upcoming show on Facebook by using an app like Songkick, maybe share some MP3s with friends through email, and attempt to interact with these bands—or pop stars—through Instagram. In other words, we now engage actively in a participatory spectacle thanks in large part to technology.

We participate differently when we go to clubs and arenas to see shows, too. Steady concert attendance in the 2010s would seem to suggest that as we devalue the worth of a recording, we continue to value the unrepeatable live event.[10] Judging by all the camera phones being held up into the inky darkness, we seem to go to concerts so we can record them. We're so conditioned by consumerism and the technology of social media that we've learned to turn even a live performance, the ephemeral live moment, into a product by mediating our experience with cell phone video cameras. Entranced by media, we turn everything into media; beholden to commerce, we turn life into a commodity. Maybe this is what we've wanted all along. If we still hunger for history and narrative—and I think we do; I think we want to create both, not just witness them—then by recording a concert we become at least documentarians of history and possible events as they happen. And we get social prestige credits for being there.

But if you've been to or performed at a concert since the proliferation of the smart phone, you know that those little blue orbs dotting the arena (or flashing in your face) also become distractions that take us out of the performance. The exceptionality of the historical moment, its web of actions and circumstances, and its specificity of place and time are standardized by the uniform limitations of the phone's camera, its narrow perspective, and its pitiful sound recording capability. And then we post the clips to YouTube. These can be fascinating assertions of ownership and commonality. They privatize what was public and then publicize what was private, though in an altered way. Or we use the app Periscope to illicitly broadcast real-time but immediately perishable live concert footage to the web as the event happens. Unlike the performer, though, we bear no sense of responsibility for the product. We're really only confirming our consumerist role.

If we get lost in documenting a live performance, we risk losing it twice. It'll disappear into history anyway. Mediating the experience, already thinking of the product we're creating, already in the future, we lose our presence as every second passes by. We participate but lose what is truly new: the unique moment of art as it's created and experienced.

All of this, from the MP3 to the cell phone camera, is what Debord predicted in the early 1990s in his slim sequel, *Comments on the Society of the Spectacle*. Here he argues that the two kinds of spectacle he'd previously defined—the "concentrated," a personality-based, violent, and authoritarian form, and the "diffuse," an egalitarian, consumerist, and absolutely American form—have been combined into the "integrated" spectacle in which authority is hidden and consumerism is overwhelmingly woven into the fabric of daily life thanks in part to "incessant technological renewal."[11] "[R]eality," he writes, "no longer confronts the integrated spectacle as alien" because we more actively shape reality to our needs, or think we do, through the spectacle.[12] If the spectacle is our church, then in the integrated spectacle we are more devout: more connected, but unable to turn away. Debord claims that "spectacular discourse leaves no room for reply," but we now live in a church in which we do talk back. What we produce, though, is the same thing we've always produced: our alienated selves, e.g. the "you" who yells at people in the comments section of a YouTube video and the "you" who would never say such things to the same person if you met them.

This was the arena into which Passion Pit stepped with *Gossamer* in 2012: a stark, confusing, and still-evolving battleground. The scene was set for them long before, thanks to these innovative technologies, old values, new effects, and the new situation to which the music industry had to adapt.

It adapted like Captain Ahab, determined to catch the whale even if that meant drowning in the whirlpool of its own stubbornness and pride.

Chicken Carcasses and Monoliths—Suing Children—Trickle-Down Economics

In 1996, everything changed before we realized it had changed, which is, you'll recall, part of Badiou's definition of the event. That year, the United States Congress passed the Telecommunications Act, which more or less unleashed corporations to buy each other up. Gone were the limitations on how many radio stations could be owned by one company, and thus: Clear Channel. Consolidation! Nothing screams "fertile ground for the new" like consolidating the ways music can be heard. The effect, as music journalist Greg Kot argues, was that radio stations began "fretting about chasing [listeners] off with new, unfamiliar music. In this environment, taking chances on unproven artists supported by underfunded independent labels was considered bad business."[13] This led to fewer openings for new records and a new method of payola which came back to bite the radio industry in a FCC ruling in 2007. The homogenization of conglomerate terrestrial radio was offset to some degree by satellite radio and internet radio, and to be fair, there's some debate about whether or not payola may have actually helped fuel crossover diversity on the Top 40 radio, particularly hip-hop.[14]

The same consolidation affected the major music labels. Before 1998, the industry was controlled by six already enormous corporations: Warner Music Group, Sony, Universal Music Group, EMI, BMG, and Polygram, each of which owned numerous subsidiary labels. Watch the dominoes fall: Polygram was absorbed into Universal in 1998, BMG was sucked up by Sony in 2004, and EMI was divided up like the carcass of a chicken and parceled out to Warner and Sony in 2011 and UMG in 2013, leaving us with "The Big Three" we have as of this writing. You say the internet led to musical democracy? Not quite. To give you an idea of how thoroughly these corporations control popular music, first a statistic: according to a Neilsen/*Billboard* report in 2012, the Big Three controlled 88.5 percent of the market.[15] By 2014, that market share had fallen ... to 86 percent.[16] Secondly, consider that Passion Pit's "Take a Walk" and its album *Gossamer* were released by the indie label Frenchkiss but distributed by Columbia Records/Sony. Is it possible that a publicly traded multinational corporation has a far different view of the bottom line than a small and truly independent label? Each is in the business of selling new music, but what "new" means to each is determined differently. It's not that Sony wasn't looking for good new music in 2012, but that its version of "new" was still and always will be ultimately measured by a commercial yardstick. The willingness of big labels to take chances has flexed and tightened for decades, but in the 2000s, like radio, these corporations spent less time cultivating new and young artists. As Kot writes, "The long-range, career-building view was out. Instant payback was in."[17] This is more or less an example of the shortening of narrative and the compression of time described by Rushkoff as symptoms of presentism. When someone like Prince or Madonna had their initial hits, we asked, "What will they do next?" Now we wonder if a new artist will be able to make a second album.

The litany of the music industry's mistakes since the late 1990s didn't help the situation. How to describe it succinctly? At the exact historical moment the industry should have been becoming more flexible, it became rigid. The corporations forgot that people, especially young people, want the new not the familiar. But as Kot points out, the newlymergeds were controlled by Wall Street, which values stability, and "in an industry supposedly devoted to creating a highly volatile and unpredictable product—music—this was hardly a sound strategy."[18] And then, naturally, the music industry ignored its chance to license a copy-protectable MP3 when it was presented to them in 1997 by its inventor, Karlheinz Brandenburg, as the internet grew like a tumor. Again with the falling dominoes: becoming increasingly monolithic, the corporations struggled to adjust to the idea of music on the web; they sued Napster, filed "educational lawsuits" against children, college students, and single mothers, destroyed their already "meh" reputation with the buying public, failed to catch the iTunes train, ignored YouTube, and missed out on streaming music services such as Spotify.[19] A 2013 report by Moody's claimed that "consolidation ... should give [the Big Three] more leverage in their negotiations with the digital music service providers" and "improved bargaining power to negotiate more favorable rates," failing to note the reason an improvement was needed: paltry royalty rates that were the result of the industry's formerly antagonistic and Neanderthal-esque attitude toward those providers while it clung to its baby blanket, CD sales.[20]

The compact disc, the album format, and the return of the single combine for the nearly *Hamlet*-like ending of our sordid tale. From the late 1990s to roughly 2010, at every step of the way, the music industry resisted change, resisted the new, and nearly destroyed itself in the process. In 2000, what was then the Big Five along with other smaller labels sold 785.1 million CDs; by 2010, that number had dropped to 250 million, and by 2014, according to Nielsen, only 140.8 million CDs were sold—a decrease of roughly 644 million CDs.[21] Beholden to the album format, the industry ignored that, thanks to the MP3, the single was making a resurgence via online streaming platforms. As the prices for a compact disc peaked somewhere close to eighteen dollars, the cheap or free single-purchase allowed listeners to get the handful of good songs they really wanted off an album without having to bother with what we might affectionately call "deep cuts."

So the irony of critiquing the American Wow from purely an anti-commodification angle is that its commodities are worth less today than twenty years ago. That said, near the end of the disastrous 2000s the music industry finally began to adjust, realizing that its best option was to monetize the internet instead of punishing its users. In 2009, Universal Music Group executive Doug Morris launched the Vevo channel on YouTube, "[taking] over thirty years of creative output from more than 10,000 artists … written off as promotional cost and transform[ing] it into a high-growth profit center."[22] You'll notice that the financial success is derived from UMG's back catalog, not new music. This is how the American Wow as a business recalibrated itself, but at least that meant the profits surely would trickle down to the musicians, eh?

No. Despite record industry executives making one catastrophic decision after another, musicians are paying the price. They're not selling as many units and they're making less money overall from the units they do sell since streaming royalty rates are so low. In 2008, *Wired* editor Chris Anderson wrote, "Free music is just publicity for a far more lucrative tour business," which is true to an extent—bands can make decent money on ticket sales and merch like t-shirts and, yes, CDs and downloads—but completely undersells how difficult touring is.[23] Musicians must tour if they're going to make *any* money, which means grueling months on the road. (Three to four per year is not uncommon for mid-level pros.) Different approaches work for different bands, but the challenges for new bands are considerable. Anderson should have written, "… a far more lucrative tour business if you're willing to sleep on strangers' couches, eat fast food, argue with booking agents, and visit the repair shop when your van's radiator melts down, which it will." Anyway, to create capital for recording, bands turn to patronage systems like Kickstarter, IndieGoGo, and Patreon wherein fans, if they exist, fund projects in return for special incentives like bonus tracks, signed merchandise, free tickets, house concerts, and so on. Undoubtedly there's some freedom in this, and more control of one's work, but it's harder to make a living.

And so, as much as I'm criticizing the marriage of "Take a Walk" to Taco Bell, I understand the band's reasons behind it.

Passion Pit's front man Michael Angelakos said of the ad, "What does Taco Bell have to do with three of my family members struggling financially … I have no idea. It's not about promoting celebrities or giant corporations or anything like that."[24] He added, with presumably some hint of excitement, that "[i]t's just airtime ... an amazing opportunity." But before I sound too rigidly ideological, let me admit that when Angelakos says in the same Q&A that "[a] lot of older artists are adamantly against the usage of their music in commercials. They can actually afford to turn that down," he's got a point, because their back catalogs are making bank.

Ground Beef Dissonance—"Milky Way"—Performing Taco Bell

Still, all of this has an effect on how we perceive the new. As much as the core of music is performance, aesthetics and interpretation will always be influenced by technology, especially when technology is welded to commodification. That's why I couldn't hear "Take a Walk" for years—literally, at least three years—without thinking of Taco Bell's seasoned beef. The song documents the trials and tribulations of an American immigrant and his wife. They start with nothing, build a family, climb the mountain of the American Dream. After bringing over his family, the man watches them disperse around the country. Investments tank, debt builds up, the man is on edge .... Angelakos' storytelling is compact, moving; the music rallies sinking spirits. But the Taco Bell commercial ruined the song for me. Ruined the entire album for me, really. *Gossamer* is anxious about its anxieties, and even though its crystalline production values and Angelakos' falsetto more often than not deflect those anxieties, songs like "I'll Be Alright" and "It's Not My Fault, I'm Happy" own them honestly and without affect. But the point is that, even if the album had been significantly new, I would've been too distracted by Taco Bell meat to notice.

When a song is licensed to sell a product—tacos, cars, lingerie, coffee, cola—the result is a kind of double product, a fused commodity that only reinforces the utilitarianism of music. Just about every definitive recording becomes a commodity, but its meanings exist in wider realms because of the variability of performance. The tying of a recording to a second commodity that has only commercial motivations constricts those realms and variables. The context of history is replaced by the context of a second product, and since we don't think much about the history of a taco, history dribbles away like juice down your chin. The variables that always exist in a performance cede to the narrow purpose of the second product; they don't disappear, but they're obscured by *we hope this catchy song makes you want to buy our tacos*. Any potential in the music is now tied to the limited potential of the second product, a potential that is usually based on an already approved cultural value like the version of freedom that comes from being able to buy a taco whenever you want.

It's probably more realistic to think of all of this as dissonance, a conflict between one meaning and another that can't be resolved. The real danger for art is that, in the end, we don't perceive any dissonance. When "Pink Moon," the title track from the English singer-songwriter Nick Drake's final studio album, was used in a commercial for the Volkswagen Cabrio in 1999, the minute-long spot made no connections to the complexity of Drake's struggle with depression, the period of improved health that made possible the recording of *Pink Moon* in October 1971, or his suicide in 1974, which may have been an accident. A commercial is incapable of such complexity or empathy. A song is very capable; "Pink Moon" is a gorgeous blue hypnosis, a sounding of hope from within the shadows of depression. That will not sell a car. The spot, dubbed "Milky Way," instead showed four new adults ditching a party to enjoy a moonlit drive along the coast in a car that would be discontinued three years later, turning Drake's dark night of the soul into a typically American Wow ode to youth and freedom. For a commercial, "Milky Way" was visually striking in 1999 and some YouTube users apparently still think it is. Wrote one not long ago, "Advertising is so often rampant commercialism, it's easy to forget it can occasionally be artwork. This surely is the latter."[25]

The internet and digital technologies have made visible what has always been visible in a highly consumerized economy: everything's for sale, even a musician's ultimately fatal battle with depression. If every musical performance is already nothing more than a product, then there's no cognitive dissonance to be had when a song is used in a commercial; there's no aesthetic dissonance, no difference, between art and commerce at all. The problem isn't that, being the savvy consumers we are, we're capable of thinking of "Take a Walk" as both a story of immigrant financial success and ruin across generations released at a time when millions were still out of work following the Great Recession, and, at the same time, a series of sounds and words used to seduce a person into spending hard-earned and hard-to-come-by cash on a taco, or a bag of tacos, or maybe a taco meal. The problem is that these two perceptions fuse into one thing: a way to sell a commodity. And if that's true, then there can be no slow burn of meaning, no unsolvable mysteries within a performance; there can be no obscure sense of personality, no hermits or outcasts, nothing that doesn't serve the social purpose of consumerism. The logical extension is that aesthetic newness becomes nothing more than commodified innovation; the new is not generated by music, but by music's function and place in the economy. Linked now to Taco Bell, "Take a Walk" becomes a performance of Taco Bell, a performance of consumerist values. And those are not very new values at all.

7

We Can Flux: Prince Queers Democracy and the New

> *There have been great American artists who have worked beyond the public's ability to understand them easily, but none who have condescended to the public—none who have not hoped, no matter how secretly, that their work would lift America to heaven, or drive a stake through its heart. This is a democratic desire ... and at its best it is an impulse to wholeness, an attempt not to deny diversity, or to hide from it, but to discover what it is that diverse people can authentically share. It is a desire of the artist to remake America on his or her own terms. This impulse powers the strongest popular artists as it powers pop culture itself. It is an urge to novelty and necessity; it exhausts most talents with terrific speed and goes on to something else.*
>
> —Greil Marcus, *Mystery Train*[1]

February 4, 2007, Another Super Bowl

The scene: Miami under siege by a typhoon. Prince strides gracefully across what must be a slippery stage in the shape of his male-female symbol. It's purple, naturally. Eight years before Katy Perry will fly around on a skyhook, I'm worried that Prince is going to be electrocuted. He seems unperturbed.

Drenched and wearing heels, he is nonetheless a supreme badass, as always. Twenty-four years after introducing "Purple Rain" that night at First Avenue, Prince slices into its solo, his guitar growling and shrieking, its tone thick, pissed off, as if *it's* worried about being electrocuted. Silhouetted against an enormous billowing sail, he runs the melody downward, hits a jarring blue note just out of key enough to remind you of Hendrix, drags it back up, plays a series of trills, and finds his way to the dignified signature melody that comes before the sing-along *ooh ooh ooh-ooh-ooh*. The music, the setting, the downpour: tonight the spectacle becomes more than usually seems possible, nothing else sounds so good, and Debord is a fool.

The night caps off a three-year comeback that started with *Musicology* in 2004. It feels like Prince has come out of hiding, like he's finished with the name-change business, like he's Prince again. But even if his live act is unbeatable and always will be, his studio work since *The Rainbow Children* in 2001 has mainly consisted of uneven reinterpretations of the music that influenced him and safe recreations of his own magnetic influence. The shocking originality of Prince's music in the 1980s and the rippling power it's had on music and culture since then are so absolute that complaining about the decline of his innovative power seems petty, almost embarrassing. As a fan, it feels like a betrayal. No popular musician has ever stayed consistently new; it's hard enough just to be good. And yet, the more inventive the artist, the more he or she is judged by those past inventions, which means Prince in the new millennium faced the highest bar possible.

That's another reason why tonight is so thrilling. It's like Prince is swatting away all of that. *Be here with me right now*, he seems to be saying. *This is all that matters.*

The Event—Flux and Democracy in the American Wow

In the 1980s, Prince was an event. He entirely changed what was possible for the situation. There was the bold ultra-fusion of his music. I can't think of any other artist who would risk playing a snippet of "How Much Is That Doggie in the Window" before seguing into "Automatic," as Prince did during the *Parade* tour, and no one else who could make it work. As his closest contemporaries, Michael Jackson and Madonna were pop modernists, honing the genre, confirming its discipline. Prince was so interdisciplinary he called the very notion of disciplines into question. As in, why bother with them?

Among them, sexual identity. Through the bracing, brazen eroticism in his songs and onstage shenanigans (stroking his guitar neck until it sprayed water in *Purple Rain*, for instance), Prince freaked the rules of identity, performing queer a decade before hardly anyone was using the term in a positive, empowering way.[2] The queer values of variability, contingency, and plurality were engrained into the ultra-fusion of Prince's music on a fundamental level: its blurring of genres, its ability to meet any occasion, any audience, its fleet improvisations, and the various ways Prince's body, voice, playing, and arrangements presented the flux of being human. When he sang "I Wanna Be Your Lover," he sounded like he could be talking to anyone; in "Sexuality" he does, fusing queerness with revolution. "Controversy" and "I Would Die 4 U" dove right into the heart of ambiguity without resolving it, as did "If I Was Your Girlfriend," which used his funky, squeezed Camille voice. Queerness intersected with race—by which I mean, here was a Black man in 1980 wearing a trench coat and bikini briefs—and those intersected with religion, an intense unorthodox Christianity in which God's presence was a perpetual conflict and the source of ecstatic joy. Much of that joy was to be found in the passionate sounds and styles of Black churches and gospel music in songs like "Purple Rain," "The Ladder," even "Play in the Sunshine."

These qualities alone might have made Prince an event even if he hadn't become a pop superstar. But he did, and so, at the highest level of American Wow stardom, at its normalizing peak, he questioned what "normal" meant. It was damn near miraculous. When I ask the question of how anything can be new in the pop spectacle, I'm partly asking about the power of the individual artist to work against the limitations, normalizations, and commodifications of that spectacle. To be new in this stratosphere of popularity and in the face of those challenges requires a level of commitment which in turn demands, I think, a belief in something greater than one's own ego. Prince was deeply egotistical; so are hundreds of other pop superstars and probably hundreds of thousands of nonsuperstar musicians. But Prince was also dedicated to the exploration of "what it is that diverse people can authentically share," as Marcus writes in *Mystery Train*. He wanted to transform the American Wow and the entire nation into the inclusive democracy he imagined they could be.

After the Event—Wandering Nostalgia

Now comes the part of the story that breaks my heart. Like the other (very few) musicians who have created events and lived long careers, Prince musically struggled under the weight of his own newness. After 1995's *The Gold Experience*—for me, the pinnacle of his decade, a kaleidoscope of urgency, humor, muscle, and sensuality—Prince dropped a handful of unremarkable albums with unremarkable songs. Meanwhile, you could listen along as the pop music on the radio caught up to him and surged ahead. When *The Rainbow Children* came out in 2001, I didn't know what to make of it. Now it stands up, a beautiful and quirky album, but it's also his last truly ultrafusionist studio recording. In the late 1990s and early 2000s, he embraced the internet as a way to release more music and connect directly with fans through the NPG Music Club; his prolificness was the main reason for his dispute with Warner Brothers which led to him scrawling SLAVE on his cheek in 1993 and changing his name to the unpronounceable symbol ☥. The internet made perfect sense for Prince, but the music he released through the club wasn't very good. Too many go-nowhere instrumentals like *N.E.W.S.*, *Xpectation*, and *C-Note*. The exception was *The Chocolate Invasion*, or at least its slightly more experimental songs like "When Eye Lay My Hands on U" and "Supercute" which showed Prince hadn't given up on melody. But soon he was repeating the record industry's mistake of taking a hard line with fans who were sharing MP3s and posting videos on YouTube.

    Prince still commanded respect in the American Wow, but he didn't chart like he used to. The fact that his supposed return-to-form was the mediocre

Musicology indicated just how far he'd slipped. A stale airlessness pervades the album; it's uptight, not tight. It laid down the predictable template for his next few albums, including the stronger *3121*: a funk grinder or two (the title track and "Black Sweat"), a few dance pop numbers (e.g., "The Word"), a rocker ("Fury"), and a few slow jams ("Incense and Candles"). Distribution stayed weird. In 2007, *Planet Earth* was released exclusively through a British newspaper, as was *20Ten*; in between them, *Lotusflower/MPLSound* was put out solely through the department store chain Target. In a way, this was all new, but it was chaotic. As an American fan, half the time I couldn't even find the music. (How in the hell was I going to get an album attached to the *Mail on Sunday*?) What I did hear was sometimes moving and wonderful—"Reflection" from *Musicology*, "Black Sweat" from *3121*, "Guitar" and "Chelsea Rodgers" from *Planet Earth*, "Colonized Mind" from *Lotusflower*—but it wasn't particularly new. When the Linn Drum sounds he'd made famous with the Revolution returned on albums like *MPLSound* and *20Ten*, a wandering sense of nostalgia only increased, even on superb songs like "Chocolate Box" and "Future Soul Song."

If you listen to Prince's live recordings from the new millennium, particularly post-*Musicology*, you hear an entirely different artist. He's more engaged, more inventive, more relaxed. Two 2007 aftershow concerts documented on *Indigo Nights*—which you could only get at the time by purchasing what was essentially a coffee-table book, *21 Nights*—prove that our man was still capable of turning a relatively run-of-the-mill Vegas-blues ballad like "The One" into a scorching, holy melodrama. And that he could still mix together wildly different styles, tossing a bit Scott Joplin's ragtime number "The Entertainer" into "3121" and following it up with about ten seconds of keyboard squelches. In a stunning set at the Montreux Jazz Festival in 2009, the sheer life-affirming energy of his music, missing from most his studio recordings, is almost overwhelming, whether it's his cover of Hendrix's "Spanish Castle Magic" or a tender, attentive reading of "I Love U But I Don't Trust U Anymore," easily the best song on 1999s *Rave Un2 the Joy Fantastic*. While so many of his studio recordings sounded unfinished, as in dashed-off, here Prince un-finishes "Little Red Corvette" into a slow, humid film noir. The choruses are full of the same old come-ons, those perfect double entendres, but the verses seethe like a framed man. In the extended coda, a synthesizer goes off like a siren. There's such a feeling of menace. In the background, the same metallic *suh-SUH-suh ... KEH-keh* drumbeat from the studio recording hisses and smacks from inside the song's deep undertow as it fades. "Yes, Montreaux, yes!" Prince says, as if he and the audience have achieved a great victory.

In recent years, I've become convinced that Prince's aesthetic was in fact an argument about newness, and that you could hear it best through his live performances. "The Event is not an end," writes my philosopher colleague Matt Mitchem, "it is not the final victory of truth, or the final solution for thought; it is rather the authorization for philosophy to declare that a new possibility for the world has appeared."[3] Having authorized this declaration in the 1980s, Prince never stopped pursuing new possibilities for music and ordinary life, understanding intuitively or consciously that they emerge through performance.

"Black Sweat"—Working the Trap

CHRIS ROCK: Early on in your career, you, uh ... the androgynous thing. Was that an act or were you searching for a sexual identity?

PRINCE: That's a good question. I don't suppose I was searching, really, I think I was just being who I was, being the true Gemini that I am. And there's many sides in that as well. And there was a little acting going on, too.[4]

Late in his career, Prince may never have penned new songs as gender-fluctuating as "If I Was Your Girlfriend," but in subtle ways he continued to perform queerness. After all, what's to say that the persona singing "Black Sweat" is male or straight? Prince's falsetto whispers to us, challenges us, and apologizes for coming on so hard, but this groove can't be helped, now can it? Over a syncopated beat marked by a quick suspension of time just before the hi-hat, Prince's voice leaps from coy to a deep soul rumble and on up into an ecstatic atmosphere, the place where his falsetto's smoothness disintegrates into a scream. Writing about Prince in 1980, the critic Ariel Swartley noted that "falsetto literally confounds sexuality" since it is "a voice like a woman's coming from a man …."[5] Swartley's conflation of sexuality and gender is the precise stability that queerness seeks to destabilize, but the point for now is that falsetto extends past the boundaries of authenticity and inauthenticity in the moment of performance. It has the ability to queer gender and sexuality, to make them contingent and variable. Through what some might call artifice, falsetto expresses a truth about identity flux.

Prince never abandoned his gorgeous falsetto. Neither did he abandon his body, by which I mean he stayed in shape and understood what his body and the clothes he put on it could communicate: sensuality, vulnerability, athleticism, and flux. Look at his doe eyes and slim smooth face in the video for "Black Sweat." His soft, loose suit. His playful coif brushed to the right. Director Sanaa Hamri often frames Prince either off-center or in maximal close-up, his presence switching between tease and fulfilment. In one shot, he passes through the frame, hilariously, as if he's on an escalator, his eyes bewildered and his nose crinkled by the "white lady scream" mimed by the model Celestina Aladekoba. She whispers to Prince, they stand near each other, but in fact they spend most of the video apart. Aladekoba dances; Prince usually doesn't even watch her. He seems more bemused by her than attracted to her; their relationship is friendly, not erotic. The video and the song never arrive at a gendered or sexualized resolution.

"For many members of the queer community," wrote Nathan Smith for *Out* in 2016, "Prince's sheer persistent resistance to being restricted by language was an exciting and provocative feat and one through which they could channel their own frustrations and identity struggles."[6] Prince's resistance depended on the languages of words and sounds (and clothes and bodies); he could sing hetero to a woman in a song like "Incense and Candles" and at the same time, with his computer-tweaked falsetto vocals and sensual rhythms, perform in a way that defied easy sexual or gender (or racial, or class) categorization. So while his presentation of queerness may have been subtler in the new millennium than it was in the 1980s, it did not vanish, and it tells us something valuable about the intersections of queerness with performance and the new.

In her seminal 1990 text *Gender Trouble*, queer theorist Judith Butler demonstrates that gender is an ongoing construction through performance rather than an essence which determines performance. But this construction often responds, Butler argues, to the various ways society compels us to conform to an idealized and impossible gender role, one we can never match because, as Butler said in a 1992 interview, "becoming gendered involves impersonating an ideal nobody actually inhabits …."[7] One's efforts become impersonations, and these performances over time construct one's sense of gender. In the same interview, Butler lamented that readers of *Gender Trouble* had taken performativity to always be a positive and free opportunity to innovate one's identity. Instead, she argued, the performance of gender is a daily grind. "Performativity has to do with repetition," she said, "very often with the repetition of oppressive and painful gender norms to force them to resignify. This is not freedom, but a question of how to work the trap that one is inevitably in."[8] The social trap is omnipresent; it exists whether we think we're performing (working the trap) freely or not, and whether or not we're assured our performance is free. Thus, performativity is mandatory, not optional, and as Butler emphasizes, for queer folks, performativity is part of an everyday life which includes threats of exclusion and violence.

One of the reasons performativity was taken to be free and positive was that Butler's main example of it in *Gender Trouble* was drag. The power of drag to work the trap is derived from its "parodic repetition of gender norms" which is capable of breaking the illusion that heterosexuality is "the original of which homosexuality is an inferior copy"—in other words, something not-new.[9] The result is a spectrum of genuine original identities that are nonetheless always under pressure from social forces. Not all drag performances will accomplish this. Neither is drag the only way to perform this kind of parody. Falsetto, for example, is a vocal technique that banishes the notion of a gendered original since its parody of the female voice blurs the distinction between man and woman, and sometimes straight and queer. Instead of being an inferior copy, at its best—e.g. Prince, whether it's "Do Me Baby" or "Black Sweat"—falsetto becomes entirely original and genuine.

Just now, I slipped into the exact thing Butler warns against: equating "performance," the romanticized assumption of the individual's unfettered willpower and expression, with "performativity," the oppressively necessitated response to social power. Butler emphatically expanded on the differences between the two in her 1993 book *Bodies That Matter*, writing that performativity "is neither free play nor theatrical self-presentation, nor can it simply be equated with performance."[10] But I'm not convinced that artistic performance is unrepetitive, unburdened, or an unconstrained presentation of self. While I don't want to ignore the numerous ways oppressive gender norms are enforced against queer persons in everyday life, this is a book about music, and the performance of gender and sexuality in music doesn't come easily or without consequence. This, in fact, is partly what I hear and see in "Black Sweat:" the effort to work the trap of gender and sexuality—race, too; it matters that it's a *Black* sweat—in a contemporary society and a specific culture which claims everything is permitted when it's not.

The Scourge of Public Authenticity— There's Joy in Repetition

For its musicians, the pop spectacle of the American Wow is the inevitable trap. You can't perform *in it* and not, in some way, be *of it*. Already so hell-bent on order and normalization, the Wow fluently commodifies even progressive identities like queer; the more popular you become, the bigger your "brand," the tighter and swifter the trap. Debord returns: "All individual reality has become social reality directly dependent on social power and shaped by it."[11] Individual performers and their art are judged by how successfully each reflects economic, political, identitarian, and other cultural values in the American Wow. (It happens in all music, but let's stay focused here.) When Beyoncé performed in front of the word FEMINIST at the VMAs in 2014, there was less discussion about what she meant or what it had to do with her music, and more discussion about whether or not she was right. In other words, the possibilities of meaning are boiled down to simple yes-or-no questions. Is Katy

Perry's work authentically feminist or not? (Did I ask that in a recent chapter? Did I give you an answer?) Is "Black Sweat" authentically Black, or masculine, or queer?

Social reality, social determinism, social mimeticism: I'll call it *public authenticity*. Tamping down imagination and play, turning music into nothing more than a mirror held up to society, public authenticity champions the self presented in public and, often, through media; it equates that public mediated self with the private self, and judges both according to ideals of public identity no person can actually live up to. Neither can their art. Insidiously, it can seem as though, as Greil Marcus paraphrases the above Debord quote in *Lipstick Traces*, "[n]othing that actually happens becomes real until it is represented in the spectacle that is social life—after which it becomes unreal, and passes into its opposite."[12] While public authenticity as practice or criticism rarely interrogates or even understands *itself* as a representation of social norms, the danger is that we take its logic for granted, crafting our lives and our art in order to seem authentic in a way determined by this mediated public reality. In short, this is how we participate in the spectacle.

This is obviously bad news for any substantial sense of newness. If music is heard as something that ought to be an accurate representation of social reality, then it cannot shape the public. Neither can it be anything more than an artist reproducing some version of what's already possible as determined by society. But since we still value newness, public authenticity itself is offered up as a kind of newness, a contemporary conversation about the arguments of the day. Its allure is the sparkle of "now." It becomes a substitute for a more complex, individual, and artistic new.

In the face of the omnipresent trap of public authenticity, can musical performance be liberating or is it doomed to conformity? Can it be new? Prince responded as all ambitious artists do: *I define what's authentic, I define what's public, I define what's new.* When he answered Chris Rock in that 1997 interview that he was "just being who [he] was," and that "there was a little acting going on, too," he all but defined a more positive view of Butler's performativity as a combination of genuineness and artifice, neither cancelling the other out, neither beholden to social norms. While he would have agreed with Butler's insistence on "iterability," the repetitiveness of performance—like the Lucretian swerve, the possibility that small differences might eventually become significant—Prince found joy in that repetition, joy in working the trap by working up a black sweat.[13] He understood, as most musicians do, that the repetitive nature of performance is actually what makes it always a matter of becoming. There was, for him, joy in the flux. Even if his music couldn't always find a way to communicate a sense of formal newness in the 2000s, it does possess an insatiable desire *for* newness.

Eventually that led somewhere artistically, and not coincidentally, it happened because he took a look at the society around him and what it considered authentic. Instead of imagining just himself, he imagined a future for all of us.

Prince Goes to the Future—Bringing Elsewhere Home

Art Official Age, released in 2014, is a confusing album. It's also Prince's best album of the new millennium, or at least since *The Rainbow Children*. Here's its story: Prince wakes up from suspended animation and finds himself in the future, which is not all it's cracked up to be. I think. To be honest, the concept is fuzzy, and the album seems to give up on it in the final act. The music, though, is distinct and fresh. "Art Official Cage" approaches the experimental pop ultra-fusion of songs like "Crystal Ball" but with some *Diamonds and Pearls*-era swagger thrown in. "Clouds" seduces me with its chorus alone. "The Breakdown" and "The Gold Standard" pretty much epitomize his late-era soul-funk nostalgia but sonically elevate that nostalgia with earnestness, even if the latter uses those deep "Bob George"-like vocals from the *Lovesexy/Black Album* era. After sagging in the middle with a string of nondescript ballads, the album springs to life again with "Way Back Home," the perplexing centerpiece. Over churning, swampy percussion, Prince's character protests this utopian society he's found himself in, declares how he's bucked the norms but perhaps at the cost of meaningful relationships, and doubts all those stories with neat, happy endings. There's a weird sense of alienation here, something our time traveler can't quite articulate. And then, the moment of the song: as he reveals that his greatest, maybe his only satisfaction comes from being able to see his path home, Prince's falsetto soars, pure and sweet. Combined with the words, it's a phrase of elation and, somehow, melancholy. He sings it again, reaching an even higher note. Whatever the concept of the album is, it's swallowed into (or freed by) this sound of hurt and self-determination.

If there is a late-era Prince album that consistently performs queerness, it's *Art Official Age*, but not in the way you might expect. The notion of utopia is crucial to queer performance and theory as a model for the political new. "The here and now," writes performance studies and queer theorist José Esteban Muñoz, "is simply not enough. Queerness should and could be about a desire for another way of being in both the world and time, a desire that resists mandates to accept that which is not enough."[14] Muñoz understood utopia as potentiality in the same vein as the philosopher Giorgio Agamben: it is here as an idea but not yet a reality. (What Agamben means by "potential" is roughly the same as what Badiou means by new possibilities, or the impossible.) Crucial to utopia and potential, Muñoz argues in *Cruising Utopia*, is the "emotional modality" of "hope" that sustains queer futurism in a present moment marked by lack.[15] But *Art Official Age*'s futurism is cautious, its optimism guarded; utopia is not liberating, it sounds cold. It, too, lacks. In "Clouds," Prince wakes up in the future just after the song dismisses the common metaphor for the internet and techno-utopia. Three "affirmations" seem like the album's obvious lessons, but as the British musician Lianne La Havas' telepathic guide instructs Prince in the album closer "Affirmation III," the swampy percussion and melody of "Way Back Home" resurface. Everything she says is answered, or contradicted, by the song's chorus hook.

Is this a resistance to futurity or a reconsideration of what it means? Prince says nothing about going back in time, but neither does it seem like he'll stay in this utopia. The self-determination in "Way Back Home" combined with La Havas' final counsel that we are our own destinations suggests that utopia is a "home" in which we find a new understanding of our own identity: the serenity of knowing who we are and the integrity of holding to that vision.

Utopia is never a place we really arrive at. The lie of futurism is that we get there and then time stops. Instead, utopia is an always-forwardness, the sense of becoming Muñoz identifies, and a peace of mind that one is headed in the right direction—which means it's a quality we can possess in the present moment. There is no way to be certain, thus the importance of hope.

It's absolutely critical that Prince's performance of utopia is adamantly tied to music as an imaginative art form that keeps hope alive for the self *and* for his audience, including the queer community. Butler came around to the importance of the imagined, recognizing that "the struggle to survive is not really separable from the cultural life of fantasy" which art brings into being. "Fantasy is what establishes the possible in excess of the real; it points, it points elsewhere, and when it is embodied"—as nearly all music is—"it brings the elsewhere home."[16]

Transfiguration—We Can Flux

To my mind, there's really only one other American musician whose cultural and musical impact has been as significant as Prince's, whose work and persona have been just as confounding and alluring, and who, as a working artist, has been as restless, prolific, and constantly evolving: Bob Dylan. On that Newport Folk Festival stage in 1965, Dylan argued that everything is permitted. Along came Prince fifteen years later, declaring that *you only think you permit everything. Let me show you what's really possible.* Through his performances, he showed that what had been considered possible was not actually possible for everyone, that we had failed to realize the egalitarian, fluxing possibilities Dylan offered, and that even greater impossibilities had appeared on the scene.

There's another connection here, one that helps me understand Prince's extended career. In *After the End of Art*, Arthur Danto says pop art like Warhol's *Brillo Box* transformed pieces of pop culture into the sacred: into art. His term is not transformed, though, it's "transfigured," which refers to the moment when Jesus, surrounded by his disciples, became, for a hot minute, holy. For Danto, this is what *Brillo Box* accomplished: an ordinary thing became divine.

An actual box of Brillo detergent wasn't divine, but the representation of it could be if art was made to look like it. This is what Dylan did on *Bringing It All Back Home* which turns the ordinary language of folk music into art. But it also turns surrealist poetry into folk music, and months later, *Highway 61 Revisited* continued to play with these different kinds of transfigurations and ended up with something more ordinary but more profane: pop music. Based on Danto's description, we might think of transfiguration as traveling from one state, the ordinary, into another permanent state, the sacred. That might work with an art work like *Brillo Box*, but it's not what happened in the Synoptic Gospels—Jesus showed his holy nature and reverted—and it can't happen in musical performance. What *is* permanent is the potential that's revealed by transfiguration. There's no erasing that. The transfigurative moment, then, is itself a moment of change but it also shows the potential for constant flux, constant possibility.

With Dylan's event in 1965–1966, we applied this fluctuation to music and cultural laws. Everything was now permitted. In truth, we looked at music more like a work of visual art: rock 'n' roll had become transfigured into rock, as if that was a permanent state in which it could stay. That's never what Dylan meant, and that's the misunderstanding Prince seemed determined to correct. Through his ultra-fusion and by bouncing between the holy and the obscene, Prince revealed that performance is always the potential for transfiguration. In addition, his performances argued that we are always in flux: our bodies, our voices, our speech, and our identities. It's an argument that transfiguration can be kept open like a two-way road, even if there are always borders, checkpoints, and tolls. The traveling is more important than the destination, the self-determination and freedom and equality more important than settling on a resolved outcome.

This potential for constant transfiguration was and remained the core of Prince's impact, his event. In fact, he exposed the flux, the variability, at the heart of what Badiou means by the event. The ceaseless flux available through performance was an aesthetic and a set of instructions on how to work the trap of contemporary American life; it had artistic and political value; it merged ordinary life with the potential of imagination, what Butler calls fantasy.

Flux isn't a resolution, it's a way of living. There's nothing final about it. It doesn't come easy. While its freedom has obvious merits, there is, too, a profound human necessity in finding *some* resolution, even temporary resolution. A kind of purposeful floating, like when you stand on those lily pads they have at water parks and try to keep your balance. In the poet and critic Maggie Nelson's memoir *The Argonauts*, which concerns in part her marriage to the gender-queer artist Harry Dodge, Nelson weighs this necessity in her palm: "On the one hand, the Aristotelian, perhaps evolutionary need to put everything into categories" and "on the other, the need to pay homage to the transitive, flight, the great soup of being in which we actually live." She goes on: "*Becoming*, Deleuze and Guattari called this flight … [a] becoming in which one never becomes, a becoming whose rule is neither evolution nor asymptote but a certain turning, a certain turning inward."[17] Becoming: see Heraclitus' concept of flux, which is somewhat debated; the Platonic reading is that you can't step into the same river more than once, i.e. all things are changing constantly, never the same, always "new." Another way to put it, found in the closest thing we have to Heraclitus' actual words, is that *a thing may stay the same by changing*.[18] Like a song, or a person. Thus, the stability of what we might call identity actually depends on flux, perhaps even more so if we accept and embrace our fluctuating nature.

Musical performance is a temporary resolution of the need for categorization and flight, for sameness and change, for definition and possibility. If, as Butler says, identity is formed through repeated acts of performance, then a performance is an instance among an implied set of repetitions. A performance particularizes and locates the performer; it says, *here, right now*. But at the same time, it retains the potential for future performances. This is what gives music its power: the way that it suspends and releases, stays and moves, becomes an instance and continues a trajectory of becoming while engaging with the intensity of bodies, emotion, social relationships, private desires, and imagination. At some point, I think, Prince said "Funk is the space between the notes;" he was probably quoting Parliament-Funkadelic's George Clinton, who may have adapted a famous one-liner by Claude Debussy. My point is that Prince's music asks us to understand that identity is the space between the notes. The notes are never absent, but without the space between them, the notes would be indistinguishable; more to the point, creativity really comes from the ways in which we manipulate the between-space.

Let me be clear: musical performance is a way of working the trap of normativity and public authenticity. Hope lies in our ability to perform as we wish, and to give this hope to the audience. That's a crucial difference from Butler's theory, what indeed separates different kinds of performances: a musical audience to some extent creates the trap of normative ideals, but that same audience also wants to be transformed. This is how the performer can spring the trap of the American Wow into something more liberating. Citing the work of Miranda Joseph, Muñoz writes in *Cruising Utopia* that "performance is the kernel of a potentiality that is transmitted to audiences and witnesses" which in turn creates "modes of belonging, especially minoritarian belonging."[19] Prince knew this. He was a generous performer who understood that his task was—and I say this in full recognition of the phrase's meanings—to get off so that the audience could get off, too. It's not coincidental that musicians talk about "getting off" as a moment (or two) of aesthetic climax, aesthetic because it's perceived as good, beautiful, transfigurative. For musicians, "getting off" usually means taking a solo, so yes, it sounds masturbatory, but its purpose is to transfigure the audience from ordinary to ecstatic, to share with them an experience that's liberating and fulfilling. It's also repeatable, but capable of feeling new every time.

Transfiguration: flux: queerness: audience: democracy—Prince laced them all together. "The momentum of democracy (of equality) (of conformity) that powers American life does not, as Tocqueville thought it might, bleed all the life out of culture," Marcus writes in *Mystery Train*; "it has created a wholly new kind, with all sorts of new risks and possibilities."[20] Prince channeled this democratic momentum and its potential for belonging through the pop life of the American Wow, through its music, fashion, celebrity, and enthusiasm, through its "vision of a world in motion," its eternal renaissance, in order to make truly possible that which the American Wow claimed was already possible: nothing less than the potential—the real newness—that all people might live their lives as they wish, as themselves, at home in their own bodies, at peace with their messy, hard to define, constantly in flux identities, equal and free. No matter how Prince succeeded or failed to create innovative music in the new millennium, he continued to live by this momentum and perform it, to chase that democratic impulse, to carry its fire and ignite his performances with it so that his audiences might imagine who they could be. It is not a fire that's gone out.

8

Kanye's Night at the Museum: The Iconoclast Goes to Work

You're standing alone in an immense hall of a museum in the middle of the night. The executive director and chief curator gave you a tour, and as they tripped over themselves—"We're honored you're visiting us, Mr. West, or should we call you *Ye*?"—they didn't realize you were memorizing the passcodes and paying off the security guards. Your shoes make no sound on the wooden floor. You're looking for inspiration, something to follow up *My Beautiful Dark Twisted Fantasy*, but this is a cold, hygienic place, sacred and clean. Each hall looks the same. Letting the escalator take you up a flight, you admire the polished stainless steel. Here is Jasper Johns' *Target with Four Faces*. Indigo and mustard-colored rings on a red background, the faces keeping watch, their eyes obscured. You're tempted to paste a photo of yourself in the center of the bullseye. But you don't have a beef with these works. They're the detritus of fallen gods. You respect them. Here is Umberto Boccioni's *The City Rises*. In person, it's less bold than the image that appears online. Feathered brushstrokes. The red horse. Is that smoke or a tornado? The revolutionary movement. Bodies pulling and being pulled. You can hear them screaming. The beauty of pain. It would have made a good cover for *My Beautiful Dark Twisted Fantasy*. Fantasies: futures. Boccioni was a Futurist. You remember Marinetti's manifesto, the promise of the young coming to kill the old, the promise of an art that was nothing but cruelty, violence, and injustice. You file that away. Here is one of Mondrian's geometric paintings, *Broadway Boogie-Woogie*. Looks like a circuit board made out of Legos. Its title is a theft. Pinetop Perkins, 1928, "Pine Top's Boogie-Woogie," named for a style of piano music made by Black Americans out of Texas as early as the 1870s. Mondrian's painting was done in 1942: Pinetop replaced by Broadway, the blues replaced by white showbiz. What the hell does a Dutch painter know about boogie-woogie music? Leave it alone, you think. There's no need to destroy or deface the art if your own will make it obsolete. But you can't help it this time. You just *do* things. Does art have to explain itself? No. In an upper right blank space you write in permanent marker: *Harlem, South Bronx*. Near the middle you write: *Chicago*. In the bottom-left you write: *Mississippi*, where Pinetop was born. Tomorrow you'll buy the painting. Maybe you'll use it for this next album. Or not. It's too recognizable. You need something radical. Some people say innovating inside of the American Wow is impossible. You know who says that? The weak. They read *The Society of the Spectacle* and it made them uncomfortable. You read Debord's book like a manual. You notice a room off to the side. Basically a stairwell. Peeking in, your breath catches. The paintings here are simple and familiar. A black block floats in a field of raw white. Underneath, a tilted red square. Such a small difference, and yet it feels unnerving, as if it's daring the viewer to put it straight. *Painterly Realism of a Boy with a Knapsack—Color Masses in the 4th Dimension*. Your eyes snap back to the painting, then back to the title. You smile. It's a dare. A prank. KAZIMIR MALEVICH. You remember the name from your time at the American Academy of Art. The next painting, *Suprematism: Airplane Flying*. Right. Malevich called his work Suprematism, you recall, not for any difficult philosophical reason but because it was the supreme answer to nature and to the art that claimed to represent nature. Minimalism as purity and domination. The end of art as it was known at the time and for all time: that's what Malevich wanted. The death of the old gods, the birth of the new. You recognize yourself. Your pulse quickens. You're an iconoclast in the heart of the spectacle of pop culture called the American Wow. Maybe the only one left. You invade its temples, desecrate its idols, create your own. That is what you do. That is what you must do. The cynics say, "He is his own idol, his own god." Maybe. But what if your god is art, and, as in Buddhism and the gnostic sects of early Christianity, you *are* god as any person is god. That'd make you the god of art. Art incarnate. Or at least, its profane avatar.

The absolute power of art is what drives you. Music journalists and critics don't get that. No one gets that. They talk surprisingly little about your music but they'll go on forever about your hubris, outbursts, your interruption of poor Taylor Swift at the 2009 MTV Video Music Awards. They focus on the chaff you throw out to see if it will distract them. LOOK AT ME. It always distracts them. In the future, a journalist at the *New Yorker* will ask, "Why are so many people fond of being mad at Kanye West? Is it his lack of control, his self-absorption, his boastfulness?"[1] These accusations are totally hypocritical in a spectacle that values boastfulness and self-absorption and a lack of control. That's what some critics seem most offended by: your absence of an internal censor. You are the ill-mannered rant, the guy who storms the stage, the guy who goes ON and ON. You can't help it. The truth pours out of you. But of course they value this quality. It's a good show that gives them plenty to write about. More hits on their sites, more clicks on their ads! The American Wow absorbs your iconoclasm as "controversy," reducing it as it reduces everything into chatter and product. The officials admire your demolitions because they think these actions are just entertainment. Happily distracted by celebrity, they miss the war you have been waging from within the American Wow on behalf of art. You are an insurgent, an aesthetic revolutionary. "Why, Kanye?" they cry. "You're already free!" But not everyone is. And you're not naïve. Even you must work the trap. Daily. Negotiate the expectations of the lightly complexioned. Of the darkly complexioned. You are only yourself. Who called you a backpacker? Who said you couldn't flow? You even have to watch the accolades, lest things get too rigid. People think of the American Wow as freedom pitted against the institutions of tradition, as if pop culture is always instable and institutions are always steady and lethargic. But you know better, don't you? Pop is not instable enough. What we call pop culture is institutional, shaped by the systems of capitalism, media, industry, government. These are the old gods. You work from within their temples. You must. That's the only way to get close to them, to drug their food, to whisper to them as they sleep, to slip radical literature to the young priests and priestesses so that, one day, the only temple that matters is art. Not the art of the old that pop corrupted, but a new art that will corrupt pop. You see it now: this is what your whole career has been about. It really began with 2010's *My Beautiful Dark Twisted Fantasy*, a maximalist noir opera that actually succeeded in turning songs about your fame and public battles into art. (Usually that shit falls flat on its face.) Until then, your music was adventurous and full of protest, but you didn't know what you were against. Maybe you didn't understand what you were *up* against. In the beginning, you were just the talented producer from suburban Oak Lawn who played a key role on Jay-Z's breakthrough *The Blueprint*. Critics thought you were too bougie. Between 2004 and 2007, you made that work in a big way: *The College Dropout, Late Registration*, and *Graduation*. You were already in love with music. You dropped surprises, like a faithful version of the gospel song "I'll Fly Away," or the Daft Punk sample behind "Stronger." When you sang more than rapped on *808s and Heartbreak*, the critics and fans all shook their heads with pity and sniffed at your use of AutoTune, the epitome of inauthenticity, and they *tsk-tsk*ed you after you spiced up the incredibly boring VMA show in 2009, enjoying all the while the spice, the glam, the gossip you provided. They valued you as a court jester, a scapegoat. This is what you reflected back at them in *My Beautiful Dark Twisted Fantasy*: that their reality is a myth, and the mythos of art is the only reality. That's Nikki Minaj's message, in her Barbie Doll posh Brit voice, on the opener "Dark Fantasy" in which you rewrote lines from Roald Dahl's *Revolting Rhymes*, which are themselves rewritten fairy tales. Swelling with warm soul and hard put-downs, the album was epic in the traditional sense of the word: a story a nation tells about itself. That story was the tangling of power, race, celebrity, and representation. Go for power and you become a pariah. Reject power and you're an outcast. You titled one song "Power" so no one misunderstood. "I'm living in the twenty-first century, doing something mean to it," you rapped. In "Monster," through Jay-Z's rap you compared yourself to a list of supernatural creatures that thrill but exist on imaginative sufferance until they cross a line, until, as Minaj rapped in her song-stealing feature, they come looking to "eat your brains." Near the end of the album, Bon Iver's isolated voice becomes a global celebration in "Lost in the World," a high note to end on, but it segues right into "Who Will Survive in America?," which sets a portion of Gil Scott-Heron's spoken-word "Comment #1" over a dark propulsive club track. "Us living as we do—upside down, and the new word to have is 'revolution,'" Scott-Heron says in New York City in 1970, echoing Debord, revealing how "revolution" had become mere fashion of the new, one more co-opting within the spectacle controlled by whites, but how despite that, "The youngsters who were programmed to continue fucking up woke up one night"—and that's it, right there, that's what happened with *My Beautiful Dark Twisted Fantasy*: you woke up. How could you not be honest? Your candidness, written off as rude—and, let's face it, written off implicitly as failing to be an appropriately professional Black man within a white power structure, a failure to commodify yourself as just a harmless trickster—threatened to be redeemed after *My Beautiful Dark Twisted Fantasy*, though. That was a problem. You teetered on the brink of what Groys describes in *On the New*: "Every profane element incorporated into culture reminds us of its wild, profane, free past, when boundless, absolute, intolerant, destructive, all-embracing claims could still be made without embarrassment."[2] That's what happened to Dylan, to Prince, to Jay-Z. It happened to anyone who got big enough. And it was happening to you.

That's why you're here tonight, looking through the museum for the profane. Sometimes, it takes the organized legitimacy of the institution to remind us of that wild, profane, free past, says Groys. You snap a photo of Malevich's work with your phone and hustle down the stairwell. The doors of the museum flutter behind you. You walk back to the hotel with a chilly industrial pulse in your head, call up your team of producers and engineers, and spend the rest of the night writing and recording *Yeezus*, an album that sounds like the sun never rises. Fusing drill, EDM, hard rock and avant-garde sampling, *Yeezus* is chilly and violent and beautiful, as hard and reflective as stainless steel. It sounds like a profane scream inside a sacred museum gallery. Only the pulsating bass frequencies and your voice provide any warmth. On *808s and Heartbreak*, sound was a struggle, a fight with technology. On *Yeezus*, the mastery of technology comes from the minimalist approach. Sound is as bold as a black square on a white background. Your Suprematism. You pull back on having typical drum tracks. Overdriven synths overwhelm the ticky-tack percussion in the album opener "On Sight" so much that the drums on "Black Skinhead" might make a listener think no one's ever used drums before. Shrieks, grimy synth blurts, bass throbs, alarms, orchestral blasts, and what sound like computer errors punctuate time, mark it, stop it, and drive the songs as much as any percussion. Even the voices become percussion: Assassin's spitfire on "I'm In It;" Nina Simone's pinched "breeze" from her performance of "Strange Fruit;" King Louie dragging behind the beat and Beenie yowling on "Send It Up;" and, on "Bound 2," samples of the Cleveland, Ohio 1970s soul group Ponderosa Twins Plus One's "Bound" paired with an "uh-huh honey" from Brenda Lee's "Sweet Nothings." They almost sound like they're from the same song. Your flow (once considered your weakness) is tight; your pseudo-singing via AutoTune turns inside out, becoming more of a computerized vocal blast and détourned art in the strategy of dada than any attempt at "mostly normal" singing, which is the mistake you made on *808s*. In "Hold My Liquor," a late-night synthwave prowl through the city, Justin Vernon's marred vocals become your id, and the hook, performed by the very young Chief Keef of Chicago, is that id rising through the water like a crab on a line baited with chicken gristle. The album pours out of you, no limits, no filters, it just pours out despite the sharp edges and minimalist limitations, it just pours out, and what are you gonna do, stand in its way? When it's done, you've created an entire world of confession, self-flagellation, public stoning, getting stoned, blues, sex, scathing social critique, implicating yourself at every turn with seriousness and humor. *Yeezus* may be your funniest record, no more so than when you're demanding your "damn croissants!" on "I Am a God." That *New Yorker* journalist will seem to take you at your word here, and granted, your interviews give anyone a reason to—but maybe that's just the spectacle talking, insisting that what the public reads in the press is the real *honest-to-gosh* truth from an artist who wants to be understood and liked. Maybe you don't want them to like you. Or maybe you're just inconsistent, like any other person, whereas they expect their products to be consistent. You refuse to be a product. The only way to do that in the American Wow is to keep upping the profanity but also mix it with the sacred. It's cliché to say you blend the sacred and profane in your music. To the dogmatic believer, it's also wrong. Blending the sacred with the profane *is* profane. That's the chance you take. Maybe you can't help it, but it's also your choice. On *Yeezus* you play with sacred icons like a cat with mice. "I'm In It" transfigures the unveiling of a woman's breasts into Martin Luther King Jr. shouting "Free at last!" and then you boast that you fisted a woman "like a civil rights sign." In "New Slaves" you sing that you "see the blood on the leaves" but compare your reaction to Bobby Boucher, Adam Sandler's doofus character in *The Waterboy*. Most radically, on "Blood on the Leaves" you put Simone's "Strange Fruit" underneath what seems like a generic song about a relationship gone wrong, co-opting the horror of lynching to serve your own personal dramas. The key line is "I gotta bring it back to the 'nolia," the magnolia trees from which bodies are hanged in Abel Meeropol's poem-turned-lyrics. You seem to be trumping up *and* dismissing the drama of "unholy matrimony" and a gold-digging mistress by flashing that one historical image. An academic-type will later claim that by referencing Simone and Billie Holiday (who sang Meeropol's song first) and by sampling the brass in C-Murder's "Down for My Niggaz," you are "keeping the voices of ancestors and the awareness of the history alive" and that "Blood on the Leaves" is your "call, formed in response to the history."[3] That's too easy. This song, like nearly every song on *Yeezus*, is a betrayal. You want the audience to stare at the build-up of misogyny and aggression and solipsism without flinching. No literary interpretation can wash all that off. You wouldn't want it to. The profanity is what forces people to rethink those icons they take for granted. Much respect to Billie, Nina, MLK, and even C-Murder, but their gods are dead. Can't speak anymore. People can't hear them. So the music has to become more profane, more transgressive. But you are not merely a transgressor, since the transgressor has no intention of overthrowing old religions; he just breaks their laws. Groys writes in *Art Power*:

The desecration of ancient idols is performed only in the name of other, more recent gods. Iconoclasm's purpose is to prove that the old gods have lost their power and are subsequently no longer able to defend their earthly temples and images. Thus the iconoclast shows how earnestly he takes the gods' claims to power by contesting the authority of the old gods and asserting the power of his own.[4]

And there you are on *Yeezus*, defending the scandalous, defending transgression. Attacking the gods of spectacle and the commodity. No one else is going to do it. They're too nice. Too afraid. It's not that icons like Simone or "Strange Fruit" are no good because they're old. Their gods of art cannot work today like they did yesterday. The American Wow is too powerful. You have to sneak into it, work within its context, and destroy it from within. That's the new context for art that matters, the shocking context it must find if it's to thrive, if it's to truly be new, if there is to be a new god of art.

9

Power Up: Persona and Anonymity Trouble the American Wow

Building a City, or Rebuilding Metropolis

They will take your name, she said. I'm telling you, they'll take your name, face, body, and put them to use. You'll need more than one of each. How do you work the trap? Show them only what you want them to see. Save a little for yourself. In 2011, Janelle Monáe is rising through the stage at the Grammys to the celestial keyboard opening of "Cold War." Her back is to the audience and draped in a James Brown cape to match her tuxedo shirt, black pants, and pompadour. The camera captures the jittery but determined this-is-happening-now-you-better-get-ready look on the singer's face, a silent pep talk she's having with herself. *How do you work the trap?* Maybe she's putting on the mask of her android persona, Cindi Mayweather. Someone counts off under their breath, the mic live when it's not supposed to be, and Monáe launches the song with a challenge: "So you think I'm alone? But being alone's the only way to be …." The first verse is shaky; her voice is just barely flat, reaching for the song as it races ahead of her. *How do you*—it's Cindi who slips the cape, grabs the second verse and chorus, and finds her footing, and when she wrenches out "cold" in the last line of the second chorus—one, two, three different vowels—we have liftoff.

In 2010 and 2011, there was no more fascinating a performer in the American Wow than Janelle Monáe. Working from inside that spectacle, she'd spent half a decade building a consistent vision by way of an ultra-fusionist aesthetic and an epic narrative crafted around her alter ego who hails from the year 2719. On *Metropolis (The Chase Suite)*, a 2007 EP, Mayweather is a top-of-the-line android who faces shutdown for falling in love with a human. The long-form video for "Many Moons" visualizes the futuristic concept succinctly: Cindi performs her kinetic blend of neo-soul-funk-punk while her sister androids, perfect replicas but distinctly dressed and named, parade down a fashionista runway and are sold to the highest bidder at the Annual Android Auction. The parallels between this dystopian public sell-off and America's history of slavery are even more chilling considering that Metropolis resembles *American Idol*. "We're dancing free, but we're stuck here underground," Mayweather sings, soon navigating a "cybernetic chantdown," a long list of labels made for and commodifications made from Black people, particularly women, and their art.[1]

In Monáe's 2010 breakthrough *The Archandroid* and its two hits, "Cold War" and "Tightrope," Mayweather has become self-aware of her power and leadership and more confident and more concerned with the collective good of her fellow androids. The video for "Tightrope" gets at the importance of this collectivity; it's one part unnerving ode to Maya Deren's 1943 experimental film *Meshes of the Afternoon* and one part African-American dance party in which every dancer has their own personality, with Mayweather loosely at the center. In 2013, *The Electric Lady* expanded the musical star maps, from the opening James Bond-esque strains of "Suite IV Electric Overture" to the martial gospel song "Victory" and its popping synths. "Q.U.E.E.N." finds Monáe collaborating with Erykah Badu on a feminist and queer anthem. Here, Mayweather has fully embraced her role as the leader of the android underground, moving through the shadows and the airwaves, her subversive pop on the verge of inciting a revolution. In both albums, Monáe and her collaborators approach Prince levels of ultra-fusion, carrying on a burgeoning trend of experimental innovation in R&B that has more than musicological significance. As one critic wrote, "Monáe's appropriation of the historically 'non-black' genres of rock, electronica, MGM musical orchestration, cabaret and folk music allows her to transcend ideological borders ...."[2] Committed to these border crossings, Monáe makes her ultra-fusion and futuristic concept more than experiments; while most pop artists bounce from one marketable persona to another like tourists, she's diligently been building a city, if not a world.

The Filter of Persona—The Wolf

How do you work the trap? Spring it. Craft your image and use it to deflect attention back to the music. Show them something familiar, say, a James Brown hairdo, then turn that around in a different direction. Show them you are more, not less. Show them the future.

Years ago, the music critic Ellen Willis described the limitations faced by women in popular music, such as the hackneyed lyrics in love songs, as "filters of pop convention and cliche." "[T]he flip side of searching for the pure utopian moment through those obscuring filters," writes Willis, "is embracing the poignancy of the filters themselves, representing as they do the condensed stories of human joy, tragedy, and resignation inadequately but insistently expressed."[3] Filters are not ideal, but they are pragmatic ways to work the trap. Willis was heartened by the fact that women had seized control of those filters and were reworking them, building new ones, claiming and "achiev[ing] more power to construct their own filters out of the cultural detritus and fool around with them, as men have always done." As Willis describes them, filters can be manipulated to tell truths, even in—especially in—the American Wow, in which identity is packaged, bundled, and sold on the Metropolis catwalk.

Persona is a filter, the aesthetic use of more than one name, face, body. All performers invent layers and masks for themselves on record and on stage; "the performer" is a type of persona, isn't it? If Janelle Monáe is even going to show up at the Grammys, she has to present herself as someone other than who she is in day-to-day life, a person who must say something artistically, with style, while millions of people listen to, watch, and judge her by their desires and beliefs, including their beliefs about how a Black female musician should act.

No pressure there. A persona can be a defense mechanism, a way of working the trap, but it can also be productive and political with the intent of breaking the trap. For musicians who work within the American Wow, personas seize control of the pop culture industry's tendency to turn identity into a product, into *the* product. Instead, personas, including the cyborg persona, may "offer a way out of binaries and solid identities, a path to utter contingency and fluidity of the subject"—the flux.[4] Monáe's use of persona argues for a new understanding of identity.

Despite the futurism of Monáe's concept, Mayweather requires no special makeup, no Aladdin Sane lightning bolt across the face. She wears the same black-and-white ensembles as Monáe, especially the tuxedo shirt and slacks the artist has called her "armor."[5] As important as this uniform is in terms of queering gender and sexuality and making a connection to the history of African-American labor, the Mayweather persona materializes just as strongly from Monáe's movements and her eyes. So often she *sounds* like she's looking at you, gauging you. The music might reach delirious heights, like in the playful final third of "Faster" or the entirety of "Tightrope," but something is always held in reserve with the wariness of a wolf.

Star Maps of the Future— Hacking the Prosthetics—False Maria— Writing the Code of the Self

Before I first heard Monáe's songs in 2010, I had no idea what Afrofuturism was—but I did. Sun Ra's cosmic jazz. Parliament-Funkadelic's interstellar grooves. Patti Labelle's outlandish late-1970s costumes (half-remembered on my part). The robotic moves in breakdancing. Octavia Butler's science-fiction novels. The predominance of Black cyborgs in comics, including the one named, well, Cyborg. Outkast's *Stankonia*. A term coined by cultural critic Mark Dery in his essay "Black to the Future," Afrofuturism recombines African cultural roots with science fiction in order to reclaim an erased history, redefine Black identity in the present, and imagine a future designed by Black people.⁶ Afrofuturism is more than a recombination of aesthetic tropes or a revival of past styles. It is absolutely a vision of the new—a revolutionary, political, utopian new. The impossible made possible. Afrofuturist artists grasp the power of art to summon this newness into thought, to summon a future potential. They leap over the revolution itself to show the desired utopian result. But there is often a necessary return to the present day to show how the new can come into being. That's why Sun Ra and P-Funk took on the role of time travelers, as Monáe has done with the Mayweather persona.⁷ The difference is that, in Mayweather's future—our potential future—a dystopian cold war is still being waged. Her revolution could be ours.

To make that happen, Monáe implies we need to think about technology not as consumers but as producers. The artist John Jennings writes with Clint Fluker that "Afrofuturism is a lens that renders reality via a *pantechnological* perspective. It views *everything* as a type of technology."⁸ That would include music. Not just some music. Not just synths. *All music*. All musical instruments are technologies: the saxophone, the drum, the violin, the electric guitar. The human body needed to play these instruments, or to be an instrument, is also a technology. Jennings and Fluker argue that:

> Afrofuturism seeks to embrace the *artifice* and fully exploit the fact that all things that we *think* define us are merely constructions that function as prosthetics that produce various effects relating to their user's needs. Afrofuturism posits that throughout history, many Black people have noticed the affordances of different types of technology while under countless forms of control. The most important affordances of these *liberation technologies* have always been freedom, equity, and agency.⁹

The prosthetic has been a method of domination, like the trap of gender norms, but since it's a technology, "it can be hacked into and rewritten." The instrument is a prosthetic in an almost literal sense. The human body can't make the exact sound of a snare drum, but by hitting one, the snare becomes an extension of the body. How you hit, when you hit, where you hit—square in the center, or on the taut edge—these are choices made in performance, and so the use of musical prosthetics becomes a matter of performance.

Persona, a filter, is also a prosthetic of performance. In Monáe's work, this is visually made literal. The album cover of *Metropolis* depicts Cindi Mayweather as an incomplete body: head, torso, and half of one arm. Being built or being disassembled? The design of her chest-plate is identical to that of False Maria from Fritz Lang's 1927 silent film *Metropolis*, an enormous influence throughout Monáe's concept. Monáe has turned the message of that film on its head, though. False Maria replaces a human woman sympathetic to the disgruntled working class; in the end, the feminine cyborg is burned alive, the "real" Maria is saved, and, but of course, the young white dude who saves her is also the one who unites the workers with the ruling classes. Cindi Mayweather, on the other hand, *is* the working class. While her tux-and-ascot "armor," often described as androgynous, is precisely the kind of parody Butler means—it repeats a gender norm and turns it into queer originality, similar to Groys' negative adaptation—it also recalls the black-and-white attire of butlers, waiters, maids, and other occupations often held, throughout the twentieth century, by African-Americans. "I picked the uniform," she said in 2013, "and I made sure to stick with it because it reminded me of my parents and how they had to put on the same uniform every day to go to work."[10] Mayweather's attire also calls to mind the attire worn by Black jazz and early rock 'n' roll musicians in order to be seen as "respectable" for white audiences. As a cyborg who dresses like a human, Mayweather represents the way racism and sexism have been used as prosthetics to regulate and justify the exploitation of Black work. But she's also the potential for the transformation of that oppression into freedom through liberation technologies as subtle as a black tux.

As much as she gives the American Wow exactly what it wants—a bold identity, fashion, celebrity, hits—Monáe's use of an Afrofuturistic persona complicates the spectacle's very narrow concept and tradition of identity. The lie of the spectacle is that what you see and hear is publicly *and personally* authentic, that there are no filters, no personas, just the artist being herself. Monáe rips that idea to shreds. This is why her commitment has mattered. Plenty of artists toy with personae but their playfulness doesn't really stick, which means it's more likely to contribute to a "what's the latest fashion?"

commodification of identity—the precise thing Butler warned against. And to be turned into a product, identity must be simplified. Products don't encourage you to ask questions, they answer them efficiently. Monáe's commitment to her cyborg persona not only shows how *any* performer struggles with the pressure to construct a simplified self, it also makes us ask more questions, questions that might lead to the expansion of what identity means in the first place. Do we always understand ourselves? Do you need to know the "real" person in order to know or enjoy her music? Should we pretend to be what others want us to be so they'll listen to us, and thus contribute to our own commodification?

These questions have special significance for Black performers who inevitably must work the trap of racialized identity. Afrofuturism resists the identities forced on Black folks by recognizing first that identity is another prosthetic, a technology. It is, perhaps, an unavoidable technology in a culture of capitalism that itself claims to be unavoidable.[11] If you gain control of that technology, you create your own identity. But the danger is that society and consumerism and, yes, art can just co-opt that identity and turn it into a product—unless, perhaps, you make it vast, so big and complex and fluid that no one can get hold of it. The sci-fi novelist Samuel L. Delaney has said the answer is *not* to "construct ... something so rigid as an identity, an identity in which there has to be a fixed and immobile core, a core that is structured to hold inviolate such a complete biological fantasy as race—whether white or black."[12] Maybe the word for it isn't "identity," but instead, "self." *Being*. A core that is mobile, free, a self that is so grand, so plural, so "pantechnological and constructed," that it is defined best by the potential of art.

This is Cindi Mayweather's story. She is enlightened and capable of being a leader precisely because she has cracked the fantasy code written into her own CPU. She knows the code is there, knows that it has designed her to be a product, and knows that it was constructed by programmers, engineers, educators, politicians who have been celebrated in the past as visionaries for their inhumane technological innovations. But Mayweather—and Monáe, as an artist—has taken control of that technology and is now writing her own code in order to write a new identity.

Negative Persona—A Wig and a Windows 95 Computer

Daft Punk wears kick-ass futuristic motorcycle helmets. MF Doom raps from behind a chrome mask. Various indie rock bands wear mascot-sized animal heads in their videos. In 2012, the bands Malefactors of Great Wealth and the Black Swans pay homage to artist Chris Burden's 1971 performance piece "You'll Never See My Face in Kansas City" in two songs with the same title; in the videos, each singer wears the same style of ski mask Burden wore as he wandered around K.C. for three days creeping everyone out. The pop singer and songwriter Sia does not show her face during her performances, live or filmed. Instead, she uses her blond bob haircut, long enough to hide her face, as a kind of shield. Performing at the 2015 Grammys, she faces the wall of a ravaged apartment as she sings "Chandelier" from her album *1000 Forms of Fear*. The young dancer Maddie Ziegler and the actor Kristen Wiig enact a drama in the foreground, each wearing the same clothes and wig as the singer, and I hardly notice Sia's body rocking as she sings the slurred tale of a clubfly bitterly reveling in her excesses and confronting them, her voice swallowing the words of the verses before they leave her mouth.

These performers use anonymity as a negative persona which says there is no identity, no product other than the work of art. It lessens the importance of a public self, of a name that can be known, a biography that can be looked up, or a face that can be seen and commodified. In the cultural economy, persona adds identity; anonymity subtracts. In the American Wow, this makes it a kind of profanity. But what anonymity takes away from the spectacle, it gives to art. Think of it as a noise-cancelling device, something that blocks all the useless static of celebrity, status, and image so we can actually hear the music.

No artist today has committed to the aesthetic of anonymity quite like the rap collective Goodbye Tomorrow. They offer no other names, no faces. They present themselves through one voice. Emerging from the Chicago scene in 2015 with the singles "JAY Z" and "100K" before dropping the full-length *A Journey Through the Mind of a Non Believer*, Goodbye Tomorrow's music is unmistakably based in drill, a midtempo, melancholy but still frenetic offshoot of Atlanta-born trap, but the group adds electronic swerves and blips, a bit of Kanye West's R&B-gospel swagger (especially on "Light One, Pour One"), and multiple vocal registers. There's an anxious, self-interrogating quality in the lyrics. Unlike the work of drill's most well-known rapper, Chief Keef, here there's no boasting about guap, no bragging about hitting. Visually, the collective speaks from behind a chaotic assembly of the glitches, lags, broken code, and conceptual 3D renders of antiquated technology. Their first general motif was a Windows 95 interface crippled by viruses; a year later, the group's website looked like a Geocities page from 1998 overflowing with cheap internet clip art.

From within this matrix of sound and image, Goodbye Tomorrow's use of technological masks rejects the commodification of identity at the heart of American culture. *Show only what you want them to see. Save a little for yourself.* Instead of outright rejecting capitalism, they expose its absurdity and reveal that it's a kind of economic technology, another prosthetic, that can be manipulated. G.T.—my way of naming the singular voice that speaks in their music—raps about getting that cash in hand in "100K," but earlier in the song claims, "I inscribe my reality/Don't talk about what's realistic." As the official audio plays on YouTube, the accompanying visual of a 16-bit city nightscape screensaver is overtaken by an error message: IF YOU WISH TO EXPERIENCE FREEDOM, TRY RESTARTING YOUR REALITY. Later a blue screen of death declares, PRESS ANY KEY TO FREE YOUR CONSCIOUSNESS. If the computer was working, you wouldn't see these messages; it's only the error codes, the "fatal exceptions," that make us rethink our allegiance to consumerism. While the lyrics play out a more familiar story of a young rapper proclaiming his talent and demanding to get paid for his work, "100K" argues for art's ability to break down and reprogram the prosthetic of capitalism.

The threat of the commodification of one's identity while pursuing success has special importance for Black Americans and other oppressed individuals and communities who are keenly aware of the ways in which their efforts are judged and co-opted. In "JAY Z," which has the subtitle "A Dissertation on the Diaspora of the Black Soul," Goodbye Tomorrow uses the comebacks of Michael Jordan and Jay-Z to fuel a story of renewal, dedication, and art's influence. "Girls on the floor going crazy," sings G.T., "In a Mercedes/Got me feelin' like I'm Jay-Z." Even if it's a dream—it sounds like a dream—it is nonetheless an affirmative dream. Once again the video complicates things. First we see a group of Black women in white high-fashion dresses. *Hard transition*: a dreadlocked tribesman being approached by slave hunters who morph into police. At the chorus, the video transforms into what looks like an unfinished late-1990s, 3D video game. A skeletal figure is running; he could be anybody, could take any shape, but he's built into the stereotype of the hoodie-wearing Black thug. He multiplies. Neon text flashes: WE WERE KINGS BEFORE THEY MADE US NIGGAZ. *Cut to*: a sneering, flesh-and-blood, white suburban kid picking up the last verse. Young Black women dance in an alley only to become images on a clean white Mac. At the end, the leader of the women from the intro is throwing ring-clad middle fingers.

The racist construction of Black stereotypes has a long history and plays out in the present: that message, from the video, is obvious enough. But the song's lyrics, in this context, become more ambiguous. Are influential African-American athletes, musicians, and businessmen like Jordan and Jay-Z to be admired for their resistance to these stereotypes? Or are they reminders of how the American Dream—and the American Wow—sells self-commodification as the only path to success, one that requires acceptance by a white mainstream audience? In a talk explaining his "Fifteen Theses," Badiou argues that "if art is not something of the market, but is something against the force of the universality of the market, the consequence is that the artist must disappear" lest he become another commodified artist.[13] The key word, though, is "universality," as in the universality of the market economy being the only way to judge success and thus the only path worth traveling. That's what Goodbye Tomorrow questions in these two songs: the absolutism and absurdity of the ways capitalism commodifies race.

All of this would be harder to pull off, maybe impossible, if either video used the typical approach of the performer in full view lip-synching along with the music, selling himself as much as his message. The musician today always bears an image which can obscure the meaning of his own work, leaving a gap for the market to step into. As Goodbye Tomorrow uses it, anonymity's negation of persona keeps the filter of public identity from getting between the listener, the music, and the message—a strategy that's contrary to the values of the American Wow, which makes it difficult to pull off. Discussing Goodbye Tomorrow's use of anonymity with the group in 2015, the host of the University of Illinois-Chicago radio show Hip-Hop Non Stop brought up how Chance the Rapper's collaboration that year with the band Donnie Trumpet and the Social Experiment on the album *Surf* was often described as Chance's solo project. G.T. responded,

> Because [Chance] has his image, every time something's put out, it's gonna to come through that lens. It's out of their control, almost, how it's gonna be perceived. They could do a project and he's on one song, and they'll still call it a Chance song in the normal press circuits just because that's the filter it's coming through. So, it's like, rather than put that filter on ourselves, we just want to let freedom be there.[14]

That freedom is theirs and the audience's. The gamble is that anonymity turns the music into a mirror. You listen and hear yourself. Not the idealized self produced by the American Wow, but your authentic self—which might be a new sensation.

Goodbye Tomorrow exists on the fringes of the American spectacle, surveying and making guerilla attacks on it, and I have to admit: it's hard to imagine their ascetic version of concealment climbing to the top of the Billboard Hot 100. Their commitment to rejecting a knowable, "branded" identity is a transgression of the highest social order in the American Wow. Those who are entrenched in the Wow are, shall we say, skeptical of anonymity. In one of those "artists you should know about" articles every site runs now and then, *Rolling Stone* crows, "It's only a matter of time before we're rewarded with the identity of this Chicago rapper and his collaborative cohorts"—because the point of being anonymous can't possibly be more than a PR stunt or experiment, right?[15] How else will they profit or enjoy fame? And yet, Goodbye Tomorrow does the most good fighting a close-range war against the American Wow from just outside its borders. Like Monáe, they treat the plastic surface of popular music and media as an artifice that can be shaped with some heat into a liberating technology, a new and empowering language for themselves and for their audiences. "We don't come into your head, *you* come into your head," G.T. said in that radio interview. "That's why it's not any type of identities. We're literally *not* Goodbye Tomorrow. Goodbye Tomorrow *is* the world, it's for everyone."[16]

A Condition of Truth—Keeping a Bad Take— The Body Politic

One more thing, she said. Do not forget your suffering. They will try to take that, too, when they take your body. This is why you need more than one body: to protect the one you can't live without. Persona and anonymity act as protective shields, armor placed between the artist and the consumerist machine's sentimentalizing of the body's suffering. Monáe uses Mayweather as a safe site to work out what that means. While Sia offsets her body, lessens its performative importance in order to preserve her selfhood, Goodbye Tomorrow severs the ties between consumerism and the body almost completely. In each of these, the protective gesture implies a perceived threat, the risk of psychological and physical suffering if identity is exposed.

One more problem with Debord's spectacle—his description and his critique—is that the body is unaccounted for, including what it wants from music: to sway, to dance, to feel every limb, to thrash headbanger style, to make love. This lack of concern is what differentiates Debord from the philosopher, music critic, and poptimist whipping post Theodor Adorno. Best known for his slim-and-grim book *Minima Moralia* and the landmark doorstop *Aesthetic Theory*, Adorno, for some, epitomizes the elitist view of pop music as a commodified distraction from reality. But the entire reason for Adorno's skepticism of mass culture, one that is so often ignored by critics and scholars alike, was the devastating horror committed by the Third Reich against Jews, the transformation of millions of bodies into ash carried out with the aid of propaganda, including the popular music of the time. As an aesthetic philosopher writing about music in a field obsessed by beauty,

Adorno insisted on the importance of recognizing suffering, so much so that in *Negative Dialectics*, he wrote, "The need to lend a voice to suffering is a condition of all truth. For suffering is objectivity that weighs upon the subject; its most subjective experience, its expression, is objectively conveyed."[17] In other words, as I read it, a person cannot be whole without being able to voice suffering. Adorno saw this as an example of the problems faced by philosophy, but it was also part of his mission, as the literary theorist Terry Eagleton puts it, "to return thought to the body"—and for Adorno, says Eagleton, "what the body signals ... is not first of all pleasure but suffering."[18] Adorno was severe in this belief, traumatized by the Holocaust; his weakness as a critic, really, was that he could not hear the suffering expressed in his favorite pop music target, jazz. That doesn't mean he was fundamentally wrong about his theory. Now, there's no reason why music should express only suffering, for God's sake—life is hard enough—but it also seems true to me that pop music tends to either sentimentalize or ignore the suffering of bodies.

Persona doesn't inherently communicate suffering or the body any more than a singer singing "I feel so bad" convinces you that he does. Through Monáe's use of an Afrofuturist persona, however, with its emphasis on prosthetics, self-design, and political dissent, the relationship between technology and the body is both painful restriction and potential liberation. In the video for "Cold War," the camera frames Monáe's face-as-Cindi's face in a close-up. Time code speeds along in the lower right-hand corner; we watch what promises to be an unedited first take, and it is. For the first minute-and-a-half, Monáe lip-synchs as Mayweather, gracefully robotic, her head panning from one side to the other. Here she seems to be performing what the scholar Robin James describes as a "robo-diva" resistance to intersecting white, patriarchal, and humanist expectations about Black femininity and sexuality.[19] Monáe is expressive but controlled, she shows only her head, not her whole body, and her gaze is in no way seductive. There's a sense that this video itself is restrictive, a document of surveillance. And then Monáe arrives at the line "I was made to believe there's something wrong with me." Her stony gaze melts into a smile and she breaks character. As the recording continues (the overlaid song and the filming itself), Monáe laughs in the way we do when we're nervous and self-conscious and trying to hold back a more serious reaction; she's on camera, knows it, says something to someone off camera, but finally the crying wins out. As viewers, we imagine the insults and stereotypes that have said, *Something's wrong with you*. At the same time, it's as if Monáe is just now realizing how much she's succeeded in overcoming those commodifications with art of her own design.

She tries to continue lip-synching, bows her head and pinches her fingers over her nose, tries to wave away the emotion, and eventually gets reoriented. A tear slips down her cheek. In another video, on another face, this would seem maudlin. Not here. Monáe's face has been so stern and dignified, some quality held in such reserve, protected, and the filming so minimalist that the suffering feels honest and unaffected. It's even more powerful because she and her collaborators let the moment stand. Technology is not used to correct a supposed deficiency; in the same way Goodbye Tomorrow's error messages hint at more accurate realities, this "bad take" shows the truth of suffering, which is not reduced despite the moment becoming a victory over it.

If the American Wow's greatest transgression, as Adorno believed, was to commodify suffering into a falsehood that sells records, then persona and anonymity take control of the body that can be commodified, duplicating a "safe" copy, defining what will be seen and what won't, or withholding it altogether. But it's possible that this control isn't just for the performer's benefit or expression. It's possible that we might begin to think about the ways in which our own bodies are commodified and monitored. We might even care more about the ways prosthetics of identity are applied to the bodies of others: the body politic.

Part Three

Shouting at the Hard of Hearing

10

On the Good Side: Antiwar Music in the 2000s

> *Art is not a mirror with which to reflect reality, but a hammer with which to shape it.*
> —BERTOLT BRECHT

The Town—A Witch Hunt—Breaking and Mending Bones

There was once a good girl who went rogue and was shamed on the public square. You probably know her story. At a March 10, 2003 concert in London at the Shepherd's Bush Empire theatre—an ominous name to say the least—Natalie Maines stood onstage with her Dixie Chicks bandmates, including the sisters Martie Maguire and Emily Robison, and said, "Just so you know, we're on the good side with y'all." It was the first night of the band's Top of the World tour and the eve of the United States' invasion of Iraq. The Texas band, which had just performed the National Anthem at the Super Bowl, was prepared to play "Travelin' Soldier," a hit song from their new hit record *Home*. Maines infamously went on: "We do not want this war, this violence, and we're ashamed that the President of the United States is from Texas." In footage of the concert included in the documentary *Shut Up and Sing*, Maines immediately laughs, maybe at the audience's positive reaction, maybe at her own nerves.

Maines' offhand comment was enthusiastically quoted in a *Guardian* concert review the next day, and before you could say "*The Scarlet Letter*," the Dixie Chicks were blacklisted from country radio by vengeful DJs and the stations' parent corporations. (Another brilliant post-MP3 move by the music industry: exiling one of your highest selling acts as your profits sank. Kudos to you!) The good folks of the town showed up to throw away their Dixie Chicks CDs and appear on television. At one demonstration, a tractor ran over a pile of the band's discs. Despite Maines' initial apology, pop country fat-cat Toby Keith disgustingly, childishly displayed Photoshopped images of Maines with Saddam Hussein during his live shows before slugging through his hit "Courtesy of the Red, White, and Blue (The Angry American)," a song so dumb it's a parody of itself. An anonymous letter delivered before a concert in Dallas promised that Maines would be assassinated if she didn't "shut up and sing," prompting the cancellation of the concert and a police escort back to the band's hotel.

All of it was an absurd public spectacle, bad enough that Merle Haggard called it a "verbal witch-hunt and lynching." And indeed, beneath all the outrage bubbled a clear misogyny: Bill O'Reilly, naturally, called the Dixie Chicks "callow, foolish women who deserve to be slapped around." One 2007 study of the media reaction summed it up succinctly, finding that a male antiwar country artist is "romanticized as a 'rebel' or 'outlaw' ... while a woman who speaks out is characterized as an irrational 'slut' and a 'traitor' ...."[1] The Dixie Chicks' response was to pose nude on the cover of *Entertainment Weekly* with slogans and insults written on their bodies—"Big Mouth," "Free Speech," "Shut Up," "Saddam's Angels," "Proud Americans," "Traitors," "Dixie Sluts"—making it clear that gendered violence always comes to bear on the bodies of actual women, not personae.[2]

The manhandling of the Dixie Chicks—I do not use that term coincidentally—set a chilling precedent in 2003 for antiwar statements and political speech in popular music, especially within the pop spectacle of the

American Wow. Despite this, a number of musicians rejected the notion that an artist should shut up and sing. For some, the answer was to craft character-driven topical songs that sounded, at best, reformative. For others, the only answer was revolution; the political institutions of America were an already broken bone that would never heal and needed to be shattered and replaced. Meanwhile, an entirely different movement emerged with tranquil and nervous music that retreated into an apolitical, pastoral dream. While Anti-Flag and Conor Oberst were launching antiwar (or just anti-Bush) missiles, the likes of Devendra Banhart, Sufjan Stevens, and Iron & Wine were singing songs about childhood, innocence, and nature—music that sounded like mending bones.

The Same Town—Being Contemporary—Lethargy and Growling—Truth Procedures

Underneath the bleachers at a football game, a teenage girl sobs. The PA announcer has just read the name of the town's latest young man to die in Vietnam. The girl knows him, loves him, but in this final verse of "Travelin' Soldier," no one else does. Imagine the crowd's chatter underneath the blaring voice, the girl silently condemning these hypocrites who plant miniflags in their yards but don't care about the young people who die in their name. "Travelin' Soldier" subtly (almost subliminally) criticizes the destructive cost of war, but it aims its anger at these ungrateful townspeople—at us—not war itself. It is a song drenched in fate, the sense of being helpless in the shadow of the powerful, and the certainty that nothing will change. The town should change, but Maines knows, the song knows, that it won't.

Released on *Home* in August 2002 with American troops in Afghanistan and the Bush administration conniving to send more to Iraq, "Travelin' Soldier" was a topical song. Despite it being set during the Vietnam War, no one could have missed its contemporary relevance. There aren't many good definitions of a topical song, but it's clearly tied to an immediate historical context even if that context is broadened, as in "Travelin' Soldier." A more straightforward example is Steve Earle's story of American-born Taliban convert John Walker Lindh, "John

Walker's Blues," released in 2002. As in plenty of topical songs, Earle inhabits a persona, Lindh, and speaks in first person. Tracing Lindh's development from typical suburban kid to would-be jihadist, Earle's performance nests within itself, so assured and cozy that it's boring. Does it need to be anything else? The topical song generally relies on its present-day relevance for its aesthetic impact. Its newness is purely the sense of "being contemporary."

I take that term from the title of a series of statements in the *Performing Arts Journal* in 2012 in which artists were asked to describe what being innovative, new, or contemporary meant. As he began finding his way through to an answer, the poet Charles Bernstein responded that "we have to constantly reinvent our forms and vocabularies so that we don't lose touch with ourselves and the world we live in. The need for change in art is prompted by changes in the social and economic environment."[3] In this concept of the new, art succeeds by being an accurate reflection of reality: a document. It has no impact on society. Like "Travelin' Soldier" and "John Walker's Blues," this kind of art mutes its own political stance and claims to simply tell it like it is.

But this capitulates art's power to the social and historical contexts in which it's made, to the whims of public authenticity, or, as the music sociologist Simon Frith puts it in *Performing Rites*, to the belief that "(real) social processes determine what music means."[4] From this perspective, "Travelin' Soldier" means what it accurately reflects about the pre-Iraq War moment and "John Walker's Blues" means the same regarding Lindh. Are those meanings valuable? Sure. Are they new? Not really. Despite their contemporary quality, the two songs follow social meaning and trail behind history, not because they're written after the historical events but because they're subordinate to history itself. Being contemporary is essentially presentism as a vaguely political aesthetic, a frantic attempt to keep up with what's going on. Rejecting social determinism, Frith writes that "a musical experience 'means' by defining (imagined) social processes" and, later, that "the question is not how a piece of music ... 'reflects' popular values, but how—in performance—it produces them."[5] It might very well produce the same popular, political values, but it might not. The performance itself matters. "Travelin' Soldier" barely moves the needle politically, but the Dixie Chicks' vocals inject the song with an urgency that insists on the relevance of its very slight protest. Earle may be singing like a lethargic American teenager on purpose in "John Walker's Blues," but the cumulative effect of his vocal performance and the song's ambling pace is, well, lethargy. The song wants to produce a reconsideration of the way Lindh has been portrayed, but as a performance, it sounds about as interested in that as the rest of the American public.

Flip the coin: Tom Waits' "Day After Tomorrow," from *Real Gone* in 2004. Composed as a letter from an American soldier overseas, the song begins as a typical late-era Waits ballad, stripped down to an upright bass, a watery acoustic guitar, and a gentle electric guitar. It's just as lethargic and growly as Earle's performance, but as the story spills out, "Day After Tomorrow" begins picking apart every myth about a soldier's experience, removing one plank at a time until there's nothing left to stand on, putting a human face on the politicized life of a soldier, and quietly diving into questions that have no answers: "How does God choose whose prayers does he refuse?/Who turns the wheel, who throws the dice …." By the end, you wonder how we could ever put anyone in this position, and "Day After Tomorrow" has nearly become a protest song.

The small but crucial distinction between music that reflects and music that produces meaning has an enormous impact on how we think about the new and the political through music, especially music that wants to create change. Politics is not just an expression of the new; it has the power to *be* the new: a different, real future. If a piece of music only reflects cultural values or certain political ideologies, then those values and ideologies are already possible and the music is D.O.A., a redundancy. If music produces popular values through performance, however, it might become an engine of social change, fueling a dialogue about who's right and who's wrong and what should be done. This is the new of *making* the contemporary instead of simply *marking* the contemporary.

And that is why some people run over music with a tractor. Music has, among the arts, a uniquely subversive political power. It can compel the listener to visualize different futures through narratives and emotion with the immediacy and internalization of a poem, working by metaphors and codes that can bypass logic and the official language of the state. The performance of music puts this thought into the air for other people to hear; a dialogue begins.

Through its performance, we hear bodies in motion, arms and legs waling on a drum set, hands pulling the guts out of an electric guitar, thumbs walking a sinister bass line, and the voice, its inflections, its breath. We might better understand, then, how the political has a real effect on real, vulnerable bodies. And if the musician can communicate her performance as a deliberate action, we might understand the political as a choice, not fate.

If political music can't change the world, why did the country music establishment and its fans shun the Dixie Chicks? Shouldn't the reaction have been laughter, derision, and a lot less "Burn 'em at the stake"? The overflowing hatred against the Dixie Chicks, the glee, the circus of it all seems out of proportion only if we underestimate the power of political music to introduce potential into a situation. The simple power of "What if?" What if we admit that we, too, are ashamed of the president? What if we demand something different? This is the potential of Badiou's event, the sudden possibility of what was thought to be impossible.

The possible outcome of the event, says Badiou, is a "truth-procedure": a new way of thinking critically. This procedure doesn't create a singular truth; it's simply a new process for finding truths, as if new stars have appeared in the sky by which we might chart unforeseen paths. Is it a letdown that an event creates only new *thought*? We demand action! But how effective will that action be? Is it only looking toward today or tomorrows? Thought is capable of imagining a future, including a political future that might be different from the options presented to us by those who value, more than anything, social order. Music has the power to then fuse that thinking with the body, to make thought sensual, anger spiritual, dissent joyful.

Anywhere USA—The Protest Singer Punches a Hole through the Noise with More Noise—Getting It Right/Wrong

While it's tempting to generalize about the topical song and the protest song, the truth is that, as performances, either can come across flat or full of energy, like a pose or a tsunami. So it's all theory, really, any song can topple the rules, but let's try this out: The topical song generally doesn't look to the future or try to create one; protest songs dissent against the present and even implicitly call for a different future. "Invention is not a matter of choice ... but a necessary probe of perception for grappling not only with things as they are but also things as they may be," wrote Charles Bernstein as he kept developing his thoughts. "For that task, words such as innovation and invention may be inadequate; perhaps better to invoke the aesthetic force of NO ...."[6] NO to today. NO to a future just like today. Imagining and demanding change in the present, the protest song seeks an event-like rupture caused by its own performance: a revolution.

The first word in the language of revolution is NO. Political scientists dither about various types of revolution, but as a model of newness, its characteristics are obvious: fundamental social change that comes swift and total. In *Novelty*, Michael North describes how, for more than a millennium, this current definition of revolution didn't exist; it morphed from the inevitable cycles of one power usurping another into the rhetoric that social or political change was natural, a "repairing of the damage done" to original balances in order "not to regain the old but to revive the new."[7] The new here is a natural, God-given potential that's been devalued and ignored by a corrupt government. And then comes the newness of the French Revolution which "open[s] out into an 'unknown future' mainly because the effect of political acts seems ... inherently unknowable."[8] Indeed, one of Badiou's favorite examples of the event is the French Revolution, which, as you may recall, started as the glorious dethroning of the monarchy and quickly devolved into a bloodbath. The unlimited possibilities of violence and more corruption that might result from a revolution are why the word remains dangerous to some.

Most of the protest music in the 2000s didn't care. More important was the deployment of "the aesthetic force of NO" like a punch in the face. The crushing NO of a distorted guitar. The frenzied NO of a drum beat. The bellowing, screeching NO of a voice. Listening to these songs even today, the intellectual in me seeks nuance—what about that unknowable future?—but the rest of me just wants the noise and rhythm. System of a Down's near-industrial "Boom!" Public Enemy's swaggering fusion of metal and rap on "Son of a

Bush," the entire song ringing with alarms. The ominous inevitability in the beat of Eminem's pre-2004 election call for insurgency, "Mosh." Most protest music in the 2000s, from rap to metal to punk, believed it needed to counter the cultural noise of distraction with musical noise shaped into a spear and capable of punching through the static. In order to force a listening, musicians had to match the political power they rejected with a sonic power of their own. Between 2002 and 2006, committed activists Anti-Flag epitomized the fast, aggressive, and doubtless music of the antiwar movement, fusing melodic So-Cal punk with old-school hardcore speed and a heavy-metal riff here and there. On songs like "You Can Kill the Protestor, But You Can't Kill the Protest," lead singer Justin Sane's vocals hammer away like the band's music: a yowl that strikes with an almost machine-like precision and repetition, repetition, repetition. In an often bewildering 2004 op-ed, music journalist David Hajdu wrote that contemporary protest songs were "idiosyncratic and individualistic works, inappropriate for group singing," calling up the ghosts of MacDougal Street and the Newport Folk Festival while neglecting to ask if protest songs need to be sing-alongs—and apparently having never attended an Anti-Flag show.[9] Or a Rage Against the Machine show. Even if the band had effectively broken up in 2000, songs like "Bulls on Parade" and "Guerilla Radio" endured as protest songs because of their repetitive-like-a-jackhammer music and lyrics that allowed the audience to chant along with them. In other words, yes there was "group singing," and from a political standpoint, there's good reason for repetitive sound structures. Fifty years from now I doubt we'll be singing Michael Franti and Spearhead's well-intentioned but lyrically ham-fisted and musically snug "Bomb the World," or Steve Earle's slog-fest "Amerika V. 6.0 (The Best We Can Do)"—arguably a protest song, inarguably a terrible title— but I'd put money on there being a crowd of protestors singing the coda to Machine's "Killing in the Name" as they did outside the Republican National Convention in 2008 when police shut down the band's concert for no good reason.[10]

But here's the big question: Does music that seeks a political new need to sound new? Listening to this body of work, it's rare to find a band pushing against its established sound while also pushing against the political establishment.

Protest in music often wants to signal clarity and commitment, and maybe it has to in the face of so much opposition. You will recall, perhaps, the list of "questionable songs," i.e. John Lennon's "Imagine," distributed by what was then called Clear Channel to its radio stations following September 11. Maybe the list came from corporate, maybe it was spread amongst the deejays—stories conflict—but it most definitely contained the item "All Rage Against the Machine."[11] And then along came the USA PATRIOT Act, which was not exactly a godsend for freedom of speech. And then we all watched the Dixie Chicks get physically threatened and ostracized from country music. (Despite this, Hajdu had the nerve to write, "There is a tentative quality to some of the recent topical music ...."[12] Indeed! I wonder why?) It seemed like a lot to ask musicians to risk dissident speech, dodge the government, figure out the internet, organize tours and political actions, negotiate the ordinary challenges of making a living and making art, and *oh, by the way, completely reimagine your sound while you're at it.*

But there's always some pressure for musicians to sound new, and as the popular music studies scholar Peter Dale argues, there exists a "significant body of contemporary thought that would dogmatically link radical art to radical politics, as if one cannot have the one without the other."[13] While this is true to an extent—Badiou is a good example of such a dogmatist—"radical" also has a cultural meaning, as in outside of the mainstream of either politics or music. Artists like Anti-Flag, Public Enemy, System of a Down, and even Tom Waits to some extent, exist on the fringes even though they have robust subcultural fan communities. What's more, many of them played drastic, bold, jarring, really really loud music that the folks at the football game in "Travelin' Soldier" would consider radical just for its sound alone.

At the same time, plenty of critics like Hajdu were looking for something more nostalgic and believed the contemporary need for newness actually worked against the Young People Today. "Popular music does attach high value to newness and originality," Hajdu wrote, channeling Harold Bloom, "and protest music is clearly a genre to which today's youth cannot lay fresh claim. It has been done before, and in their parents' time—facts that undermine young people's sense of cultural proprietorship and threaten their generational identity."[14] To buy this, you have to forget that the protest singers of the 1960s valued originality, too, but did not exactly invent protest music whole cloth. Those of Dylan's generation quite knowingly built on the work of the Weavers, Pete Seeger, and Woody Guthrie, to name a few, and Dylan borrowed the tune of an ancient ballad called "Nottamun Town" for "Masters of War," one of *the* protest songs. But the ghosts of the 1960s loomed large in the 2000s. As late as 2009, a befuddled Stephen Walt in *Foreign Policy* admitted twice that he was "not as plugged in as [he] used to be," and concluded anyway that no recent antiwar song seemed "likely to become a standard anthem," as if standard anthems are necessary or even possible anymore.[15]

Dale argues that political music doesn't need to be innovative in order to be politically or musically effective, and to some extent I agree. He offers up an excellent example of the Beastie Boys' 2004 back-to-basics and politically explicit album *To the 5 Boroughs*, an affirmation of their late-1980s sound and, in a sense, their integrity. Pearl Jam attempted the same thing on their 2006 eponymous album and the solid if unimpressive "World Wide Suicide." The old-school muscularity of rapper Paris' 2003 album *Sonic Jihad* took nothing away from the scathing protest of "Field Nigga Boogie" or the call-to-arms "Tear Shit Up." Really, the list goes on and on. Inarguably there's a kind of protest music which has no desire to be misunderstood; for it, aesthetic possibilities are always subservient to political possibilities, and the degree of innovation is dictated by what's needed for the song to reach its audience. This approach—Dale's approach—is utilitarian, and maybe in this new millennial America, if the protest singer had to punch through a wall of complacent noise, any kind of artistic ambiguity *was* a risk, maybe even a luxury or a cop-out. And if the music isn't just sonically redundant like a drill in order to make its point, but clearly identifiable and familiar to the point of being derivative, then it's still true, as Dale says, that "we have heard it before—but not in this particular moment ... from these individuals with this particular passion."[16] Which sounds an awful lot like nothing's been done before.

The problem with this approach is twofold, and let me bring up Conor Oberst's "When the President Talks to God" in order to explain it. Employing the talking blues form used by Guthrie and Dylan and countless other folkies, the Bright Eyes singer's voice quivers, beaten and contemptuous, as he lists off all the commander in chief's enormous flaws. Yes, it's ridiculous that Bush claimed he bounced ideas off of God, who, as you might expect, in the song just confirms everything the president already thinks. In response to every punchline, Oberst plays a two-note twang on his acoustic's low string that's just as hickish and negligent as the president he's imagining—which by 2005 was the president a great deal of the country already knew it had. That's problem number one: timing. The potential of the unique historical moment doesn't guarantee newness, just the potential for newness. Passion alone isn't enough. In fact, passion can expose the second problem, which is that the singer is just singing to the choir that is his audience. This is satisfying in a number of ways—I laughed the first time I heard "When the President Talks to God"—but it's not new. Oberst repeats what his audience already thinks. Dale writes that for him, as a leftist listening to leftist music, "the question ... is always whether the music and politics seem to be *right*," and while he means something like the rightness he quotes from Barry Shank's book *The Political Force of Musical Beauty*, a sense of completeness, the ultimate good is the edification and reassurance of the left to keep on keepin' on.[17]

Like Swift's entrenchment of what we already know about the 1980s in *1989*, this sense of rightness is fun, even thrilling—way more thrilling, for instance, in the punk band NOFX's single "Idiot Son of Asshole," a B-side about George W. Bush, than it is in Oberst's tune. Deeply committed to voter registration and protest organization, lead singer Fat Mike looks like a harmless dude you'd expect to see toting around a bong, but here he transforms that persona into Bush in a song that's as gleefully ridiculous and politically scathing as anything out there. Listening to it, I imagine that America in the 2000s had become as juvenile and inept as its president, a satire of what the country should have been. So there's maybe a slight shift in what I already think, but not much.

I want to agree with Dale, I really do, but the artist in me is just as adamant as the critic. If the protest singer seeks a newness of thought, then his greatest mistake is to assume the audience already agrees with him. Such a song speaks from within the cultural archive—or, to be more precise, the subcultural archive of the protest movement which like any tradition can be nothing more than a bunch of people who've decided that everything's already been decided. If we're talking about a truth procedure that opens into unheard-of possibilities—admittedly a tall task—then art has to at least make the reach, and to do this, it has to keep one foot, or both, in the profane realm of ordinary experience devoid of slogans and predictable conclusions.

This demands a certain amount of surprise, not capitulation. I hear it in a song Dale mentions, Against Me!'s "White People for Peace," a protest song from their 2007 album *New Wave*. At all times, the band has been driven by Laura Jane Grace's raw, remarkable voice. Grace most often summons a full-throated howl that seems to have no limit, as desperate as it is unswerving, as flexible as it is genuine. All of that comes to bear in "White People for Peace." Conflicting forces lock horns, the people are screaming for peace, war will last so long as there's money to be made—none of the lyrics will shock you. It's a protest song about protest songs, a meta-protest, but despite this heady self-referentiality, the way Grace snaps off the words, the way she and guitarist James Bowman bend down the chorus melody by a half-step, these will push you out of your seat. So much tension and dissent generated by small musical choices.

The protest songs of the 2000s that stick with me possess a sense of disruption. Blow Up Hollywood's "W.M.D." from *The Diaries of Private Henry Hill* is so unassuming as it follows a recruit from basic training to the front lines in Iraq where he's given the task of searching for roadside bombs, this acronym he's never heard of, that none of us had heard of until the Iraq War. There the story ends, its drop-off ominous. But what gets me is, in the middle of this tight, almost pop-rock number, a guitar solo that sounds note-for-note like a George Harrison solo circa 1968–9, maybe "Something" from *Abbey Road*. In a few seconds, it ties a rope between the Vietnam War and the Iraq War. This temporal displacement is blatant in the Black Angels' 2006 debut full-length, *Passover*, an album that blends psychedelic rock, the Doors, the Velvet Underground, and a haunting sense of the Vietnam War. Filled with fuzz tones, reverb, and droning, *Passover* only offers subtle lyrical connections to the war in Iraq on songs like "Young Men Dead" and "The First Vietnamese War," but the connection grows on you. In the hidden final track, "Fighting in Iraq," the Black Angels finally fuse the two wars together; the song sounds like a folkie in a 1960s coffeehouse singing about a soldier heading to Iraq as the audience looks at each other in confusion. This is some extreme artistic, historical, and political dysphoria. I can't shake the feeling there's something *wrong* with these two time periods speaking to each other.

That sense of something being wrong is destabilizing, and if we're looking for the new, disruption wins out over stability. It could be as messy and confusing as Green Day's sprawling concept album *American Idiot*, in which our antihero Jesus of Suburbia must choose between St. Jimmy, the nihilist, and Whatsername, who I guess is supposed to be a revolutionary figure of some sort. He chooses her and her integrity; St. Jimmy dies; Whatsername vanishes and our hero's alone, abandoned by both sides of the punk rock spectrum. In his book *33 1/3 Revolutions*, Dorian Lynskey describes lead singer Billie Joe Armstrong as someone who "does not like to pretend he knows more than he does. He writes songs from the perspective of an anxious spectator, swamped by dismaying information, and wondering where to go from here," which is a good description of the album.[18] As political protest—well, Robert Christgau complained that the album's politics weren't explicit enough, containing only "vague references to Bush, Schwarzenegger, and war (not any special war, just war)," as if anyone had to explain what war was on.[19] While "Holiday" is as pointed a diatribe against Bush as any other, what the album mainly communicates is confusion, mediated alienation, and the risk of choosing a path—including the possibility of choosing what seems like the right path and still ending up nowhere.

One of the most honest and surprising pieces of political speech came early, Nas' song "Rule," from *Stillmatic*. The single was released less than a month after the World Trade Center towers fell and as everyone knew American troops were headed to Afghanistan. Lyrically, the song itself isn't as pointed as the one that follows it on *Stillmatic*, "My Country," but its arguments about power and violence are impossible to miss over a repurposing of Tears for Fears' "Everybody Wants to Rule the World." The speech I'm talking about isn't rapped, though, it's spoken at the end of the song over a generic bugle and drums playing a martial tune. Black Americans have long memories of the injustices done to them, argues Nas, and the impending war proves to him that

America is a country where you have to take what you need or want, regardless of the cost. The drums and bugle drop out. The speech seems over, but then he adds, "This is what my country is"—his throat tightens, maybe out of regret for what he's about to say, maybe bitterness—"and my country's a motherfucker." The words have no complexity, but the way they're said does.

Maybe Nas was wrong. The thing is, very few people are willing to risk being wrong. Everybody wants to be on the good side. Somebody's good side, at least. It's easier to speak politically when you know your audience will agree with you, which means the difference between the jingoistic "Courtesy of the Red, White, and Blue (The Angry American)" and "You Can Kill the Protestor, But You Can't Kill the Protest" isn't as great as we might think.

Of course, it's easier to say nothing political at all, though sometimes we can mistake a whisper for submission.

The Woods—First Day Forever—Knights of the Twentieth Century, or, Pony Feet

One day as I listened to Iron & Wine's placid 2004 album *Our Endless Numbered Days*, I had a hunch: Dealing with the trauma of September 11 and the two wars that came after it, a lot of young Americans wanted to retreat to the safety of the woods, and this album was the sound of that desire. Iron & Wine epitomized the pastoral remove of a new folk movement in the early 2000s comprised of two friendly camps, one populated by hushed singer-songwriters who sounded like virtuous lumberjacks and another by experimental wild children with sticks in their hair. Despite the differences between indie-folk artists like Sufjan Stevens (lumberjack) and freak-folk musicians like Devendra Banhart (sticks), the music of each sounded like it was driven by a common motive of receding from the corrupted world of politics back into the purity of nature and spirit. This new folk revival, only distantly related to the one centered around *O Brother, Where Art Thou?*, shocked me at the time because of its sudden concentration—there were tons of artists, it seemed, including Vetiver, Coco Rosie, Joanna Newsom,

Akron/Family—and also because, in the aftermath of 9/11 and during the wars in Afghanistan and Iraq, its sudden cohesive expression sounded both hopelessly naïve and seductively perfect.

The regressive impulses of the new folk revival are expertly described by the ethno-Americanist scholar Robert Cantwell in his seminal book about the 1950s–1960s folk revival, *When We Were Good*. There he describes how "a number of 'progressive,' alternative, or oppositional styles and ideologies ... have ridden the waves of generations of youth recoiling from the real world as it confronts them after domestic and scholastic protections have receded, often adopting the more genuinely angry styles and postures of excluded ethnic, working-class, or minority youth."[20] There was no anger in the new folk movement, and neither was it particularly working class, but there was plenty of recoiling from progressive society and all the mayhem it had caused in the world, which was on fire.

Utterly rejecting modern culture and the new-as-progress, Devendra Banhart was the vanguard of the freak-folk movement. At times on 2002's ridiculously titled *Oh Me Oh My ... The Way the Day Goes By the Sun Is Setting Dogs Are Dreaming Lovesongs of the Christmas Spirit*, he sounds so far ahead of the pack that he's gotten lost. Imagine pushing away slender tree branches as you traipse toward a campfire from which ooh'ing voices and handclaps emanate; you breach the clearing and only Banhart is singing over the fire, alone, aglow, the multiple voices of "Roots (If the Sky Were a Stone)" coming from his mouth. Elsewhere: yowls, shrieks, and on "Nice People," a voice I can only describe as belonging to a seething druidic madman. If there is one freak-folk artist who literally sounds like he's recoiling, serpentine and dangerous, it's Banhart—and it's this danger that distinguishes him. Banhart's music sounds outside of time and yet wholly possessed of an uncivilized future based entirely on primal laws that bind man and nature. Banhart's early music has often been described as childish—meant, in some cases, as a backhanded compliment—but on *Oh Me Oh My ...*, on *The Black Babies* with its terrifying "Old Thunderbird," and on *Rejoicing in the Hands* and songs like "See Saw," Banhart sounds adolescently free, immature but far from innocent. Like Joanna Newsom, his wild-child ally and a musician he championed early in her career, Banhart finds the tension between the archaic and the freshly born, or those who'd like to consider themselves freshly born, maybe reborn, which is the real drama of the American wilderness.

The same year Banhart released *Oh Me Oh My ...*, Iron & Wine released *The Creek Drank the Cradle*. Music critic Amanda Petrusich describes how, upon its release, the album became "the kind of record that gets passed between friends like dog-eared copies of Rilke or Robert Lowell, pressed into hands, slipped into mailboxes, tucked under pillows," which sounds unnervingly quaint but also precisely captures the intimacy and sacredness of Sam Beam's whispered acoustic music.[21] Like Banhart and the freak-folkies, Beam chased a dream of starting over, but his newness sought a Christian rebirth and pursued the restoration of man's intimacy with God. (I remember thinking back then that you apparently couldn't get right with an electric guitar. The devil's music!) You're halfway through *The Creek Drank the Cradle* before "Upward Over the Mountain" strikes into the heart of things. Blending visceral coming-of-age memories with a farewell to the past, the song performs a covenant between a young man and his mother that sounds like it has holy stakes: the creation of a "new man," that crucial idea running throughout the New Testament and most of *Creek* and *Our Endless Numbered Days*.

Traditionally Christian, the idea of the "new man" is also traditionally American and, it turns out, an example of a traditional model of newness: restoration. In his book *The New Being*, Paul Tillich dwells on the claim made by Paul in the New Testament that (in Tillich's words) "[n]o religion matters—only a new state of things."[22] Tillich's reading of this shocking statement is that a hidden new state of being exists within the old state in which we live, invisible but accessible through reconciliation and reunion with God and then resurrection—in other words, a potentiality very similar to (and totally different from) Badiou's event. Setting aside that enormous conundrum, what matters for Tillich, and what seems to matter in these early Iron & Wine albums, is the possibility of the restoration of our relationship with Christ, "a renewal of the Old which has been corrupted, distorted, split, and almost destroyed."[23] In *Novelty*, North finds the same sentiment expressed by medievalist and art historian Gerhart Ladner, who claims the ancient Christian church "conceived of [its] very newness as making possible the *restoration* of that newness which was man's part of the first glorious day of his creation"—newness as an eternal situation, a first day forever.[24]

What does this have to do with America? We return to Cantwell. At one point, he discusses the folklorist John Lomax's rather romanticized notions of the cowboy as a synthesis of the heroic qualities of European myths and the rugged character of the American frontier. This virtuous hardworking outdoorsman has an ambivalent, that is, quasi-political at best, relationship with society; his individualism trumps any communal ties. The cowboy is "[d]auntless, reckless, without the unearthly purity of Sir Galahad," Lomax wrote in a 1915 article, "though as gentle to a pure woman as King Arthur"—how does he act toward an impure woman?—and is "truly a knight of the twentieth century." Riding away into the sunset, "the thud of his pony's feet mingling with the jingle of his spurs," the cowboy is a "careless, gracious loveable figure" whose "faint and far, yet cheery still" song echoes over the prairie.[25] The mere thought that such a person might be capable of wrongdoing, let alone sin, seems like an abomination. More to my point, the cowboy as Lomax describes him is a symbol of successful restoration, a new, modern man who's connected to nature and God before social responsibility or politics.

Sam Beam sounds too hermetic to be a cowboy, but the innocence is there. It absolutely shines through Sufjan Stevens' music and his harmless sweet candy of a voice. Strictly speaking, Stevens is neither an indie nor freak-folkie; his sonic ambitions, multi-instrumentality, and polyglot styles dwarf what you hear in early 2000s freak- or indie-folk. But despite the diversity of sounds on albums like the sprawling *Michigan* from 2003, the equally sprawling but more interesting (and sometimes ridiculous) 2005 album *Illinois*, or the album sandwiched between them, the more restrained if overtly Christian *Seven Swans*, Stevens is an innocent, withdrawn character who sounds more at home on the range than in the city. Probably a bit closer to Galahad, admittedly. *Seven Swans* in particular sets up camp on the good side; filled with meditative hymns to love and restoration, its protagonists claim mortal sin but sound venial. Nonetheless, Stevens' search for lost innocence represents the possibility for everyone to find that first day forever.

There's something poignant about searching for this kind of newness in the 2000s. Reynolds includes freak-folk in *Retromania* as an example of hauntology but never considers why it happened when it did. For that you can turn to *Present Shock*, in which a young woman who wants to affect political change has found her generation disengaged because, she tells Rushkoff, it was "traumatized by 9/11 and now [it's] incapable of accessing the greater human projects." She goes on to tell him that millennials "need … to connect with people from before that break in the story in order to get back on track."[26] A break in the story: what a perfect way of describing it. Trauma is a fracturing of self, society, and the narratives we use to hold things together, and it echoes through the new folk revivals like the reverberations of a passed storm. Artists like Banhart, Beam, Newsom, and Stevens reach back to *before* the trauma, back to a playful weird, and back to an imagined time before politics.

The new folk movement spoke a gentle "No," a protest that found newness only in the restoration of old, natural promises; its future was personal and tribal, hushed and secretive. Sounding completely the opposite of antiwar revolutionary music, its apolitical aesthetic was just as radical.

The Grotesque Mask—Flattered Audiences— Words Are Abandoned

The problem with the new folk movement was that its cherubic voices and pleasing adolescent tenors sounded as pure and smooth as milk, especially on the indie folk side of things. Where was the "corruption, the distortion, the split, the almost destroyed"? Where was the suffering? Even when it's overcome in the story a song tells, suffering matters, has to be felt; without it, a restoration project becomes a lie. What is there to restore if we sound essentially innocent and untouched?

Adorno was right. The condition of truth requires that suffering must speak. But this silence, or absence, can just as well be a problem faced by the political singer if he speaks about the *idea* of suffering rather than performing it with his whole body. Suffering must be physical, felt bodily, not just as emotion or argument. That is its political power, to show how the ideological, the rational, the policy, the law always affect a physical vessel that can be punctured, mangled, executed, used, or ignored by those in power. Where there is no body in the political, the political is not the whole truth. The same can be said of political songs. "Music will be better," wrote Adorno, "the more deeply it is able to express—in the antinomies of its own formal language—the exigency of the social condition and to call for change through the coded language of suffering."[27] So rather than listen for a certain kind of ideological rightness, do we hear suffering in "John Walker's Blues," or "Mosh," or in anything by Rage Against the Machine or NOFX? Not a shred (maybe in Rage), but I do hear it in "Day After Tomorrow," in that catch in Nas' throat in "Rule," in that single half-step drop in the chorus of "White People Against Peace," and in the heart of darkness that is the Black Angels' *Passover*. In these performances, sometimes just in a single moment, the political emerges from the body as a howl from the throat, as the grotesque mask of an enraged face, the neck taut, the head banging, the whole body flailing. Whatever such performances say or don't say about a political future, revolution, or the event is overshadowed by the genuine newness of their embodiment of suffering and their rejection of it as commodified art that flatters the audience or as an acceptable political outcome.

Such a performative moment happened on the unlikeliest of stages in February 2007: the Dixie Chicks' return to the Grammys to play "Not Ready to Make Nice" nearly four years after that night at Shepherd's Bush Empire. (I still can't get over the name of that place.) The band had released *Taking The Long Way* the previous year; its singles were ignored by country radio, the band's Accidents and Accusations tour avoided the South, and meanwhile the album was on its way to selling 2.5 million copies. As a studio performance, "Not Ready to Make Nice" is slickly produced. Maines' voice sounds thin as it walks a knife's edge between righteous anger and self-righteousness; when it cuts loose near the end, it's pushed to the back behind her own multitracked singing of the chorus. And those *strings*. Too heroic. But it is a protest song, given the situation; with swagger and melodrama, it says NO and imagines a better future.

So here they are onstage at this awards show, their most direct confrontation to date with the industry that turned its back on them. Because let's remember: the shunning of the Dixie Chicks wasn't just a country music problem; pop country was in 2003 a massive crossover genre and the Chicks had just performed the National Anthem at the Super Bowl. Framing the controversy as a country music issue allowed the nation to pretend like the silencing of political dissent in music in 2003 wasn't the status quo, as if Clear Channel hadn't released its list, as if Congress hadn't passed the PATRIOT Act, as if CMT editorial director and former *Rolling Stone* editor Chet Flippo hadn't said of the Dixie Chicks in 2004, "You're an artist? And you have a message? Hey, put it in a song. We'll listen to that. But, otherwise—shut up and sing," simultaneously questioning the band's artistic authenticity and spinning the myth that Americans may not tolerate musicians making political statements in England *but they sure do love political songs*.[28] Anyway, it's 2007 now, the war in Iraq has been a proven disaster at the expense of thousands of American and Iraqi lives, and the Grammys audience has the Chicks' backs. The band doesn't play "Not Ready to Make Nice" any differently; the tempo is the same, the arrangement is the same, the melodrama and the strings are the same. Maines' voice, though, is up front and imperfect, riven by anger and acceptance as she faces down the nation that scapegoated her. She launches into the tirade of the second verse, the words spitting out and running together. Hands are raised, clapping, cheering. It's something, I guess.

Still, that isn't the moment that gets me. It's in the final chorus, when Maines sings the first two lines then abandons the rest, abandons words, really. There is no multitracked vocal to get in the way. She channels her voice as hard as she can into two sustained cries, a guttural moan, and then a swoop into a refined note without purity, a note of suffering and anger that becomes a weapon.

11

Shouting at the Hard of Hearing: Springsteen Finds a New Audience

Wringing the Neck—One Wrong Move— Righteous Rock As Usual

March 5, 2012: The first sounds on Bruce Springsteen's *Wrecking Ball* are resolute drums and the nervous siren of a lead guitar processed to sound as if it's emanating from Mars. Cue a wall of guitar and a chiming melody soon doubled by what might as well be a trademarked glockenspiel. Quickly, "We Take Care of Our Own" fills a space as big as "Born in the U.S.A." albeit more orchestral and, because it's been staring for too long at the unfulfilled promises of America, not as surprised by what it sees. "Easy Money" lopes along, free and vicious, an answer to the question in the next song, "Shackled and Drawn," before it's asked: When you've been abandoned by the rich after a lifetime of honest working, what are you supposed to do? (The answer involves a gun.) The spry and reckless tone of those two songs plummets on "Jack of All Trades," wherein a desperate man begs for work. Another victim of the 2008 economic collapse fueled by corrupt Wall Street bankers and CEOs, the man waxes philosophical about surviving misfortune and then adds, with hardly a hitch of emotion in his voice, "If I had me a gun, I'd find the bastards and shoot 'em on sight." Threat, boast, or fact? Soon after, "Death to My Hometown" jigs along to its bitter end: a shotgun blast. Breaking all rules of the theatre, here in the first act of *Wrecking Ball,* the gun has already gone off.

It's hardly needed. These first five songs constitute the most sustained bout of anger and violence Springsteen has put to record since the four-song sequence on *Live 1975–85* which began with a furious version of "Born in the U.S.A." recorded in 1985, well after President Reagan attempted to hijack the song's meaning for his re-election campaign. In the song's final minutes, Springsteen and the E Street Band strangle the song's neck so there will be no misunderstanding. This segues into a brutal version of "Seeds," a performance so good the song never needed to be recorded for a studio album, then a touching, bitter rendition of "The River" and a stomp through Edwin Starr's "War."

Together those four songs told the story of a young man who goes to war, survives, and comes home to a lack of jobs, a lack of resources, pervasive desperation and depression and rage. Eventually, he turns against the war itself.

In 2012, it was still a familiar story.

I took immediately to *Wrecking Ball*'s anger. For whatever its aesthetic misfires, the album spoke to the despair, confusion, frustration, and drift in our lives, including my own: work lost, unavailable, and scrounged for; medical conditions uncovered, untreated; bills unpaid, bill collectors dodged, tightropes walked between responsibility and reality. It's embarrassing to talk about one's own economic status, particularly in our materialistic, glamour-of-success culture. And there are limits to what I'm willing to share, and most likely, what you're willing to read. I will say this: For many years, I lived in a constant state of tension. Even when my income was relatively secure, I felt that one mistake or one day of bad luck—a car breakdown, a slip on the ice, a misplaced word—could ruin me. Next thing you'd know, I'd be walking through traffic like Michael Douglas in *Falling Down.*

This is the kind of personal narrative Springsteen has always excelled at: songs about frustrated working-class men and women who don't have the time or energy to consider the political forces shaping their lives and who instead lash out in self-destructive, self-alienating ways. Yet most of *Wrecking Ball* is unabashedly pointed, broadly drawn, public, and deeply political. It speaks to the nation; it names the criminals. Critics who claimed it was just Springsteen's typical brand of righteous rock-as-usual missed that what had changed was not the subject—he'd been singing about that for years—but instead, the strategy. On this album, Springsteen set aside his more nuanced storytelling in favor of social jeremiads for desperate times.

The new strategy on *Wrecking Ball* fascinates me, but so does Springsteen's journey to that point. If you look for protest songs, or even topical songs, in the jazz–R&B operas of his earliest albums, you won't find any. If there's a shred of political newness, it's in the optimism and propulsion of songs like "Spirit in the Night" and "Born to Run," in the romantic utopia of a democracy that's always formed and judged in the urban streets. By the time Springsteen released *Darkness on the Edge of Town*, he was clearly attuned to a wider landscape of change, a lonelier place but one filled with even more potential for an artist willing to embrace it all. And then catastrophe strikes. Our story picks up there.

South of Harrisburg, Trouble—Saint Flannery— Large and Startling Figures

March 28, 1979: Everything goes to hell at the Three Mile Island nuclear power plant in the middle of the Susquehanna River in South Central Pennsylvania. A valve sticks, man can't talk to machine, and how-do-you-do: partial nuclear meltdown. A jeremiad almost comes true.

Living less than five miles from the plant, my father manages a local wastewater treatment plant and has to stick around while thousands evacuate. Many years later, he writes that days after the incident and "to my utter amazement, [the plant's corporate owners] GPU continued to report that there had been no leak of radiation material. By that, I took them to mean that there were no uranium rods laying out in the front yard."

April 3, 1979: Less than a week later and at a different Power Plant, Springsteen and the E Street Band record the manic "Roulette," which sounds like the soundtrack to a realistic horror film someone has yet to make. Is it about Three Mile Island? Written within days of the meltdown, the song sports a protagonist whose fear turns into paranoia and lyrics about a talking river, roadblocks, and toys abandoned on the lawn like in one of those nuclear holocaust educational videos. So, yes, I'd say so. "Roulette" is Springsteen's first topical song, if not protest song. I can only hear it as a NO. Maybe there comes a time when you can't afford to be subtle. Or maybe the anger and dread just spring up. Anyway, "Roulette" is left off *The River*—"I may have just gotten afraid," Springsteen says years later, "it went a little over the top, which is what's good about it. In truth it should have probably gotten put on"—and, in fact, the song won't be performed live until 1988 when Max Weinberg beats the hell out of the drums to rein the band to a tempo Springsteen can sing over.[1]

September 21–22, 1979: Well-intentioned musicians perform at No Nukes: The MUSE Concerts for a Non-Nuclear Future at Madison Square Garden in NYC. As captured on film and as heard on the inevitable live triple-album, the performances seem oblivious to the terror and displacement months prior in rural Pennsylvania. Everyone has a good, easy time of it, and they look fab doing it. James Taylor, Graham Nash, Carly Simon, and John Hall mime their way through, what else, "The Times They Are A-Changin'," by now the standard we're-not-gonna-take-it song that seems impossible to sing with any fresh, visceral impact. Lots of applause, though. Then the Doobie Brothers perform something.

Springsteen wades into the Cool Whip of rock-star political consciousness for the first time at No Nukes. Until now, he has infused his music with politics in the most primal sense of the word: politics as the meeting place between the individual and society. It's a rough part of town. Like many songwriters, he's used character and story, only with more acuity and honesty. But now he's on stage for a cause, and he responds with "The River" more than a year before it will be released on the eponymous album. Dedicating the song to his brother-in-law and sister, Springsteen conjures up the fears and bitterness of so many people besieged by forces greater than themselves. At first, it's a fragile, tentative performance. In his suit, Springsteen looks like a greaser who's cleaned himself up for the big dance but can't go along with the good vibes, so he clings to his harmonica. Eventually, the song finds its way; it's too good a song not to. "Is a dream a lie if it don't come true, or is it something worse?" he sings—worse as in the forced evacuation from your home near a potentially destroyed river in the wake of a partial core meltdown, or having to stay because that's your job.

For Springsteen back then, politics meant primarily the economic dangers in which his characters found themselves, from the hopeful, embittered people in *Darkness on the Edge of Town* to those folks living along *The River* who drifted but searched for home and gambled on love, and were often disappointed by what they found. His strategy was to make sure that ideals like freedom, dignity, and the common good emerged from songs that worked like short stories: precise shards of narrative filled with keenly observed details about ordinary people. As Chekhov advised, these stories asked questions and offered few answers. Rock 'n' roll demands some answers, though, and Springsteen's storytelling ambitions worked because he knew how to throw a musical punch. Recalling the making of *Darkness on the Edge of Town*, he wrote, "I knew the stakes I wanted to play for, so I picked the hardest of what I had, music that would leave no room to be misunderstood …. Power, directness, austerity were my goals. Tough music for folks in tough circumstances."[2] There's your answer: the music itself. But *Darkness* and *The River* were not "We Shall Overcome." The lyrics were not explicitly political. The sounds punched, the words jabbed, but Springsteen's politics were contained within stories that, on record, maintained a degree of ambiguity. It was up to the listeners to make the connections, even if, on startling songs like "Stolen Car," the connection between the story and the American Dream circa 1980 was all but obvious.

I've always found it compelling that beginning in the late 1970s and especially close to the time he recorded *Nebraska*, Springsteen was reading the American and very Catholic fiction writer Flannery O'Connor. Known primarily for her odd, brutal short stories of grace and violence in a South divided by race and class and tradition, O'Connor cared less about her characters' politics than she did their salvation. These are recognizably normal people whose strangeness seems to be the great American secret. Despite and perhaps because of their relentlessly terrible decisions, blind ignorance, comfortable smugness, and simple bad luck, their salvation is real, even if it's horrifying to witness. In comparison to the clear directives of protest folk,

O'Connor was subtle, but in literary terms, she was a shouter. There is a rage to much of her writing, rage at the hypocrisy of the religious and the apathy of everyone else, a shrillness that goes hand in hand with her utter weirdness and the unanswerable mysteries inside her characters. Her work is thrilling and confrontational and unapologetic. (It is my goal to get O'Connor canonized as a saint, even if I'm not Catholic.) In *Mystery and Manners,* she writes that a Christian writer voicing dissent might need to disturb her audience and its sense of what is natural. She continues:

> When you can assume that your audience holds the same beliefs you do, you can relax a little and use more normal means of talking to it; when you have to assume that it does not, then you have to make your vision apparent by shock—to the hard of hearing you shout, and for the almost-blind you draw large and startling figures.[3]

There aren't many overt examples of O'Connor's influence on Springsteen's work. The title of "A Good Man Is Hard to Find (Pittsburgh)," recorded in 1982, echoes one of her most famous short stories, and maybe Springsteen was inspired by her darkly redemptive tale "The River," but O'Connor's narratives are quite different from each of those songs. There was, however, a much more obvious connection looming on the horizon. Describing how he'd read her work in his late twenties, Springsteen observed in 1995 that O'Connor "got to the heart of some part of meanness that she never spelled out, because if she spelled it out you wouldn't be getting it. It was always at the core of every one of her stories—the way that she'd left that hole there, that hole that's inside of everybody."[4] That's what showed up in the form of large and startling figures on the album which followed *The River, Nebraska.*

A Man Goes Down the Well—Three Versions of "Atlantic City"—The Audience Tunes Out

Looking for new ways to speak about the nation and speak to it—which is to begin speaking politically—an artist might shift gears stylistically, take on new influences. "I was interested in finding another way to write … about people, another way to address what was going on around me and in the country," Springsteen recalled in 1995, "a more scaled-down, more personal, more restrained way of getting some of my ideas across. So right prior to the record *Nebraska*, I was deep into O'Connor."[5]

Nebraska descends as far down into the well of American blankness as you can go and still get back out. O'Connor would have appreciated its cast of killers, drifters, con artists, the archetypal son in "Mansion on the Hill," and the two brothers in "Highway Patrolman," all of them filled with meanness and holes, all of them larger than life. The music journalist Geoffrey Himes makes a fine point that on *Nebraska* Springsteen adopted O'Connor's use of child narrators in songs like "Mansion on the Hill" and "Used Cars," a tactic that forces the listener to caulk the cracks of meaning.[6] But Springsteen has never in one of his songs drowned a child looking to recreate the magic of his own baptism, as O'Connor does in "The River." Grace arrives pitilessly for O'Connor's characters. Describing the end of her story "A Good Man Is Hard to Find," in which an old woman has an epiphany just before she's murdered by a serial killer named the Misfit, O'Connor said she'd discovered "that violence is strangely capable of returning my characters to reality and preparing them to accept their moment of grace. Their heads are so hard that almost nothing else will work."[7] *Nebraska* shares O'Connor's severity. Even in a gentler song like "My Father's House," epiphany comes to the narrator like a two-by-four to the jaw. But if violence wakes up people who think they're innocent in O'Connor's stories, in "Nebraska" and "Johnny 99," random violence is the murderer's desperate ploy for grace, a ticket out of this broken meaningless world, a sinister method of transforming oneself into the "new man" described by Paul in the New Testament.

Before any of this, however, you're confronted by *Nebraska*'s barren sound. Even compared to the stripped-down clarity of *Darkness on the Edge of Town* and sections of *The River*, *Nebraska* is unnervingly desolate: stark rockabilly rhythms, plainsong melodies, muted 6/8 arpeggios fingerpicked on an acoustic guitar, a distant bell, a forlorn harmonica, and most of all, Springsteen's red-eyed voice. The album is as quiet as Iron & Wine's *Our Endless Numbered*

Days, but its intimacy actually creates a sense of alienation. Except for a few terrifying, high-pitched barks, Springsteen doesn't shout at the hard of hearing, he mutters with a barely contained rage, the kind of shouting-through-a-whisper done by people who've given up talking in an America where no one is listening: protest songs for a nihilistic country.

At the time, *Nebraska* seemed like a detour in Springsteen's art, albeit an important and successful one. Fresh off the tour supporting *The River*, then his most successful album, Springsteen sat down in his home in Colt's Neck, New Jersey with a Teac four-track recorder and an Echoplex mixer, composed the stunned tunes that make up *Nebraska*, and laid them down as demo tracks in late 1981 and January 1982. After a torturous process of trying to record the songs in the studio with the E Street Band in the spring of 1982, Springsteen finally released them as they were that autumn, complete with hiss and chairs creaking. By that point, he and the E Street Band had already recorded a number of takes that would end up on *Born in the U.S.A.* in 1984.

End of story, right? Nope. In the years that followed, O'Connor and her large and startling figures lingered as Springsteen's politics continued to evolve, his activism increased, and his relationship with his audience and the nation grew even more complex. Tracking the story from 1982 into the new millennium, all the way to *Wrecking Ball*, you can hear how a strategy and its potential might lie dormant until the performer realizes it, how history is a randomizer in the spectrum of chance, variability, and potential that music already contains, and how songs can be unfinished, shaped and reshaped, suited to their times, fashioned against their times, and eventually, perhaps, lead to a new way of employing that old strategy with an even more explicitly political voice. And we can follow that story with a single song—"Atlantic City."

1981/1982, New Jersey and New York: "Atlantic City" begins its performed life as a topical song so grim it's already sliding into protest. That said, coming after the blank horror of "Nebraska," it sounds like a pick-me-up. Springsteen hollers, the song's signature riff hooks you, and even that opening line about a mobster's house getting blown to hell makes it seem like we're in for a good story. Set in the netherworld of organized crime and the depressed economy of the early 1980s, "Atlantic City" is about renewal, the possibility of a future for people who've tried to do everything right but have "debts no honest man can pay" and can't find work no matter what they do. Our hero has a plan—well, at the very least, a scheme. "Maybe everything dies, baby, that's a fact," he sings, "but maybe everything that dies someday comes back." By the end of the song, he's set to do some favors for a guy he's just met. What could go wrong?

O'Connor, dead for eighteen years, smiles grimly.

1985, Paris: Here we are on the *Born in the U.S.A.* tour. Max Weinberg starts "Atlantic City" at a brisk tempo with a heavy beat, but Springsteen slows it down as he starts singing. The E Street Band's arrangement presumably harkens to the unsuccessful recording attempt during the May 1982 studio sessions. "'Atlantic City' was the one song that seemed like it wasn't gonna be any problem," Springsteen's manager Jon Landau later said, "[a]nd *that* was goin' nowhere."[8] In Paris, the signature riff of "Atlantic City" is present and accounted for, but whereas the syncopation of the *Nebraska* performance is light because it's being performed with an acoustic guitar played to sound like a mandolin, here the rhythm is a burden. The performance works, but something is missing. In the context of *Born in the U.S.A.*, "Atlantic City" and the rest of *Nebraska* are less absolute; they fit roughly with the other songs of the era, but they're now another side of the story instead of the only story, and so they're less startling and less political.

July 1, 2000, New York City: A heavy drum beat slaps back across the cavern of Madison Square Garden with the force of a hammer driving steel beams into place. As Springsteen's embittered voice begins telling the song's story, the reunited E Street Band waits to pounce, and when they do, it's clear that sixteen years after first playing "Atlantic City" live, they've all finally found the song. It swaggers with a stately menace. At the end of the bridge, which repeats the chorus—"Everything dies, baby, that's a fact/But maybe everything that dies someday comes back"—Springsteen mutters, "Yeah, maybe someday." As in, *yeah, right*. There is no hope for redemption in the future, only in the togetherness and communion of tonight. The final verse and chorus are quiet— that is a key to this version, its dynamics—and slide into a build-up gospel call-and-response between Springsteen and the band. He unleashes a precise but ragged melisma that connects the song to the 1960s soul singers who've influenced him. The song feels more alert than ever before. But its topical point of reference, the decay and corruption of Atlantic City circa 1981, has receded. What's it about now? Like I said: togetherness, community. Springsteen seems to recognize the bonds of family, friendship, and community that slowly add up to a nation.

Another development crucial for our story happens when Springsteen and the band play what is undoubtedly a protest song, the new "American Skin (41 Shots)" which is about the shooting of Amadou Diallo, an unarmed West African immigrant, outside of his Bronx apartment in February 1999 by plainclothes NYPD officers. Performing the song, Springsteen and the band are met with boos. Years later, in his memoir *Born to Run*, Springsteen will recount how a few men surge to the front of the stage and do a little protesting of their own.[9] It's the first time, to my knowledge, that Springsteen is booed for his politics.

The ghost of Flannery O'Connor is licking her chops.

2006, Dublin: Touring with the Seeger Sessions Band, Springsteen significantly reworks "Atlantic City" into a rollicking marriage of bluegrass, Dixieland jazz, and zydeco. The signature riff is simplified into phrases of three horn blasts. The cartwheeling rhythm, the pinched blues figure on acoustic guitar, the rolling banjo, the backup singers, the brassy horns—how far this song has traveled from its *Nebraska* incarnation, and how much this performance yet again unfinishes it. The struggle for hope and togetherness in the 2000 version here seems unnecessary; this is already a carnival. In the song's bridge, the desperation of needing to commit to someone is trampled by the breathless pace. The performance has nonetheless been placed in a new context: the American folk repertoire inspired by the recordings of Pete Seeger that Springsteen has put to record on *We Shall Overcome: The Seeger Sessions*, songs like "Ol' Dan Tucker," "O Mary Don't You Weep," the title track, and "John Henry." Explicitly tying "Atlantic City" to this tradition, the two-bit loser in the song becomes another in a long line of desperate Americans descending into the underworld of organized crime, a quasi-heroic figure in the tradition of Jesse James—

And suddenly we're back to large and startling figures. O'Connor has returned, probably by accident, though who can say. She is a saint, after all.

There's another change in strategy, though. Despite its antihero, this "Atlantic City" is nothing like the alienated, seething performance on *Nebraska*. The bonds of friendship and citizenship that have been forged over the years result in music that's jubilant, chaotic, communal, and national. The performance celebrates the history of America's rebellious spirit at a time when it's needed most.

The nation isn't that interested, though. While the Seeger Sessions Tour sells out across Europe, it performs less well in America.[10] Even in the midst of two wars overseas, we find little to hear in our own musical traditions, including the tradition of protest folk symbolized by Seeger. More than at any other time in its performance history, "Atlantic City" becomes a protest song. As much as I hear in it the celebration, I hear, too, a voice of dissent and warning about a mean future. What matters more at this moment, though, is that Springsteen's American audience isn't listening, which means to some extent that it doesn't agree with him.

O'Connor has returned.

Shouting at the Hard of Hearing—A War of All Against All—Taking the Risk

More than any other musician who's spoken politically in the new millennium, Springsteen has been willing to change his sound and his strategy to reach his audience. It isn't that uncommon for artists to seek new styles to address the nation—Gillian Welch and David Rawlings on *Time (the Revelator)*; Bob Dylan on *"Love and Theft"*; the Drive-By Truckers, who abandoned a certain amount of goofiness on *Southern Rock Opera*; even, to some extent, Taylor Swift on *1989*, Prince on *Art Official Age*, and Kanye West on *Yeezus*—but often in the 2000s, the more explicitly political the artist, the more consistent their sound remained. When Neil Young dove into the fray with 2006's *Living with War*, he brought back the rhythm section from his 1989 album *Freedom*; musically, it just sounded like a sharper Crazy Horse album, albeit with horns.

For most of the 2000s, Springsteen's range of sounds remained familiar, too. *The Rising*, which responded to September 11 mainly without sentimentality or condescension, and the underrated *Magic* in 2007 both spoke politically in a rock vein. *Devils and Dust* picked up in 2005 where the mid-1990s album *The Ghost of Tom Joad* left off: topically acute, often relying on a kind of historical displacement akin to *Nebraska*, or what the Black Angels do on *Passover*. The importance of *We Shall Overcome: The Seeger Sessions* can't really be overstated, then, for its development of a raucous and more participatory way Springsteen could tap into the traditions of folk protest and populism—the kind of populism that's actually inclusive. As a musical language, the album put some swagger into his protest, allowed him to be more overtly political in his performances without abandoning his storytelling, and created the sense of a massive diverse family behind him while he spoke to a nation he clearly loved.

All of those elements came together in a rock 'n' roll setting on *Wrecking Ball*. The musical differences weren't subtle, but what's most important is how they served a new strategy. On *Wrecking Ball* more than any of his previous albums, Springsteen was shouting at the hard of hearing within the nation—and within his own audience. He no longer seemed to take for granted that we held the same beliefs he did, which might be the most dangerous and exciting thing an artist can think. This perspective ups the ante on each performance, on every recording; a monologue that seems like a dialogue is replaced with a sense of real dialogue between the audience and performer, the energy of which can ignite the performance. This volatility is even more important in protest music. It's precisely what allows the performer to keep one foot in the profane realm, to avoid condescension no matter how rich or successful he might be, and to avoid the threat of performer–audience self-congratulation. *Wrecking Ball*'s methods have less in common with the kind of protest in "When the President Talks to God" or *Living with War* and more in common with the political profanity, the ordinariness, the unvalorized transgressions of Nas' "Rule," Green Day's *American Idiot*, and the rap group the Coup's excellent 2006 album *Pick a Bigger Weapon*—music that presents itself as *this is what I think, what do you think?* Most importantly for the new, this assumption of different or undecided beliefs and the search for common ground creates the potential for a change in value, action, and thought which might actually lead to new art *and* new politics.

Wrecking Ball sets O'Connor's large and startling characters into the raucous atmosphere of the E Street Band and the Seeger Sessions Band combined, a muscular and communal space. Voices shout, fiddles keen, and the drums are fat and fill the room. The spirit of "Atlantic City" shows up in "Easy Money" and "Shackled and Drawn"; in fact, the combination of fiddle, guitar, backing vocals, accordion, and a thick brass section is enough to make me feel like the Seeger Sessions Tour version of "Atlantic City" may have even lead directly to this wedding of frustration and jubilation. But the O'Connor connection cinches with "Death to My Hometown": the bluster, the penny whistle, the cacophony, the shotgun blast, and the absolute conviction of narrator's well-deserved anger. "I have spent my life judging the distance between American reality and the American dream," Springsteen said prior to the album's release, and it was clear the distance had never been greater.[11] The title song defies the wrecking ball of capitalism that swings through tradition and people as easily as it will demolish the football stadium/concert venue Giants Stadium, which here becomes the epicenter of defiance. The end of "Wrecking Ball" is one of clearest examples of how, just through its music, a song can put a future into the air: the whirling rhythms not too far from the Seeger Sessions Band's "Atlantic City," the horns blaring, the backing vocals summoning the freedom in "Thunder Road."

If the political future is not obvious enough on "Wrecking Ball," you can't miss it on "Land of Hope and Dreams," a rallying cry of protest, suffering, anger, hope, and spirit that lives up to the predecessor it sound-checks, the Impressions' "People Get Ready." Written in the late 1990s and first appearing on the E Street Band reunion tour with "Atlantic City," "Land of Hope and Dreams" nonetheless sounds like Springsteen wrote it with all the other songs. Its vision of America is almost utopian in its scope and grandeur, and tellingly, it's built on the central metaphor of a train that includes "saints and sinners" and "whores and gamblers." Usually in American music, the dream of upward mobility and change—the self-evident truth, so we've been assured, that all are equal to chart the course of their own lives—is centered on the car, which makes the dream private, a fantasy. Train songs, by comparison, are more communal and thus more political; you can still escape on a train, but you're less likely to be alone doing it. In its tempo, in the poignant sax solo by the late Clarence Clemons, and in its central metaphor, "Land of Hope and Dreams" pushes toward a future in which America has finally lived up to its promise of equal opportunity for everyone. The pain of reaching for that future is voiced in the gospel song "Rocky Ground" and in the ghosts of striking railroad workers, Civil Rights protesters, and modern-day Mexican immigrants in "We Are Alive"—and, really, in every infuriated voice from the album's first half.

Springsteen shouts for the dispossessed and angry on *Wrecking Ball*, but he's also shouting that we have abandoned an idea central to the American character: the common good.

Talking about the aftermath of the 2008 economic crisis in his memoir *Born to Run*, Springsteen puts it bluntly: "If this much damage can be done to average citizens with basically no accountability, then the game is off and the thin veil of democracy is revealed for what it is, a shallow disguise for a growing plutocracy that is here now and permanent."[12] In this corrupted ecology, the collective good is more than endangered, it's nearly extinct. As the economic noose tightens, we fight over scraps. The wealthy have succeeded in driving a wedge between the middle class, the working class, the working poor, and the poor. Politics is often presented as if its only question is, "If you had to choose, which would you get rid of, capitalism or democracy?" We often choose the latter, forgetting the more nuanced question the late historian Tony Judt asks in *Thinking the Twentieth Century*: "How do you stop capitalism from creating an angry, impoverished, resentful lower class that becomes a source of division or decline?" Without a sense of public common good, Judt writes, "[w]hat gets lost … what is corroded in the distaste for common taxation is the very idea of a society as a terrain of shared responsibilities."[13] If those responsibilities evaporate, we're closer to what the philosopher Thomas Hobbes called in *Leviathan* "a war of all against all." (He got the diagnosis correct, if not the treatment.) At times, *Wrecking Ball* sounds like that war. Springsteen dramatizes the results of a country disinterested in being a civil society, from the rage in "Death to My Hometown" to the sorrow in "This Depression." Compared to his previous work, these are unsubtle blasts of characterization and story; the nuances are lying in the mud outside the gates of a shuttered factory.

Why was it necessary for Springsteen to shout? He dared to suggest that we'd gotten complacent, that we took the common good for granted. Maybe he thought his conservative base of listeners had misinformed or narrow ideas about it. Springsteen implies on *Wrecking Ball* that a common good cannot be achieved solely through family, town, and church, no matter how worthwhile those are. Instead, the state and its laws exist to ensure fairness and to protect us from not being loved by people in power. Maybe centrists and neoliberal Democrats needed reminding of this, too. Maybe they needed to remember that politics of race, gender, and sexuality cannot be separated from class. Maybe the left needed to remember its commitment to the working class. But the real strength of Springsteen's vision was his recognition that most of his audience does not fall neatly into categories like left or right, that most people hold conflicting beliefs and find themselves challenged by the distance between their ideals and their circumstances.

On *Wrecking Ball*, Springsteen seemed to re-imagine his audience, or rather, come to terms with its diversity. Accepting this, he took the big breath and addressed the widest audience he could imagine. When you do this and aim for the loftiest ideals, the risk of political speech in music is the risk of getting things wrong. Whether or not *Wrecking Ball* was right about what it saw in America (it was), I didn't hear many other artists in 2012 taking that risk.

That's why it was crushing to read in *Born to Run*, published in September 2016, that Springsteen was disappointed *Wrecking Ball* didn't have more impact. He recounts how, as with the Seeger Sessions tour, the politics of his music was more enthusiastically discussed in Europe than in America. "I came to terms with the fact," he writes, "that in the States, the power of rock music as a vehicle for these ideas has diminished. A new kind of super-pop, hip-hop, and a variety of other exciting genres had become the hotline of the day, more suited to the current zeitgeist."[14] He's got a point. The situation is always evolving. Nothing is guaranteed except that the artist who wants to speak politically must always be listening, always adjusting, always shifting tactics, reconsidering old strategies, and scheming up new ones.

12

Living in the Interval: Political Hip-Hop, Rap, Revolution, and To Pimp a Butterfly

1.

Sandra Bland, Jermaine Reid, Clementa Pinckney, Philip White, Eric Garner, Sean Bell, Freddie Gray, Aiyana Jones, Kimani Gray, Walter Scott, John Crawford III, Michael Brown, Miriam Carey, Sharonda Singleton, Tommy Yancy, Amadou Diallo ... and in Cleveland, Ohio, another Black American killed by police, this one a twelve-year-old boy named Tamir Rice, who has been waving around an airsoft gun with the orange safety tip removed, who has been reported to a 911 dispatcher by a caller who twice says the gun is "probably a fake," words that are supposedly never relayed to the actual officers; in the two seconds between the police car's arrival and officer Timothy Loehmann opening his door, Rice has barely stood up from a picnic table with the gun in his waistband when Loehmann shoots him twice, after which he is sprawled on the ground dying as Loehmann and his partner neglect to perform first aid; Tamir Rice dies the next day, November 23, 2014—[1]

"Alright"—Unfinished Newness

On July 26, 2015, demonstrators break into chants of "WE GON' BE ALRIGHT! WE GON' BE ALRIGHT!" during the Movement for Black Lives national conference at Cleveland State University.[2] It's the hook of rapper Kendrick Lamar's "Alright" from his 2015 album *To Pimp a Butterfly*. "Alright" is a protest song without slogans; it doesn't say one specific word about social change, but the urgent need for such change energizes every word, every line, the rhythm of every line, the jazz sax, the stacked cold jazz vocals, the heavy drum fill into the hook, and the insistence in Lamar's raspy voice as he says, "Wouldn't you know, we been hurt, been down before, nigga/When our pride was low, lookin' at the world like 'Where do we go?'"

To Pimp a Butterfly interrogates every subject that it takes on, including the one it never names: revolution. What does that word mean, really? How does the Black community make it happen? How does a Black musician continue the project of revolutionary social justice in an American culture in which anything can be co-opted and commercialized? (Revolution always pumps up an ad, like when The Beatles' "Revolution" was used by Nike to communicate the vitality of new shoes, no doubt the change-from-within message John Lennon envisioned.) What happens to revolutions that fade? At the end of the album, the ghost of Tupac Shakur tells Lamar that even a failed revolution fails leaves a scar, a reminder of the potential that was, which today is an unfinished newness.

2.

—"*A young black man arrested by police in Portsmouth, Virginia, has been found dead in jail after spending almost four months behind bars without bail for stealing groceries worth $5,*" reads a report in *The Guardian; his name is Jamycheal Mitchell, he suffered from schizophrenia and bipolar disorder, and he was "accused of stealing a bottle of Mountain Dew, a Snickers bar and a Zebra Cake"*—

An Event in the South Bronx—Two Revolutions

The unfinished newness of revolution is embedded in hip-hop. There is no debate: hip-hop was an event, a seismic shift that emerged from the Bronx in the 1970s. It was almost inarguably the result of one person, DJ Kool Herc, a Jamaican-born immigrant raised from the age of 12 in the West Bronx whose music would largely go unrecorded. By August 1973, Herc was blasting his breakbeats on two turntables through monstrous Shure speakers with two Bogart preamps.[3] Early DJing was wildly recombinative, drawing from rock just as easily as funk.[4] No matter where things went from there, from the preeminence of the DJ to the rise of the MC, the core of hip-hop would remain this effortless and sustained remixing of a massive sound. Afrika Bambaataa worked to unify the communities and the gangs in the South Bronx, and soon after encountering Herc, he was fusing hip-hop with the educational politics of what became the Universal Zulu Nation. Meanwhile Grandmaster Flash mastered the technology of the turntable, including backspin and scratching, as he transformed passive listening into creative action and eventually amplified the role of the MC.[5] Together, Herc, Bambaataa, and Flash engineered an aesthetic and political revolution from the circular spinning of used vinyl records. Hip-hop radically changed the possibilities for the situation: what counted as music, what language of words and sounds could be used, what technology could be utilized, how all of that might appear in every musical genre, and what new ways a person might live in the world—a hip-hop culture with its own history, archive, and traditions.[6]

    Hip-hop at first said what any music says: *Listen*. It was music that reached out across communities; it was for dancing, showboating, romance, and fun. That said, negotiate between what an audience wants and what you want them to hear, and maybe they'll begin to listen to what's being said. Revolutions themselves, hip-hop culture and particularly rap music from their inception continued the unfinished project of social justice revolution for Black Americans. Even when it wasn't explicitly political, hip-hop was protest. It denied the stereotypes, the pathologizing of Black urban life; it celebrated

Black innovation and creativity even as its MCs started to overlay rhymes about street-level struggles. A revolutionary impulse coursed through songs like Grandmaster Flash and the Furious Five's "The Message" and Brother D and the Collective Effort's "How We Gonna Make the Black Nation Rise?" In 1982, Cornel West wrote that rap articulated "the paradoxical cry of desperation and celebration of the black underclass and poor working class, a cry that openly acknowledge[d] and confront[ed] the wave of personal coldheartedness, criminal cruelty and existential hopelessness in the black ghettos of Afro-America."[7] This was hip-hop's dissent. *Despite the pain, we keep on pushin'.*

3.

—Amadou Diallo, an immigrant like DJ Kool Herc, is shot at forty-one times by NYPD undercover officers in plain clothes when Diallo, in shadows, pulls a wallet from his pocket on February 4, 1999; struck nineteen times, Diallo dies; Springsteen writes "American Skin (41 Shots)" about Diallo and is boycotted by the NYC Patrolmen's Benevolent Association; in 2016, Mary J. Blige sings a bit of "American Skin (41 Shots)" to Hillary Clinton and we talk about awkward hand-holding; Blige releases a cover of the song, which includes a Kendrick Lamar feature in which he imagines reversing time—

Forcing the Count—Demolition Crews—Being the Interval

Badiou's event is the emergence of a new set of possibilities once thought impossible within a historical situation. Say, hip-hop in the Bronx in the 1970s. According to Badiou, we can't know if it's an event as it happens. What he means is that the current situation can't determine if the event and its newness *are true.* The situation has no language for the event, no concept for it. *What is this that doesn't sound like the music we recognize and call "music?"* (And who is "we" anyway? Who doesn't recognize?) This is an obviously important, fragile stage. "An event is not by itself the creation of a reality," writes Badiou; "it is the creation of possibility."[8] If that possibility is not seized, then it falls into the void—which is just what it sounds like: zero, zilch, nothingness.

What's required first, then, is the interpretative intervention, which names the event. This literally happened when the *Village Voice* came to Afrika Bambaataa in 1982 and asked him what this new culture was called. He responded, "Hip-hop."[9] The event is still undecidable, but the intervention has created a subject, a person who acts, and this person can attempt to force the variables of the event to be counted. As Badiou explains in *Philosophy and the Event*, forcing the count requires action, exertion, and commitment even when (especially when) official institutions deny that any new possibility has been revealed. For this to happen, Badiou suggests that the individual must "incorporate" the event, take it into himself, put himself into it—essentially, to take the chance of demonstrating *a new truth that already is*.[10]

This is exactly what the second wave of rap did. Artists like Run D.M.C., Eric B. and Rakim, and Big Daddy Kane forced the count in such a way that the public would hear the event of hip-hop and know it wasn't a novelty (essentially a zero, the void) but a new truth. The dancehall celebrations of empowerment by KRS-One and Boogie Down Productions on "Stop the Violence" and "Why Is That" made crucial connections to hip-hop's Jamaican roots. And then there was Public Enemy: Chuck D's booming voice and Flavor Flav's bitter comedic relief spitting rhymes over the Bomb Squad's screeches, alarms, and industrial grooves. "Bring the Noise," "Black Steel in the Hour of Chaos," "Fight the Power," and "Welcome to the Terrordome" intervened on complacent culture, white and Black, the way a demolitions crew intervenes on a derelict building.

Since this music was also tied to the potential for a social revolution, its aesthetic innovations forced a new count artistically and politically of the Black American, a person who, when this nation's constitution was written, was counted by the state as three-fifths of a human being. That revolutionary project continues today; political hip-hop attempts to force the counting of the bodies, the names, the lives of Black folks and other people of color of yesterday, today, and tomorrow. Its core political truth is that a dark-skinned complexion doesn't mean one counts as less than one, whole less than whole, or human less than human. This *truth that already is* is new only because it's still not fully accepted or fully realized in America today.

The count still needs to be forced.

Thus the need for what Badiou calls "fidelity," or commitment, the necessity of "remaining faithful to a past event." The event of yesterday reverberates toward the event of tomorrow, the fulfillment of a revolutionary truth. "[P]olitical subjects are always between two events," writes Badiou. "They are never simply confronted with the opposition between the event and the situation but are in a situation upon which events of the past still have an impact. The political subject, then, is the interval between the past event and the coming event."[11]

4.

—in April 2015 in Tulsa, Oklahoma, an unarmed Black man named Eric Harris runs from police, is tackled, and then is shot by a seventy-three year-old reserve deputy named Robert Bates; handcuffed, Harris says, "I'm losing my breath," and a non-reserve deputy replies, "Fuck your breath"; Harris dies—

A Blackness Way Too Vast

Even more sonically ambitious than Lamar's 2012 breakthrough *good kid, m.A.A.d. city*, *To Pimp a Butterfly* tells the story of a young Black man struggling to stay faithful to the potential of past events while being caught in the conflicts of his life. To be faithful to a project of newness, of revolution, is not easy. (To say it's easy is the political and aesthetic lie of a bad protest song, and it's not a lie that *To Pimp a Butterfly* tolerates.) Lamar never doubts the unfinished newness of the past or the goals of the event to come, only his role in the interval between them. In this present moment, the possibilities exist, but they need to be forced. How?

The album answers the question before it's even posed with the scratch of a record needle and a sample from the Jamaican singer Boris Gardner's "Every Nigger Is a Star." Musically, the album pays respect to the past because its promises remain unfulfilled and because its events offer wisdom. After the Gardner sample, "Wesley's Theory" jumps off into a serious funk beat and some Bootsy Collins' Rubber Band bass guitar from Thundercat; distorted vocals probe Kendrick's ego before he starts proclaiming all the things he's going to do when he gets signed to a fat record contract. In just this sequence you begin to hear the truly awesome density of *To Pimp a Butterfly*'s Black history and culture—what music critic Clover Hope means when she writes that the album's "blackness is way too vast"; her list includes "40 acres and a mule, Gators, cotton picking, Richard Pryor ... [m]aster, chains, jigaboos, queens, Africa, naps, and that Brazilian wavy 28-inch."[12] True to the past though mixing it in his own way, Lamar raps about the problems of authenticity, belonging, and tradition created by that same past, the high bar set by past innovators, the trap of your old neighborhood and your old way of thinking compared with the need to do right by the place and people you call home, and the responsibility and stress created for the ambitious musician who loves and accepts the sheer weight of his culture.

That includes the weight of past revolutions, political and aesthetic. All revolutions begin as the creation of the potential for change through a new political imagination, a new way of thinking that must exist and continue before the change actually succeeds. But throughout history, as those ways of thinking accumulate, the unfinished newness and potential of past revolutionary models and ideologies begin to conflict: the nonviolent ideology of the incremental legal revolution of the Civil Rights movement led by Martin Luther King Jr. as opposed to the militant, "by any means necessary" approach of Malcolm X and the Black Panthers, both sides pursuing the clashing ideals of W. E. B. Du Bois, Booker T. Washington, and Marcus Garvey. In other words, the revolutionary impulse isn't singular; it reflects the plurality of Black history itself—the plurality you hear in *To Pimp a Butterfly*. Hip-hop has always been part of this multiplicity of ideals, a site for conversation and debate within Black communities: the spoken word of the Last Poets and Gil-Scott Heron; the educational goals of Bambaataa's Zulu Nation; Public Enemy's controversial connections to the Nation of Islam; rap's fantasies about and realizations of the accumulation of wealth and power from the earliest days of Herc, Flash, Kurtis Blow, and Kool Moe Dee through to N.W.A., Dr. Dre, Biggie, Tupac, and Jay-Z—all of them entwined, all of them agreeing that Black people like any other human beings should be equal and free to determine the course of their own lives, but all of them envisioning different ways forward.

The journalist and activist Bakari Kitwana writes that the late 1980s criticism of gangsta rap "forced a dialogue that revealed one of the Black community's best kept secrets, the bigger generational divide between hip-hop generationers and our civil rights/Black power parents."[13] The issue, he says, was "Black cultural integrity," meaning the community's morality and its cohesiveness, which is needed in the face of systematic prejudice and violence. How do you keep the revolution together? Well, which revolution do you mean?

Are we even really talking about revolution?

Two Turntables (Two Microphones)

In 1970, Frank Jones, a former editor of the Black Panthers' newspaper and a bookstore owner in Oakland, testifies before the House Committee on Internal Security; congressman L. Richardson Preyer of North Carolina, who is white, asks Jones "whether the Panthers are a revolutionary group or whether they are really reformists" (you can guess which is worse) and cites a *Washington Post* op-ed which claims that the Panthers' "vision is not—or at least not yet—one in which an underclass forcibly seizes power from a ruling class. Rather, they seek a society more congruent with the vision they heard in grade school, one that offers to Blacks 'life, liberty and the pursuit of happiness.'" Preyer presumably looks at Jones, who no longer claims any affiliation with the Panthers, and asks if he agrees with that assessment.

> JONES: In a sense I do. I would again like to deal with the words "reform" and "revolution." The only difference I see in the two is the

time span involved. Reform, of course, might take place over a long period of time and revolution implies an immediate change. The past history of the Panthers has indicated that they are, in fact, reformist because there has been no real confrontation on a class basis or a race basis. So I would agree they are reformers, yes.[14]

To an extent, the entire history of the struggle for civil rights in America is contained in this brief exchange: the intersections of race, class, force, and the *pace* of change. Revolution is feared and adored not just because of its goals, which are absolute, or its methods, which are imagined to be violent, but because of its tempo. Revolutionary rap most often voices immediacy, haste, NO MORE RIGHT NOW. Reformation is the slow process of change, deliberate, careful, and often expressing a supreme confidence in the inevitability of progress so long as we're committed to it. While reformists like Martin Luther King Jr. aimed to end institutionalized racism, their methods and pace signaled to revolutionaries like Malcom X an inclination to conform, not confront, and a belief in pragmatism and self-respect, not rebellion and social upheaval. Because the promises of the past have not been fulfilled, these debates continue today, the dialogue between two turntables.

5.

—February 26, 2012: George Zimmerman is in possession of a 9 mm semi-automatic pistol and Trayvon Martin is in possession of a fruit drink and a bag of Skittles—

One Line Flips the Song—Respectability Politics— The Return of Public Authenticity

No song from *To Pimp a Butterfly* caused as much debate as "The Blacker the Berry," probably because it drills right into the heart of reformation versus revolution. Backed by a menacing, propulsive beat and punctuated by a hook from the dancehall rapper Assassin in his Jamaican patois, the song is on fire. Its first two verses defiantly call out white supremacist hatred of Black people, especially Black men, taking on every angle of institutionalized racism from prisons and education to politics and capitalism. The man in the song, this hypothetical Kendrick—the version of Kendrick Lamar in the song who we shouldn't so easily equate with the real person—proudly embraces being Black. But as the final verse builds a list of all his fidelities, it hits a wall of self-described hypocrisy: that this Kendrick cried when Trayvon Martin was killed even though he himself murdered a gang rival with a complexion darker than his own.

With one shocking line, Lamar flips the entire song. He injects a social equation that lingers, and it goes something like this: revolution focuses on the abolishment of systemic institutionalized racism while reformation emphasizes self-respect and self-improvement. These form the crucial dynamic of the entire album, which is one more reason why the line goes off like an alarm. Is Lamar a revolutionary or a reformist? Is he, as plenty of critics argued, just promoting respectability politics, Black pathology, and the specter of Black-on-Black crime? Fuel to the fire: a few months before "The Blacker the Berry" was released as a single, Lamar was asked by *Billboard* about the killings of Michael Brown and Eric Garner. He responded:

> I wish somebody would look in our neighborhood knowing that it's already a situation, mentally, where it's fucked up. What happened to [Michael Brown] should've never happened. Never. But when we don't have respect for ourselves, how do we expect them to respect us? It starts from within. Don't start with just a rally, don't start from looting—it starts from within.[15]

It isn't a careful answer. Why should it be? But it did inform the way listeners responded to "The Blacker the Berry." In a frequently cited article, Stereo Williams wrote, "If there is a hypocrisy, doesn't it fall on those who would use gang violence to silence public outrage against oppression while ignoring the fact that the gang violence is also a product of that same racist oppression?"[16] Like other critics of the song, Williams assumes Lamar is telling the Black community what it should think—Williams calls it a "finger-wagging session," a ridiculous image when paired with the intensity of Lamar's performance—and suppressing debate. Except he isn't. Lamar frames the moment in the song as a question; he isn't silencing outrage, he's voicing it. And I don't know how you could think Lamar ignores the connection between gang violence and systemic racism if you've listened to the whole song—but that's the thing: the shock of that final line hits so hard it almost wipes out the previous lines.

Here we find public authenticity critiquing art, reading a song as an uncomplicated political statement instead of a dramatization of the complexities of life as it's lived. The critics who claimed Lamar was playing into respectability politics were looking, I think, for a clearer protest song instead of what "The Blacker the Berry" is, a political song that's so personal it mucks up any categorization. "I'm not speaking *to* the community, I'm not speaking *of* the community," Lamar responded to his critics, "I *am* the community."[17] He is fully aware that the legalized brutality against Black Americans and violence within the Black community are in fact part of the same system in which young Black men, in particular, are counted and taught to count themselves as less than one.

Lamar knows this truth. Kendrick knows this truth. That's what the first two-thirds of the song are about. The ending is about the betrayal of that truth, an act of ethical infidelity to the potential of the revolution that catches up with Kendrick as a profound contradiction. Intensely personal and political, his hypocrisy speaks from the politically profane realm of the ordinary: reality, not idealism. The first job of revolutionary art is to voice this reality in all its complexity, not to resolve its contradictions.

6.

—*Carnegie Hall, 1964: Less than a year after Medgar Evers, a Black veteran of Normandy, is killed in Mississippi, Nina Simone pauses during "Mississippi Goddam" and calls her song a "show tune," adding in her syrupy deadpan voice, "but the show hasn't been written for it yet"*; Mother's Day 2014: five California Highway Patrol officers beat Black US veteran Tommy Yancy to death—

Standing at the Door—Truth Procedures

The key question in *To Pimp a Butterfly* is asked in "Alright" when Lamar raps about past injustices, when Black Americans were low on pride and wondering where to go. Not just, *Where else can we go?* but also *Where do we go from here?* "Alright"—all of *To Pimp a Butterfly*, really—is a Saturday night song of anxiety reaching for Sunday morning's certainty. At the beginning of the song, Lamar raps into the hook that if God has the backs of the Black community, then the future will work itself out, but quietly that *if* lingers. The problem for some critics is that there's not enough church up in this protest, not enough dogma in the revolution. Instead, the album is what Cornel West calls "the Afro-American spiritual-blues impulse" in rap.[18] Or what scholar Tricia Rose describes in *Black Noise* as "travers[ing] the crossroads of lack and desire in urban Afrodiasporic communities."[19] *To Pimp a Butterfly* takes place at these moments of conjunction and hyphenation, moments where doubt and faith meet, but which nonetheless require decisions.

This crisis of *To Pimp a Butterfly* is the crisis of what Badiou calls the truth procedure, that new way of thinking critically which is an outcome of the event. Since this procedure doesn't create a singular truth, it's definitely not a resolution of the need to think. Instead, it's a new way to push forward to that event to come and to push back against "official" versions of the truth, which might be the laws of the state or the laws of public authenticity regarding art. (I can't find any critic who accused Lamar of respectability politics in "The Blacker the Berry" while also interrogating what that term means, or how musical performance complicates it. Do Assassin's accusatory, hard-as-concrete hooks suddenly vanish because of the song's final line? Is Assassin "buying into" respectability politics?) Thinking in a new way, or even just trying to, marks an authentic political subject, and Lamar is indeed a political subject living in the interval between the past event and the future event. On *To Pimp a Butterfly*, he presents his persona-self, Kendrick, as someone who's become aware of himself as part of history and society; his actions have more importance because they affect others. Lamar raps in "Alright" that he's standing at the door of a minister, maybe in a confessional, full of doubt, frustrated, considering violence, seeking faith about the future. Truly though, he is the minister, and he's standing at his own door, banking on the promises of the spiritual without letting go of the doubt and despair of the blues.

7.

—*April 4, 2015, in North Charleston, South Carolina, the unarmed Walter Scott runs after being pulled over for a broken taillight and Officer Michael Slager hits Scott with a Taser; the fifty-year-old continues to run, Slager shoots him in the back, Scott dies—*

"Listen!"—Crossing Over—Nowhere to Run

On the track "Listen!!!" from his 2007 album *Eardrum*, the political rapper Talib Kweli spits out, "Real hip-hop is missin' from the shelf/It's what you felt when you listened to yourself." He means the affirmation of hearing a voice like your own, but he also means the power of what you yourself might say and the possibility that you might say something politically new. But now, for Kweli, all of that is missing. Why? What's happened?

The story goes like this. In the 1990s, hip-hop and rap drifted away from truth procedures, away from the door of doubt, faith, and political thought, and into the highly commodified, glamorous world of the American Wow. It wasn't unexpected; every fundamentally new genre of music has followed a similar path, even those with strong political motives. Nor was anyone too surprised. The appropriation of hip-hop had been a concern as early as "Rapper's Delight." When journalist and historian Jeff Chang writes that "[h]ip-hop had been reduced to a kid-friendly Broadway production, scrubbed clean for prime-time …," he's talking about the *mid-1980s*.[20] Asked during a

1987 interview, "Where will rap end up?" Cornel West responded, "Where most American postmodern products end up: highly packaged, regulated, distributed, circulated and consumed."[21] In 1988, MTV debuted *Yo! MTV Raps*, widely regarded as the day the real crossover began, but as Chang points out in *Can't Stop Won't Stop*, the technical innovation of Soundscan in 1991 showed that "[w]hat the industry thought were niche markets ... were in fact the biggest things going," and that included rap.[22] The following year, Dr. Dre of N.W.A. released *The Chronic*, and all bets were off.

Hip-hop's commercial success undoubtedly happened with the blooming of West Coast G-funk: a romanticized, lush, laid-back version of harsher gangsta rap that made the genre more palatable and attractive to a mainstream white audience. For some, West Coast rap gave in to regressive stereotypes about Black masculinity, but the accumulation of money and property rapped about in G-funk had political meaning: the economic empowerment—*real* power, some would say—of a disenfranchised people. Scholar Todd Boyd describes it bluntly: given that "there was never any intention whatsoever that a Black person in this society, especially a Black man, was supposed to make any money," the numerous rappers and producers who were "quite viable financially" in the 1990s were success stories, not sellouts.[23] Presumably this material gain was supposed to lead to political leverage and social change. Would it be a slow-burn revolution or just middling reform couched within the dominating culture of the American Wow and capitalism?

A decade later, politically conscious rap was as rare as political consciousness in any popular American music. Despite that, rappers were among the few who stood up and shouted at the hard of hearing after September 11: Nas on "Rule" and "My Country," Paris on "Tear Shit Up," the Coup, Lupe Fiasco, Eminem, the Beastie Boys, Jay-Z, and many others. The most popular artists wove their overt political dissent into albums populated by more typical hip-hop subjects since, to reach the most people—and already reaching millions—political rap like any other genre had to operate within the limitations of the American Wow, a spectacle that excels in silencing the political. And if it can't, it'll commodify and glamourize it, turn into a *lifestyle choice*. It was almost as if any revolutionary rhetoric had to strike fast and under the radar if it was going to be effective.

Four years after his breakthrough on *Mos Def & Talib Kweli Are Black Star*, Kweli is walking this line on his 2002 debut solo album, *Quality*. He brags about his mic style from the start on "Rush," promises hot DJs and killer parties on "Waitin' for the DJ," and calls out lame emcees on "Guerilla Monsoon Rap." On "Get By," the album's modest hit written with Kanye West, Kweli enacts an awakening that foreshadows Lamar's, a recognition of how the system that works against Black Americans is interwoven with personal choices—going to the clubs, smoking weed, drinking, worshipping celebrities—that either reject that system or play into its hands. And then the album's last third turns loudly political, starting with "The Proud," which is also the most personal, the most conflicted song, another precursor of Kendrick Lamar's approach. Kweli calls out the institutionalized racism that makes guns easier to obtain than an education, argues that the 2000 election was fixed, and voices his disappointment and disillusionment with the Civil Rights/Black Panther generation. These are not easily digested revolutionary words. Kweli's pinched voice and spitfire delivery hammer into the contradictions of political life for Black Americans after September 11. On the next song, "Where Do We Go?" Kweli paces around the song as if it's a room. His voice as worn as the floor, he asks the same questions Lamar will ask thirteen years later:

Where do we go? What do we say? What do we do?
Nowhere to turn, nowhere to run, and there's nothin' new.

Where do we go for inspiration?
It's like pain is our only inspiration.

8.

—*May 16, 2010: Mertilla Jones reaches for her seven-year-old granddaughter Aiyana as Detroit police swarm the house looking for a murder suspect; Aiyana is shot and killed by Officer Joseph Weekly; he blames her grandmother for grabbing his firearm; years later, evidence proves Mertilla left no fingerprints on the gun—*

Broken Contracts—Two Homes—Double-Consciousness

To Pimp a Butterfly is filled with broken contracts. Our hero, this Kendrick who is a lot like Kendrick Lamar but not exactly the same, at first doesn't realize he's the one who's broken them. In the opening trio of songs, especially "King Kunta," an allusion to the slave Kunta Kinte from Alex Haley's novel *Roots*, Kendrick is as confident as it gets, thinks he's on balance, confident, successful but woke, able to negotiate the contracts of the music business and avoid the temptations of inauthenticity and romantic infidelity. All of this, it turns out, is a lie. In "Institutionalized" he realizes he has symbolized his home, West Compton, as a prison while using it to cultivate his image in the rap game. His success has allowed him to set up a charity in Compton, but is that enough, he wonders; is it more about that image? To return home is an act of fidelity, but it also has a way of showing you up, and when Kendrick does go back home in "Momma," the affirmation and appreciation are undercut when a young boy tells him that if he's going to leave Compton behind, he should at least advocate for it. In "Hood Politics," he interrogates his younger self and finds that the same power plays from his youth inform his adult thinking. Before any of these problems are resolved, the album abruptly sends Kendrick abroad to South Africa, a spiritual home, in a sense, where Kendrick fares no better. A bad screenwriter would pitch this as an uncomplicated "finding yourself" movie, but Lamar avoids anything so easy—well, except for the homeless man who turns out to be Jesus in "How Much a Dollar Cost." Kendrick confronts his own internalized racism when he, a wealthy revolutionary Black American, can't give a dollar to the guy.

For every familial and ethical contract he's been breaking, Kendrick has been chipping away at the promises he's made to himself. These betrayals course through the album. Kendrick turns on his own morals in "These Walls," a confection of R&B enveloping the bitter story of a man who sleeps with a woman whose baby daddy is in the pen for killing the man's friend: revenge-by-sex. The song "u" is the basement of the album, its dark night of the soul. Doubt turns into self-hatred. If he's so influential, Kendrick asks himself in "u," why couldn't he stop his teenage sister from getting pregnant? If he's so faithful, why couldn't he find the time to be at his friend's bedside in the hospital before he died? Earlier, on "King Kunta," he blasts that he doesn't need to execute his rapper enemies because they're all death-driven anyway, but by the end of "u," our hero is just as unstable.

This is the self-loathing that shows up in "The Blacker the Berry," especially the opening in which Kendrick admits to sometimes enjoying watching the streets of Compton burn. A *Genius* annotation on the song makes a fitting connection to W.E.B. Du Bois' concept of double-consciousness, the split self created by racism in which Black people see themselves twice: in their own eyes and in the eyes of whites.[24] "One ever feels his two-ness," Du Bois wrote in 1909, "an American, a Negro; two souls, two thoughts, two unreconciled strivings; two warring ideals in one dark body, whose dogged strength alone keeps it from being torn asunder."[25] This twoness is what critics of the song miss. As a condition of Black American life today, this double-consciousness only gets more disorientating and destructive when Kendrick breaks promises to his home and to himself.

9.

—*in a Beavercreek, Ohio Walmart on August 5, 2014, John Crawford III carries a pellet gun sold by the store; the man who calls 911, Ronald Ritchie, says Crawford is "pointing" the gun at customers, which video surveillance later disproves; Crawford is killed on sight by police*—

Lucy Takes Kendrick to the Mall— Revolutionary Comfort

The only pact Kendrick doesn't break is the one he doesn't make. It's offered by Lucy, a feminized Lucifer who's on him from the start of the album. He's Faust, she's the Devil eager to sign an accomplished rapper to a new contract. He's already great; she can make him the best there's ever been:

artistic success, revenge, peace of mind, total power—and money. Lots of it. *To Pimp a Butterfly* is a lesson in the intersections of double-consciousness and economics. "Wesley's Theory" details how young Black men are pulled up into the neoliberal world of the American Wow wholly unprepared to understand complex finances; they'll make their money and then watch it be taken away. (The song turns Wesley Snipes into a verb, like the Dixie Chicks were turned into a verb.) In the hilarious and frenetic "For Free?-Interlude," Kendrick commodifies his own sexual self, as if there is nothing that isn't for sale. Halfway through "Institutionalized," Kendrick's friend is casing an awards show, sick of the wealth being flashed in front of him. The double-consciousness created by America's obsession with wealth appears again and again, but it reaches a fever pitch in "For Sale?-Interlude," in which Lucy takes Kendrick to the mall. Consumerism, bling, getting mine: all of it is a sort of personal revolution, in this case the sudden change from poverty to having that million-dollar check from "Wesley's Theory" in your pocket. Feminizing temptation is a cliché, but at least Lamar makes it clear Lucy is internalized, a dream, when he raps *as* Lucy. (He kind of sucks in his voice and widens it at the same time.) Neither is Lucy a stereotypical femme fatale; she's sweet, and her temptation is as innocent as a first kiss—a fitting metaphor for the eternal novelty of the American Wow.

While *To Pimp a Butterfly* is ambiguous about many things, it isn't ambiguous about rejecting the glorification of excess wealth. As the album evolves toward enlightenment, Lucy vanishes, though she may not be vanquished. This isn't to say the album rejects economic equality, material gain, or better opportunities for the Black working class, working poor, and those living in poverty, just the lure of the aspirational view that every problem can be solved by wealth. This is another argument against an isolated ideology of self-improvement since racism is not solved by money alone. In the end, buying into American consumerism would seem to only increase the disorientation of double-consciousness and lead the committed activist (or political artist) away from the unfinished newness of revolution—which is made clear when "Alright," the closest thing to a revolutionary anthem on the album, is immediately followed by "For Sale?-Interlude."

This suspicion of consumerist assimilation reminds me, strangely, perhaps, of Gil Scott-Heron's "Comment #1" from *Small Talk at 125th and Lenox*, recorded in New York City in 1970 and sampled by Kanye West on *My Beautiful Dark Twisted Fantasy*. Scott-Heron talks about having revolution, as in owning or buying it. Or renting it. Taking aim at the Rainbow Coalition of the late 1960s, an attempt by the Students for a Democratic Society (mainly white college students) to unite with the Black Panthers and the Puerto Rican gang-turned-civil rights activists the Young Lords, Scott-Heron is, let's say, skeptical. West's sampling of "Comment #1" cuts out a withering indictment of the young whites who can afford to play at revolution like consumers and retreat when the shit gets real. What they want, says Scott-Heron, is more comfort. While he's looking to fulfill basic needs like a home, a family, and food, the SDS revolution is about excess liberty. If the word "revolution" doesn't appear once on *To Pimp a Butterfly*, maybe that's because there's a justifiable suspicion of the way the concept has been redefined and commodified by whites at the expense of the real crises faced by Black people.

10.

—*August 2015: Janelle Monáe and artists from her Wondaland Records label release "Hell You Talmbout," a protest song that consists of furious drums, a unified chorus, and singular voices shouting the names of Black American victims of racist violence and murder, mostly at the hands of police: "SEAN BELL, SAY HIS NAME, SEAN BELL, SAY HIS NAME, SEAN BELL, SAY HIS NAME, SEAN BELL, WON'T YOU SAY HIS NAME, SAY HIS NAME, SAY HIS NAME, SAY HIS NAME, SAY HIS NAME, SAY HIS NAME, SAY HIS NAME, SAY HIS NAME, WON'T YOU SAY HIS NAME"; it's 2006 and Sean Bell leaves his bachelor party, unarmed, and is shot four times by five officers who unload fifty rounds into his car; Sandra Bland, about to begin a new job as a professor, is pulled over for a traffic stop; she enters a Waller County, Texas jail cell on July 10, 2015 and never comes out alive; four days after Bland's death, nine parishioners including Clementa Pinckney, a pastor and state senator, are meeting at the*

Emanuel African Methodist Episcopal Church in Charleston, South Carolina when they're gunned down by Dylann Roof in an attempt to start a race war; Nas is saying in late 2001, "My country's a motherfucker"; on April 12, 2015 Freddie Gray is put into a Baltimore police van and one hour later is admitted to the hospital in a coma, his spine broken; he dies seven days later; April 2014, Dontre Hamilton is killed in Milwaukee; July 2014, Eric Garner is killed in Staten Island; August 2014, Michael Brown is killed in Ferguson, Missouri; Tyre King, thirteen, Black, armed with a replica BB gun, is shot dead on September 14, 2016, three bullets piercing his back as he runs from police in Columbus, Ohio; Scott-Heron in 1970, about twenty-one this night but sounding like he's sixty, thunders to his conclusion: "WHO WILL SURVIVE IN AMERICA? WHO WILL SURVIVE IN AMERICA? WHO WILL SURVIVE IN AMERICA? WHO WILL SURVIVE IN AMERICA?"—

The Crowd Is Onstage—There Is No Single Method

Loosened from time and place into a constellation of pain and resistance, "Hell You Talmbout" goes on for six minutes, entirely composed of drums, a xylophone, voices, the names of the dead, and the feeling that nothing changes, that this has been going on for decades, centuries, which is yet one more reason why it has to stop. The minimalism and monotony of the structure force you to hear each shouting voice, some of them raw, some desperate, some on the edge of breaking, all of them determined, and to hear each name as it's shouted. It is literally a song that forces the count of Black Americans, their bodies, their lives—including the performers'. Their voices form a loosely cohesive choir, a sound of democracy and the common good. The space the song creates is ordinary but sacred, unbreakable by commerce because it has no commercial value and immovable by ego because the emphasis is on a community of singers. Unlike other protest songs where the singer and the band are onstage and invite the crowd to sing along, in "Hell You Talmbout," the crowd is already onstage, already singing. And it's mobile. All it needs is a drum.

"Hell You Talmbout" is the strongest unadulterated protest song I've heard this century. Nothing from the new canon of anti-Iraq war songs comes close.

But it matters, and is perhaps inevitable, that it's one song, a burst of voice and drums, and not an entire album. I don't think it'd be possible to fill an album with songs like that.

The minimalism of "Hell You Talmbout," the maximalist, ultra-fusionist sweep of jazz, R&B, funk, and rap in *To Pimp a Butterfly*: each urgently picks up the thread of unfinished newness to see where it leads. All Black American music, from slave spirituals to the blues, from Miles Davis to Motown, has played its part in weaving this thread. With such a diverse musical ancestry, there can be no single aesthetic method for political rap today, which has blossomed again. Talib Kweli uses a kaleidoscope of sounds, from hard rock to orchestral strings, while Lupe Fiasco has stuck close to a heavy R&B–pop blend. Atlanta-based duo Run the Jewels keeps it laser-sharp, mixing frenzied beats and electronic noise. Other rappers integrate political consciousness into their work more subtly as a coming-of-age story, like J. Cole on *2014 Forest Hills Drive*, or in shrewd lyrical jabs and arresting visuals like Goodbye Tomorrow. What they all have common is the constant rethinking and renewing of their fidelity to the revolutionary event of tomorrow.

New Contracts—Two Poems and a Conversation— Faithful Even to Ghosts

It wasn't until I'd listened to the album many, many times that I finally understood that *To Pimp a Butterfly* calls for revolution by asking how a revolution can be sustained, and that its answer is the importance of signing the right contracts, offering the right agreements, and staying faithful to the right promises. The irony for this book, I guess, is that fidelity seems like the opposite of the new; it requires an essentially unchanging relationship. But as I've listened to the album even more, I think this is wrong. Fidelity is entirely about the renewal of vows.

Near the end of *To Pimp a Butterfly*, broken pacts and promises are revived, beginning with "Complexion (Zulu Love)," an ode to the beauty of all skin tones; it's one of the few times Lamar doesn't implicate himself very much in the critique, focusing instead on the internalized racism within the Black community—which then segues into "The Blacker the Berry" and Kendrick's double-consciousness. From there, the album ends on a trajectory of affirmation, beginning with a meditation on authenticity in "You Ain't Gotta Lie (Momma Said)" and continuing with one of the best songs on the album, and also one of its most pop-sounding: "i." Each is a contract of appreciation, the first between Kendrick and a wannabe who keeps exaggerating himself, the latter between Kendrick and himself. As a single released in September 2014, "i" was even brighter, with Lamar's voice higher and squeezed; months later on *Saturday Night Live*, with black contact lenses over his eyes, Lamar and his band found a deeper groove in the song that made the single seem like a demo, especially with its powerhouse turn at the end—an ending that was removed, a few months later, on *To Pimp a Butterfly*. Here the song is staged as a live performance that almost devolves into a fight. Kendrick steps in, reminding the audience how many young Black men have been lost to violence and going on to explain something he may have learned in Africa: "n-e-g-u-s," he spells out—the Ethiopian word, in Amharic, for a king. What was a declaration of self-love becomes also an argument for love within the community.

The relationship between the two is put bluntly by Lamar in the final song, "Mortal Man": "If I respect you, we unify and stop the enemy from killing us." Here at the end is one final ethical agreement between friends, family, lovers, and citizens. Lamar measures the ambition and commitment required to be a leader like Nelson Mandela against the inevitable temptations and dangers. And they are inevitable. Doubts, self-contradictions, defeat: they're unavoidable, and when they happen, the question for going forward becomes, "When the shit hits the fan, is you still a fan?" Is there still a bond? Are we still faithful to each other? How else will we realize the event to come? And what will we do once it happens? *To Pimp a Butterfly* ultimately rejects the idea that self-love is enough. A necessary precondition for loving others, it has to be fulfilled by new contracts, pacts, and agreements if any kind of social revolution is going to happen. These aren't to be entered into without some serious thinking, or rethinking; in fact, they'll require constant rethinking. That's what this album is: the difficulty of the truth procedure. But for the promise of the past to survive on the interval between the old event and the new, Lamar argues that Black individuals must find a way, despite differences, to be faithful to each other, to home, family, friends, community, and those who have come before.

If there's been any doubt that *To Pimp a Butterfly* looks toward the future, change, the new, and revolution, the sequence at the end of "Mortal Man" answers that doubt. The music fades as Lamar reads the entirety of the poem that's been accumulating—that's been written, it seems—during the album, ending with a message of Black unity. Suddenly he's asking someone a question, and it turns out to be Tupac Shakur. Maybe it's a dream, a fantasy, an imagination that only art can create and make real—and it quickly gets real. As writer Michael Namikas points out, "Kendrick reprises his *good kid, m.A.A.d. City* role of a Hip Hop journalist, probing Tupac for a glimpse into America's future."[26] In response, Shakur calls up the ghost of Nat Turner and his failed 1831 revolution. Shakur sees it as unfinished newness, the origin of a coming revolution when the poor will murder the rich. Lamar seems stunned; he counters that the only hope left is music, that he feels the spirit pushing him as he raps, and Tupac says those are the spirits of the dead telling the stories. On "Mortal Man," Shakur is Lamar's link to hip-hop's revolutionary promise, his way of staying faithful to its music and politics.

Lamar turns to another poem he's written, one that explains the album's title. Both the caterpillar and the butterfly—one just trying to survive in the dirt, the other taking flight, having "made it"—share a need for continued transformation, one that depends on breaking the thin but tough walls of the institutional and internalized racism Black Americans face every day on a journey of becoming. "Although the butterfly and caterpillar are completely different," Lamar says, "they are one and the same"—their roots, their obstacles, their potential. The angular jazz behind Lamar swells as he asks what 'Pac thinks, but the ghost is gone.

But we must be faithful even to ghosts, suggests Lamar without saying another word. After all, the revolutions of the past and their unfinished newness are ghosts, here-but-not. They are most present when their names are spoken, or shouted. "Silence is our enemy," reads part of the statement that accompanies Monáe and Wondaland's song. "Sound is our weapon." Silencing the truth is easy. Speaking it is hard. You have to make people listen. The drums have to be loud. The sweep of the music has to be striking. The names have to be shouted: *Walter Scott, Jermaine Reid, Philip White, Eric Garner, Trayvon Martin, Sean Bell, Freddie Gray, Aiyana Jones, Sandra Bland, Kimani Gray, John Crawford III, Michael Brown, Miriam Carey, Sharonda Singleton, Emmett Till, Tommy Yancy, Jordan Baker, Amadou Diallo, Tyre King, Tamir Rice—*

13

Bodies in the River: Tradition and "The Body Electric"

Working Memory—Delia Green—Whitman Touches the Hands of Wounded Soldiers—The Real of the Idea

The axe. The shovel. The .44 Special. The knife. The river.

He chooses one. Does what he does. Goes on with his life and leaves the woman's body behind.

It's just the brush of an acoustic guitar that he hears some time later, a strum, a *chkk*, a strum, a *chkk*, followed by a woman's voice tender as dusk: "Said you're gonna shoot me down, put my body in the river." Maybe his shoulders tense. Say that his jaw tightens. "While the whole world sings, sings it like a song/The whole world sings like there's nothin' going wrong." Who is this woman speaking? Who gave her the right? Her voice unlocks a door that a woman is not supposed to be able to unlock. It opens up into a massive, clean, sunlight-saturated factory where men in business suits, men in suspenders and pork pie hats, men in t-shirts and jeans, men who look common, men from across all time and from all places work tirelessly at the destruction of bodies that are not male, weaving their vicious social imaginations into reality on awful machines.

In the two minutes and forty-five seconds of "The Body Electric," Hurray for the Riff Raff and its leader Alynda Lee Segarra expose and critique more than a century of popular music's expression of violence against women. In many ways, it's a familiar song and not at all formally innovative, but by using recombination and the newness of being contemporary to protest a litany of dead American women, "The Body Electric" will grab the breath in your throat and hold it there. I've listened to it twenty, maybe thirty times now and the performance can still disrupt whatever else it is I'm doing, which is the most direct way to describe the initial potential for the new that a song possesses: it possesses you.

At the center of the band's 2014 album *Small Town Heroes*, "The Body Electric" speaks immediately to the present day, to women like Sandra Bland and Miriam Carey, to women like the pregnant Laci Peterson who was murdered by her husband in 2002, to women like Tameka Lynch, Shasta Himelrick, Tiffany Sayre, and Timberly Claytor, all from Chillicothe, Ohio and all murdered sometime between 2014 and 2015, to the sexualized violence committed against young women whose rape and molestation aren't taken seriously by the police, to the emotional and psychological violence committed against women by online terrorists like Gamer Gate—women whose stories might briefly make the news and always fade away. But the song also turns its gaze to the past, to an old musical tradition that continues in the shadows: the murder ballad. It only takes one phrase to hammer home the connection: "Delia's gone," a lyric and a title belonging to many songs based on the 1900 murder of Delia Green. The point is not just to critique the murder ballad genre—by most standards, the oldest genre mentioned in this book—but to fling open the door wherever violence against women is spectacularized: blues, country, R&B, rock 'n' roll, punk, rap, pop; from Robin Thicke's "Blurred Lines" to Eminem threatening to rape the Australian-born rapper Iggy Azalea on the track "Vegas."[1] Popular music is an opportunity for performances of misogyny, and there's a tradition of men getting away with saying the worst things imaginable while women like the Dixie Chicks are crucified for taking a single verbal jab at the president.

Hurray for the Riff Raff aims to make the old new again, to retrieve this forgotten genre of the murder ballad so that we understand it as a tradition that's been culturally created and accepted rather than just a reflection of "the way things are." This in turn forces the count in favor of women and makes the violence against them shockingly new but part of a historical pattern. In a political way, this is the epitome of Boris Groys' "negative adaptation," to use something valorized by the cultural archive but to turn it on its head. The song is somewhere between reformation and revolution; it's not a rejection of the folk-country genre the band excels at, or even of the murder ballad genre, but the political impact of "The Body Electric" is a firm and unambiguous NO. As in, NO MORE. The political new is often presented as a break from traditions, but it can succeed, and probably must succeed, as an interrogation of the traditions we've taken for granted. I agree with Groys: in the economy of cultural exchange, the archive-tradition cannot be dismantled. But it is an exchange—one value accepted, one value rejected—which means certain values can be reduced to dust. "Every more or less radical innovation reorganizes cultural memory, removing from it things previously preserved there," he writes. "A culture's memory, like a computer's, may be divided into a permanent and working memory."[2] The murder ballad is somewhere in between these memories; the songs themselves reside in permanent memory, but their legacy of sensationalized violence against women is part of our cultural working memory. Rather than erase what's in the permanent memory, "The Body Electric" calls attention to both memories, calls into question the way one informs the other, and calls for something different: a song where women speak, where their experiences are not erased or reduced to a single line, as in the Kingston Trio's jaunty folk ballad hit "Tom Dooley." The plot of that song revolves around a woman's murder but the song is all about the murderer's fear of being hanged. The woman in the song doesn't even get a name, let alone speak.

Segarra and the woman speaking in "The Body Electric" have been watching and listening for as long as they've been alive. *So I'm being watched?* the song seems to say. *Let me tell you what I've seen you do.* The narrator reports this right away to the man in the song, recounting his threat to shoot her down and "put [her] body in the river," the word "put" as gentle as Segarra's soft alto. The worst of it isn't that the world keeps going, but that it's entertained by the man's threat, which becomes high drama and is then discarded. (In their most powerful performances, the murder ballads *are* high drama, creepy and sickening. They're not meant to pass by you gently.) Then Segarra turns to a woman who's already been killed in the same way, maybe by the same man; the singer retrieves her, undoing in some small sense the negation of the woman's history by unearthing it and retelling it. Segarra's tone dips lower in the next line as she vows in a whisper to stop the violence.

Like Janelle Monáe and Wondaland's "Hell You Talmbout," "The Body Electric" names the victims, even if it names only one: "Delia's gone," sings Segarra, her voice momentarily like sweet tea on a summer day, "but I'm settling the score." If you haven't recognized the images and attitudes connected to murder ballads before this—the gun and the river, the man's casual way of disposing of the body—then "Delia" might at least spark the memory of Johnny Cash's song "Delia's Gone," the first track on his 1994 return-to-form album *American Recordings*. Behind that chilling performance is an entire history of performances, a catalogue of versions of just that one song in the enormous corpus of the American murder ballad.

Who is Delia? In "The Body Electric," she's every young woman in every murder ballad; she's Frankie from "Frankie and Albert," the virginal "Pretty Polly," the naïve "Omie Wise." But we know more about her than we do most of these other women, even if the path to that knowledge is circuitous. In November 1940, in an Atlanta hotel room with John Lomax and his wife Ruby, who are collecting songs for the Library of Congress, the blues singer Blind Willie McTell—for whom Bob Dylan will create a mythic hymn some forty years later—sings a version of "Delia" that will become a standard. A different version of the song circulates years before that and pops up in a 1935 recording by the Nassau String Band in the Bahamas. McTell likely heard that variant, but it isn't popularized in the United States until a 1949 recording by Blind Blake and his Royal Victoria Calypso Orchestra. (Not Blind Blake the blues singer.

Different guy.) This second but perhaps original version is the one picked up by Cash, while Dylan includes McTell's version, naturally, on his 1993 album *World Gone Wrong*. All of the early versions have a few things in common: their performances are spry and "almost jaunty," as Sean Wilentz will later write of McTell's version, none of them are told from Delia's point of view, and none of them are sung by women.[3]

None of them tell the story of what happened to Delia Green in 1900, either. Versions of the song percolate through the South but are lost to history until a professor named John Garst traces back the details and finds the story: Delia Green, 14 years old, a young Black woman shot and killed by her 14-year-old lover Moses "Cooney" Houston on Christmas Eve, 1900. Houston is convicted but the jury suggests mercy and the judge sentences him to life in prison instead of execution. Twelve years later, he's paroled. According to the best evidence available, he dies in 1927, before the most popular musical recounting of his crime begins to surface.[4] As Wilentz points out in his chapter about "Delia" in *The Rose and The Briar*, all the versions of the song leave out Green and Houston's age and that both were Black. They leave out that Delia Green reportedly called Houston a "son of a bitch" and claimed that she was "a lady," not the slut he accused her of being. In McTell's version of the song, the scene of her murder is never described. Delia's murder creates an absence in the lives of her parents and in the heart of the singer who cries, in a fascinating bit of compressed language, "She's all I got is gone." Except that she was a gambler, Delia isn't really brought to life in the song. Neither is her suffering. As a person and a character, all that matters is her absence.

When Segarra sings Delia's name, her voice slows down and stretches out the word. The name is what unlocks and pushes open that door, revealing the not-so-secret history of dead women, murdered women, women who are made blank, stripped of their motivations, their wit, their cunning, and often, in the oldest versions of the songs, the ones that originated in the British Isles, their supernatural powers. In the mid-eighteenth century ballad "The Gosport Tragedy," a precursor of "Pretty Polly," the dead woman reappears as a ghost with lightning flashing in her eyes and haunts her killer's getaway ship until he confesses.[5] In "The Body Electric," the supernatural is a grace note—Segarra communing with the dead—perhaps because Delia's grave is everywhere you look in America, if you bother to look, and her face appears in the face of every woman gunned down by a lover, husband, father, neighbor, or police officer. Having opened the door to show the man in the song the hellish factory of murder to which he belongs, Segarra turns to him in the final seconds as the tempo slows down. You can hear the sad gleam in her eyes as she warns him, "Tell me what's a man with a rifle in his hand gonna do for his daughter when it's her turn to go?" And you might imagine this man seeing his daughter on this disassembly line, just another name to the mid-level killers working this particular factory, just another body in the river where they dump all the dead girls.

Through quiet but powerful dissent, Hurray for the Riff Raff shows why the political-as-new is most effective when it makes connections between the present and the past. In fact, history is a necessity. Institutionalized racism, misogyny, homophobia—these didn't become systems overnight. It took time. To reveal that interconnected system for what it truly is, a commonplace and orderly network of unspoken and spoken rules and customs and not just a momentary weakness, a gap, a blunder, a tragedy, a "few bad apples" that never seem to get picked and thrown away, you have to talk about its patterns throughout history. Especially in our presentist culture, the revelation of history is new, and thus politically new, because it retrieves the unfinished promises of past revolutions and reverses their betrayals.

That is what Segarra and Monáe/Wondaland do: carry forward the voices and the names of the dead on the interval between the past event and the event to come. How much power that gesture has depends on the performance itself, which in turn depends on the voices of the singer(s), Segarra's resolute hush or the thunderous clamor of "Hell You Talmbout." In the summer of 2015, Rhiannon Giddens of the Carolina Chocolate Drops released "Cry No More," a response to the murders committed by the white supremacist Dylann Roof in the Emanuel AME church in Charleston, South Carolina. In the song's video, Giddens faces a choir and beats on a hand drum that sounds at first like a deep-toned bell as she digs deeper into America's history of racism and the terrors committed today. Her voice is as resolute as Segarra's but lower, more expressive, wide as a sunset. Like "Hell You Talmbout" and "The Body

Electric," the structure of "Cry No More" is simple and repetitive so that you must hear the history it sings about. Its call-and-response creates between the singer and the choir a dialogue—the one the song demands, the one we as a nation are still not having.

To talk about the performance of a song, the action taken at a specific moment in time, is to affirm the importance of the body. How the hips sway. How the mouth stretches open at the junction of the lips, and how the muscles in the back of the neck respond by tightening. How the spine stiffens or slacks. In this instance, an irreplaceable person takes a gamble or succumbs to the predictable. It's hard to hear the body in some performances, whether they're designed to sound that way or not, but you hear it in "The Body Electric": Segarra's voice, her wrists bending over acoustic guitar strings, the tension in violinist Yosi Perlstein's arms, the tremor across the torso as the drummer beats on a floor tom. Performance encourages the listener to hear and visualize who is performing. For some performers, this is filled with risks. Say nothing and you have a better chance of staying safe, but you will also stay silent. Speak, sing, and you're more likely to draw attention to yourself, but you will have taken an action.

In an interview with Ann Powers for NPR, Segarra said, "[S]ometimes I want to do songs that everybody knows, because they haven't heard someone like me sing them yet," and when Powers asked what she meant by "someone like me," Segarra replied, "A Puerto Rican from the Bronx who went to the South, who also feels queer, who also loves classic country and rock 'n' roll."[6] Riff Raff violinist Perlstein is a transgender man who identifies as queer. His playing on "The Body Electric," like Segarra's singing, is subdued and mournful. Together they communicate the resolve and courage of bodies at risk, bodies targeted by misogynists and transphobes who expect the kind of conformist performativity Judith Butler describes. To work the trap of gender and sexuality onstage or off can be dangerous and it often comes with the potential for violence, especially for transwomen of color. 2016 was yet another record year for transgender homicide victims in the United States.[7] At this point in the book, I don't think I have to explain the added risks of explicitly political speech, including openly queer speech.

Who knew more about those risks than Walt Whitman? The locus of American poetry, our Shakespeare, was gay. Probably, in my estimation, queer. Whitman's sexuality has been a source of quiet controversy for almost a century, as if it would, for some, undo the power of his newness, which was nothing less than the cobbling together of an original American poetic voice. The controversy stems in part, it's true, from Whitman's own working of the nineteenth-century trap, his evasions and denials—performances of gender and sexuality—pitted against coded documentation in letters and journals and the robust same-sex eroticism in his poems, particularly the "Calumus" section of *Leaves of Grass*. In one of his most famous works, "I Sing the Body Electric," there is a frank love for all bodies, male and female, white and Black, that cannot be ignored if you truly give yourself to the poem, to its performance of the poet's body, his weathered eyes lit with joy, his bony hands that touched the mangled bodies of soldiers of the Civil War. Here, suffering is joined with a sensuality that is erotic at times but also an ethical contract between people, a contract that creates the event of America.

"The Body Electric" takes its title from Whitman's poem, picking up the unfinished newness and revolution of his work while critiquing and attempting to undo the power of other traditions. Even if most of the performances on *Small Town Heroes* are what I've come to think of as NPR roots music, an enjoyable and contemporary but far from sonically innovative blend of folk, country and the blues, the album still swells with the expanse of the United States, the psychogeography of its ghosts and its future ideal as a place where there's room for everybody to live as they please in peace. "We'll play in dive bars, or in country bars," Segarra told Powers, "and for the first time maybe ever, a lot of queer people feel like they can go there and hang out. And they can listen to that music because it doesn't have the connotation of being sung by people who hate them."[8] The songs on *Small Town Heroes* are sometimes ambiguous about who the object of the singer's love is, as on "I Know It's Wrong (But That's Alright)," and sometimes not at all ambiguous, as on "Good Times Blues (An Outlaw's Lament)" when Segarra sings that "there's a girl in South Louisiana, and she's always on my mind."

The band's reclamation of roots music for women and LGBTQ audiences is most obvious in the visceral and textured video for "The Body Electric." Segarra rides in a car as she sings, and we cut between three scenes. Spilled bullet casings rise from the ground; like Kendrick Lamar, Segarra is attempting to reverse time. Katey Red, a transgender star of the New Orleans bounce hip-hop scene, takes on the persona of Venus in a recreation of Botticelli's *Birth of Venus*. Midway through the video, we begin to see glimpses of a hanged young woman with a stock around her neck. As the painting comes together, the casings rise and are gathered into a blanket nestled in the arms of a Black woman. As Segarra sings the song's alarming final couplet, the video cuts back to the hanged woman staring at the viewer in what could be a wedding dress. She could be your daughter. For Segarra, who named her band after the young and old travelers she called her community, the self-exiled and the outcasts, to name Delia Green is to gather all the victims of gendered and sexualized violence into a blanketed embrace of compassion and remembering..

In "I Sing the Body Electric," Whitman proclaims that all bodies are one body, that despite our differences, there's a unity in our bodies that makes us the populace, the body politic. Here, gender and sexuality—and race, class; *all* difference—meet democracy, Whitman's greatest love. And yet, Whitman surely knew—as Segarra knows, as the Dixie Chicks, Springsteen, Lamar, Monáe, and Giddens know—that not every American believes in the radical potential of democracy, and that even those who say they believe are often all too willing to cast aside or extinguish anyone who gets in their way. "I Sing the Body Electric" is a protest poem that becomes prophecy by shouting amidst the political and ideological that the body matters, that suffering matters, that life matters. Whitman understood that dissenting art must make the performer and audience feel one another so it's clear that the political and the bodily truly cannot be separated. What a musician he would have been today.

Bodies inevitably disappear into the river of history. The danger for today and for the future is that their disappearance allows us to forget the suffering they experienced. If the body first of all signifies suffering, and if the condition of truth is to allow suffering to speak, as Adorno argued, then the flow of time works against truth. Time is not necessarily the revelator. The future, the revolution, and the event to come are never guaranteed.

If truth is to guide the present, then popular music must intervene. If it does, it might produce rather than reflect what we accept as truth. Music has the power to join past and future at the present moment in a tangible way, in a way that does not lose the body to the currents, a way that proclaims instead, *Here, at this moment: this moment begins the potential for a future that will be different.*

"The Body Electric" is, as Ann Powers writes, Segarra's "intervention."[9] In this one-song revival, Hurray for the Riff Raff perform the interpretative intervention's task of naming, but here, as opposed to the songs of Gillian Welch, the early 2000s folk revival, and the freak-folk movement, the naming has an explicitly critical and political force. It both names and lays blame at the feet of what can be considered an event for music—the invention of the murder ballad. At the same time, "The Body Electric" calls back and is faithful to the event that was Whitman: his own breaking of the chains and contradictions embedded in the history of the nation, in its founding documents, in their words, words like "democracy," "liberty," and "justice," the words Gil Scott-Heron mistrusted in 1970. Like "Hell You Talmbout," like "Cry No More," like *To Pimp a Butterfly*, like *Wrecking Ball*, and like a handful of other protest records of the new millennium, "The Body Electric" puts into the air a tangible though imagined political future. Badiou names this the "Idea," defining it as "the possibility in the name of which you act, you transform, and you have a programme."[10] If the new possibilities of the event are to be realized, then along the way, Badiou argues, a person must essentially take the risk of accepting and being faithful to the Idea. This is what he means by "incorporation": a person takes the work of art into themselves in order to become "the real of this Idea."[11] This, in turn, is what sustains the Idea and the new during the interval between the past event and the event to come, and what gives us the courage to act in that interval, to force the count of ourselves and others, and to wrench old values away from the tradition and inject new values.

Why might there need to be a second event, as Badiou suggests, if the first is so earthshaking? Because institutions are built to withstand earthquakes. An event is the point at which the possibility of disrupting a tradition emerges, like a crack in the wall. Over hundreds of years, the wall might finally collapse, but if it's to be any sooner, then it'll take more than a few people to stand outside or inside and push. What they might create is what "The Body Electric" seeks: a new and more humane tradition.

Epilogue: Nothing Has Been Done Before, Again

The Kid Goes Home—Menace—A House Concert

It is April 21, 2016. Prince has been found dead in a Paisley Park elevator. His sudden absence is as tangible as the power going out. Like you, maybe, I pore over his albums. As "Purple Rain" is posted online again and again, I grumble to myself that *he made other hits, you know*, and then I listen to the debut of the song that August night in 1983. Within days, though, fans flood YouTube with live performances and studio outtakes that a week earlier Prince would have blocked: obscurities like "Avalanche" and "Empty Room," well-worn jams like "Kiss" and "Diamonds and Pearls." Across the nation, Black, queer, white, teen, trans, Latino, retired, Christian, middle-class, gay, Asian, poor, straight, Muslim, lesbian, dressed-to-the-nines, just-got-out-of-bed, young, leftist, and maybe even some Far Right conservative Americans go out to the clubs and into the streets and dance and sing along to his music, doing what we do when great artists die: mourn and celebrate the newness they created. If it's true that nothing has been done before, then it's equally true that what has been done will never be done again.

That's when I have a bizarre thought. Maybe Prince has taken the new with him. Not just the possibility that he might unfinish a song like he did to "Little Red Corvette" in Montreux in 2009, or the new artistic territory he might have discovered, like Bob Dylan, as he approached age 60—not just his own potential to be new, but the very thing itself.

Many months later, there's a pessimism and a sense of menace that I'm trying to shake off and keep out of this book. The election of Donald Trump to the presidency in November 2016 may not be the end of America—though who knows; we kept saying *it can't happen here*—but, when it did happen, it felt like the end of a project of newness, one that was flawed under the Obama administration (everything's flawed, purity's the problem) but nonetheless was inching us closer to the fulfilment of what America is supposed to be. For all of the unprecedented debasement Trump has brought into the Oval Office, for all of the new ways in which facts have been corrupted, integrity has become a hologram, privilege has become victimization, and reality has become television, the base ideologies Trump campaigned on and won with are not new. They are revivals of the American urges toward isolationism, authoritarianism, identitarianism, and an emaciated populism founded on white straight male supremacy. But it is these values, in power at this point in history, with this technology, this media, and this collection of ravenous egos which make the situation truly unprecedented. Like every revival, this surge of neofascism marks an event in the past in order to name it, to force it to count, but it also seeks to obscure history and rely on nostalgic myths. Any resistance to this revival will at least have to name a different past event without obfuscation and seize upon the reality of this nation's unfinished promise of newness.

Why does any of that matter in a book about music? On the one hand, our current political situation is another example of how the new is really a relationship between the present, the past, and the future. But there is also the inescapable tendency of the new, in music as in anything else, to be defined by society and its standards. The event. Groys' cultural archive and the profane. The commercial and populist values of the American Wow. The allure of being contemporary. The power of revolution. This is the same conclusion Michael North arrives at in *Novelty*, writing that language itself, a social system, tends to define the new. Thus "novelty, which was once linked inextricably to the individual, to originality, and which has often been defined in terms of a tension *with* the social, actually seems more feasible as a social phenomenon."[1] It's not just feasible, it's the way things generally are. The danger for political change as well as aesthetic newness is that the individual feels alienated from society, swamped by its power, confused by a sameness that declares progress, and silenced by its seemingly natural definition of the new. But the tension between a single person and her society is in fact the potential for democracy, and we cannot let it evaporate.

What I've found myself doing in these pages is not only sifting through music to find the new, but also searching for the role of the individual musician in making the new happen. If music is performance, then performers must claim their constant potential to make the new. The theater director Peter Brook once wrote, "I can take any empty space and call it a bare stage," echoing the phrase Bruce Springsteen used to describe the site of a concert.[2] Every performer knows, or senses, that the new is in the gaps and the empty spaces, in the variables and contingencies at the heart of Badiou's event. Everywhere else, we find what already *is* or what society claims is the only thing possible. The performer's job is to seek out those gaps and empty spaces.

When I'm low about the prospects for the new, I think about a house concert my friend puts on every year. Not long ago, with all of this book's big ideas swirling around in my head—the abstract stuff, the philosophy, the concepts—I sat down with my wife and watched the night's guest unpack her twelve-string guitar, check its tuning, and begin to lay out her harmonicas. She was a traveling musician from, I don't know, Portland or Chicago or Texas; I'd never heard her and I had no idea what she'd play. I was reminded that even here, in a living room packed with friendly people tipsy on chocolate beer, the new was possible. It is, for the musician, an ordinary impulse. Whether the musician gets tired of what she's been singing, or out of curiosity she tries a tune on the piano instead of the guitar, or she hears for the first time her own recorded voice singing back to her, or she stops in the middle of a verse and changes direction, and whether or not a hit song is abandoned or a hit is all that matters, whether or not she speaks with blunt honesty or theatrical chicanery, plays from within the spectacle or outside of it, seeks revolutionary change or finds it by accident, and whether or not the only thing left after all the thinking, rewriting, rehearsing, debating, recording, and performing is a desire to take a chance and hear what happens next, the new is always waiting.

Notes

Prologue

1. Tosches, *Unsung Heroes of Rock 'n' Roll*, 10, 11.
2. Reynolds, *Retromania*, 404, 405.
3. North, *Novelty: A History of the New*, 22.
4. Smith, "Why Country Music Was Awful in 2013," YouTube.
5. Groys, *On the New*, 1.
6. Danto, *After the End of Art*, 132.
7. Ibid.
8. Marcus, *The History of Rock 'n' Roll in Ten Songs*, 26.
9. Gracyk, *Rhythm and Noise: An Aesthetics of Rock*, 36.
10. Davies, *Musical Works and Performances*, 8.
11. Frith, *Performing Rites*, 211.
12. This objectification happens primarily in the market and in popular music criticism, and is countered by academic interest in performance as it relates to music and more generally. See Butler, Marcus, and Muñoz later in this book. See also Frith and Zagorski-Thomas, *The Art of Record Production*; Small, *Musicking*; Auslander, *Liveness*.
13. For Badiou, there's no such thing as just a "site," there are only eventual sites. I've gone against his terminology to clarify his concepts at this point in the book.
14. Springsteen, Interview with Stephen Colbert, September 23, 2016.
15. Badiou, *Being and Event*, 183.
16. Ibid., 188.
17. Ibid., 190. (This paragraph and those that follow summarize *Being and Event* 181–192.)
18. Thank you to Matt Mitchem for this clarifying example.

19 Badiou only considers a situation historical if it contains an event. See *Being and Event*, 185. Throughout this book, I refer to the "historical situation" in the more commonplace sense for the sake of clarity and concision.

20 Badiou, *Being and Event*, xxvii.

Chapter 1

1 Rushkoff, *Present Shock*, 10.

2 Ibid., 11.

3 Ibid., 2.

4 Oppelaar, "Roots Still Strong," 6.

5 Wilkinson, "The Ghostly Ones," 78.

6 North, *Novelty*, 159.

7 Ibid., 7.

8 Alden, "Quicksilver Girl," 84.

9 Schneider, "Gillian Welch," *Exclaim!*

10 North, *Novelty*, 7.

11 Ibid., 31.

12 Lipsitz, *Time Passages*, 99.

13 Ibid.

14 Badiou, *Being and Event*, 208.

15 Giddens, Interview with R.L., February 13, 2012 (including all quotes in this paragraph).

16 Sacks and Sacks, *Way Up North in Dixie*, 171–173. (My recounting of the Snowdens' story relies on the Sacks' text.)

17 Leggett, "Genuine Negro Jig," *AllMusic.com*.

Chapter 2

1 Dylan, "Bob Dylan Unleashed," *Rolling Stone*.

2 Groys, *On the New*, 63.

3 Ibid., 64.

4   Dylan, *Chronicles*, 161.

5   Groys, *On the New*, 64.

6   Ibid.

7   Ibid., 64, 139.

8   Ibid., 66.

9   Welch, *Britannia: The Roman Conquest & Occupation of Britain*, 107.

10 Marcus, Email to Author, July 2015.

11 Wald, *Dylan Goes Electric!*, 307.

12 Muldar, *No Direction Home*, 2005; Heylin, *Behind the Shades*, 214.

13 Filene, *Romancing the Folk*, 215.

14 Wald, *Dylan*, 284.

15 Heylin, *Behind the Shades*, 216.

16 Danto, *After the End of Art*, 12.

17 Filene, *Romancing the Folk*, 217.

18 Danto, *After the End of Art*, 131.

19 Heylin, *Behind the Shades*, 212.

20 Dylan, *Chronicles*, 150.

21 Ibid., 153.

22 Marcus, *Bob Dylan by Greil Marcus*, 201.

23 Dylan, *No Direction Home*, 2005.

24 Dylan, Press Conference, KQED; *No Direction Home*.

25 Gordimer, "Lust and Death," *New York Times*.

26 Miers, "A Good Thing," *Buffalo News*.

27 Groys, *On the New*, 135.

28 Ibid., 103, 104.

29 Eig and Moffett, "Did Bob Dylan Lift Lines," *Wall Street Journal*.

30 Willis, *Out of the Vinyl Deeps*, 3.

31 Kinney, *The Dylanologists*, 161. For more thorough details of Dylan's repurposing on "Love and Theft," *Chronicles*, and *Modern Times*: Kinney, *The Dylanologists*, 149–180; Wilentz, *Bob Dylan in America*, 305–319; and the superb Dylanchords.info.

32 Pareles, "Critic's Notebook," *New York Times*.

33 Vega, "The Ballad of Henry Timrod," *New York Times*.

34 Deley, "Bob Dylan and Plagiarism," *Dissident Voice*.

35 Kinney, *The Dylanologists*, 164.

36 Francescani, "Bob Dylan's 'Da Vinci Code' Revealed," *Daily Beast*.

37 Wilentz, *Bob Dylan in America*, 276.

38 Kinney, *The Dylanologists*, 160.

39 Dylan, "Bob Dylan Unleashed," *Rolling Stone*.

40 Dylan, "Bob Dylan, at 60, Unearths New Revelations," *Rolling Stone*.

41 Groys, *On the New*, 156.

Chapter 3

1 Coyle and Dolan, *Modeling Authenticity*, 23 (for perhaps the first use of the term "meta-rock").

2 Bloom, *The Anxiety of Influence*, 5.

3 Ibid., 19.

4 Ibid., 5–16.

5 Ibid., 7.

6 Azerrad, *Our Band Could Be Your Life*, 498–499.

7 Reynolds, *Retromania*, 140–141.

8 Christgau, "GGGB," *Village Voice*.

9 Reynolds, *Retromania*, 176.

10 Ibid., 416.

11 Meltzer, "A Literature of Secular Revelations," 108.

12 Tillich, *The Courage to Be*, 27 (my italics).

13 Bakhtin, *Speech Genres*, 170.

Chapter 4

1 Reynolds, *Retromania*, 140.

2 Greenberg, "Modernist Painting," 101.

3   Danto, *After the End of Art*, 9.

4   Hood, "The South's Heritage," *New York Times*.

5   North, *Novelty*, 29.

6   Greenblatt, *The Swerve*, 12.

7   Marinetti, *The Founding and Manifesto of Futurism*, originally published in *Le Figaro* in 1909, incl. all subsequent quotations in this paragraph.

8   VJ Vendetta, interview with RL, incl. all subsequent quotations.

9   Neuman, "The Nostalgic Allure of 'Synthwave,'" *Observer*. Both quotations in this paragraph are from the same article.

10 Rossocorsarecords.com.

11 Surico, "Spotify Shoots Down," *Spin*.

12 Eells, "Taylor Swift Reveals Five Things," *Rolling Stone*.

13 Groys, *On the New*, 55.

14 Meyer, "Innovation, Choice, and the History of Music," 518.

Chapter 5

1   Gallo, "Katy Perry's Halftime Show," *Billboard.com*.

2   Billboard, The Hot 100: 2/7/15, *Billboard.com*.

3   Willis, *Out of the Vinyl Deeps*, 112.

4   Morley, *Ask: The Chatter of Pop*, 5.

5   Debord, *The Society of the Spectacle*, #1. (Unless otherwise noted, I'm quoting and referring to the 1977 revised edition. There are no page numbers; I refer throughout to its numbered theses.)

6   Ibid., #4.

7   Ibid., #17 (emphasis mine).

8   Debord, *Spectacle*, 3rd French edition, n.p. Or as Badiou puts it in *Being and Event* (xiv), "'Freedom' reduced to the freedom to trade and consume."

9   Rushkoff, *Present Shock*, 167–169.

10 Debord, *Spectacle*, #20.

11 Marcus, *Lipstick Traces*, 94, 95.

12 Adorno, *Aesthetic Theory*, 44.

13 Debord, *Spectacle*, #6.

14 Ibid., #181.

15 Groys, Interview with RL and Mitchem, October 12, 2016 (including all quotes in this section).

16 Dockterman, "Watch Taylor Swift," *Time*.

17 Greenblatt, *The Swerve*, 10.

18 Lamere, "Exploring Age-Specific Preferences," *Music Machinery*.

19 Debord, *Spectacle*, #192.

20 Chase, "Katy Perry," *USA Today*.

21 Aswad, "Why Missy Elliott?" *Billboard*.

22 Billboard, "Missy Elliot—Charts," *Billboard*.

23 Rushkoff, *Present Shock*, 4.

24 Ibid., 6.

25 Ibid., 23–34.

26 Danto, *After the End of Art*, 12.

27 Badiou, "Fifteen Theses on Contemporary Art," Lacan.com. (Here I refer to the lecture accompanying the theses.)

28 Debord, *Spectacle*, 3rd French edition, #9.

29 Ibid., #60.

30 Badiou, "Fifteen Theses," #13. (As with *Spectacle*, I refer here to section numbers.)

31 See *Philosophy and the Event*, 79–81.

32 Badiou, "Fifteen Theses," #15.

Chapter 6

1 Henke, James, "Neil Young: The Rolling Stone Interview," 239.

2 Whatsongisinthatcommercial.com.

3 Pearis, "LCD Soundsystem," *Brooklyn Vegan*.

4 Google Books, Ngram Viewer.

5 Among others, Milner, *Perfecting Sound Forever*.

6 Katz, *Capturing Sound*, 204–206.

7   Heylin, *Bootleg: The Rise and Fall of the Secret Recording Industry*, 47.

8   Byrne, *How Music Works*, 265.

9   Katz, *Capturing Sound*, 220, 221.

10 Pollstar, "2015 Year End Business Analysis," Pollstarpro.com. Between 2011 and 2015, tickets sold fluctuated between a low of 51.3 million and a high of 63.3 million.

11 Debord, *Comments on the Society of the Spectacle*, 12.

12 Ibid., 9.

13 Kot, *Ripped*, 11.

14 Weisbard, *Top 40 Democracy*, 259, 260.

15 Nielsen and Billboard, "2012 Music Industry Report," *BusinessWire*.

16 Christman, "Music in 2014," *Billboard*. The figures in this note and the one above count major-label distribution of "indie" labels. Counting label *ownership* instead, major labels accounted for 64 percent of the market in 2014.

17 Kot, *Ripped*, 8, 9.

18 Ibid., 7.

19 Witt, *How Music Got Free*, among many other sources.

20 Moody's, "Music Industry Consolidation," Moodys.com.

21 See Caulfield, "US Album Sales Volume," *Billboard*; Christman, "U.S. Album Sales Fall 12.8 percent in 2010," *Billboard*; Nielsen, "2014 Nielsen Music US Report," Neilsen; Witt, *How Music Got Free*; DeGusta, "The Real Death of the Music Industry," *Business Insider*.

22 Witt, *How Music Got Free*, 233.

23 Anderson, "Free!," *Wired*.

24 Angelakos, "Passion Pit Address Controversy," *Fresh 102.7.CBSlocal.com*.

25 "Milky Way/Pink Moon," YouTube link (defunct).

Chapter 7

1   Marcus, *Mystery Train*, 97.

2   Eng, Halberstam, and Muñoz, "What's Queer About Queer Studies Now?"; Hilderbrand "Luring Disco Dollies,"; Halperin, "The Normalization of Queer Theory," among others.

3   Mitchem, "True Life," 177.

4   Prince, Interview with Chris Rock, VH1, 1997.

5   Swartley, "This Prince Is No Pretender," 235.

6   Smith, "The Queer Legacy of Prince," *Out*.

7   Butler, "The Body You Want," 85.

8   Ibid., 83–84; see also Nelson, *The Argonauts*, 15.

9   Jagose, *Queer Theory*, 85.

10 Butler, *Bodies That Matter*, 95.

11 Debord, *Spectacle*, #17.

12 Marcus, *Lipstick Traces*, 131.

13 Butler, *Bodies That Matter*, 95.

14 Muñoz, *Cruising Utopia*, 96.

15 Ibid., 98.

16 Butler, *Undoing Gender*, 216, 217.

17 Nelson, *The Argonauts*, 53.

18 Stanford Encyclopedia of Philosophy, "Heraclitus."

19 Muñoz, *Cruising Utopia*, 98, 99.

20 Marcus, *Mystery Train*, 97.

Chapter 8

1   Frere-Jones, "Black Noise," *The New Yorker*.

2   Groys, *On the New*, 121–122.

3   Kaufman, "Kanye West's 'Blood on the Leaves,'" MTV.com.

4   Groys, *Art Power*, 68.

Chapter 9

1   Gipson, "Afrofuturism's Musical Princess," 98.

2   Calvert, "Janelle Monáe," *The Quietus*.

3   Willis, *Out of the Vinyl Deeps*, 162, 163 (incl. subsequent quotation).

4   English and Kim, "Now We Want Our Funk Cut," 222.

5   Monáe, "Gimme Some Monáe!" 45.

6   Dery, *Flame Wars*, 180.

7   Womack, *Afrofuturism*, 74–76.

8   Jennings and Fluker, "Forms of Future/Past" (forthcoming).

9   Ibid.

10 Monáe, "Gimme Some Monáe!" 45.

11 English and Kim, "Now We Want Our Funk Cut," 218.

12 Dery, *Flame Wars*, 190.

13 Badiou, "Fifteen Theses," Lacan.com.

14 Goodbye Tomorrow, Interview by Hip-Hop Nonstop, November 11, 2015.

15 *Rolling Stone*, "10 New Artists," RollingStone.com.

16 Note 14.

17 Adorno, *Negative Dialectics*, 17, 18.

18 Eagleton, *The Ideology of the Aesthetic*, 343. (Zabel, "Adorno on Music," 199.)

19 James, "Robo-Diva R&B," 417, 418. (James is critiquing the titular term coined by *Village Voice* critic Tom Breihan.)

Chapter 10

1   Pruitt, "Real Men Kill and a Lady Never Talks Back," 88.

2   Kopple and Peck, *The Dixie Chicks: Shut Up and Sing*, 2006. (Nearly all events described in this opening section can be found in the documentary.)

3   Bernstein, "Being Contemporary," 94.

4   Frith, *Performing Rites*, 250.

5   Ibid., 250, 270.

6   Bernstein, "Being Contemporary," 95.

7   North, *Novelty*, 44, 45.

8   Ibid., 45.

9   Hajdu, "Where Has 'Where Have All The Flowers Gone?' Gone?," *The New Republic*.

10 Love and Michener, *Sounds Like a Revolution*, 2010.

11 Hilburn, "Judging Songs by Their Titles," *Los Angeles Times*; Strauss, "After the Horror, Radio Stations Pull Some Songs," *New York Times*.

12 Hajdu, "Where Has," 34.

13 Dale, *Popular Music and the Politics of Novelty*, 149.

14 Hajdu, "Where Has," 34, 35.

15 Walt, "Where Have All the Political Songs Gone?" *Foreign Policy*.

16 Dale, *Popular Music and the Politics of Novelty*, 156.

17 Ibid., 159, 160.

18 Lynskey, *33 Revolutions Per Minute*, 523.

19 Christgau, "Green Day: *American Idiot*," RobertChristgau.com.

20 Cantwell, *When We Were Good*, 53.

21 Petrusich, *It Still Moves*, 235.

22 Tillich, *The New Being*, 16.

23 Ibid., 20.

24 Qtd. in North, *Novelty*, 38.

25 Qtd. in Cantwell, *When We Were Good*, 71, 72.

26 Ruhkoff, *Present Shock*, 18.

27 Adorno, "On the Social Situation of Music," 393.

28 Flippo, "Nashville Skyline," *CMT.com*; qtd. in Pruitt, "Real Men Kill," 91.

Chapter 11

1 The "Backstreets Liner Notes" for *Tracks* and also Brucebase for "Roulette" recording date. In *Born to Run* (275), Springsteen says "Roulette" was the first song recorded for *The River* but then says it was recorded after the MUSE concerts. Since the recording sessions began in March 1979, all evidence points to an April 3, 1979 recording date.

2 Springsteen, *The Promise: The Darkness on the Edge of Town Story*, liner notes.

3 O'Connor, *Mystery and Manners*, 34.

4 Springsteen, "Rock and Read," *DoubleTake*.

5 Ibid.

6 Himes, *Born in the USA*, 61–63.

7 O'Connor, *Mystery and Manners*, 112.

8 Marsh, *Glory Days*, 115.

9 Springsteen, *Born to Run*, 435.

10 Sony Legacy, "10 Facts," *WeareSonyLegacy.com*.

11 Gibbons, "Bruce Springsteen," *TheGuardian.com*.

12 Springsteen, *Born to Run*, 469.

13 Judt, *Thinking the Twentieth Century*, 358.

14 Springsteen, *Born to Run*, 470.

Chapter 12

1 Throughout this chapter I refer to numerous well-known incidents where police have either shot and killed a Black person or otherwise contributed to his or her death. The reader is encouraged to visit *The Washington Post*'s "Police Shootings" database, *The Guardian*'s "The Counted" database; See also Juzwiak and Chan, "Unarmed People of Color Killed by Police, 1999–2014," *Gawker* (archive). Full citations provided in bibliography.

2 Gordon, "Kendrick Lamar's 'Alright,'" *Pitchfork*.

3 Chang, *Can't Stop Won't Stop*, 68–70.

4 Rose, *Black Noise*, 51, 52.

5 Ibid., 53.

6 Again, Badiou does not consider popular music capable of being new except in the sense that it reflects the newness of "serious arts." This is a major flaw in his thinking; hip-hop exposes it as ridiculous.

7 West, *The Cornel West Reader*, 482. (From an essay written in 1982 and later revised and published in his 1988 book *Prophetic Fragments*.)

8 Badiou and Tarby, *Philosophy and the Event*, 9.

9 Hager, "Afrika Bambaataa's Hip-Hop," *The Village Voice*. "Hip-hop" was a common term by this point; Bambaataa never claimed to have invented it, and most evidence points to Keith "Cowboy" Wiggins from the Furious Five as the term's originator.

10 I'm drawing from two sections of *Philosophy and the Event*, 9–12 and 68–74. Most of this is covered in the last third of *Being and Event*.

11 Badiou and Tarby, *Philosophy and the Event*, 12, 13.

12 Hope, "The Overwhelming Blackness," *Jezebel*.

13 Kitwana, "The Challenge of Rap Music," 455.

14 Jones, "The Only Good Pig," George Mason University.

15 Edwards, "Kendrick Lamar on Ferguson," *Billboard*.

16 Williams, "Who Exactly Is Kendrick," *Daily Beast*.

17 Markman, "Kendrick Lamar Has Strong Words," *MTV.com*.

18 West, *The Cornel West Reader*, 482.

19 Rose, *Black Noise*, 35.

20 Chang, *Can't Stop Won't Stop*, 194.

21 West, *The Cornel West Reader*, 289.

22 Chang, *Can't Stop Won't Stop*, 416.

23 Boyd and Nuruddin, "Intergenerational Culture Wars," 441.

24 Genius, Annotation of "The Blacker the Berry," *Genius.com*.

25 Du Bois, *The Souls of Black Folk*, 3.

26 Namikas, "(Im)mortal Men," HipHopDX.com. Tupac's appearance is accomplished by splicing together clips from his interview with Swedish radio station P3 in 1994.

Chapter 13

1 Tan, "Eminem Rape Lyrics," *TheGuardian.com*.

2 Groys, *On the New*, 130.

3 Wilentz, "The Sad Song of Delia Green and Cooney Houston," 156.

4 My account here is drawn from Wilentz's chapter (above) in *The Rose and the Briar* and listening to various versions of the song. See also John Garst's slim monograph, *Delia*, published in 2012 by Loomis House Press.

5 Bodleian Libraries, "Broadside Ballads Online," Oxford University.

6 Segarra, "Hurray For The Riff Raff's New Political Folk," *NPR.org*.

7 Advocate editors, "These Are the Trans People Killed in 2016," *Advocate.com*. See also the National Coalition of Anti-Violence Programs (ncavp.org).

8 See Bodleian Libraries, "Broadside Ballads Online," Oxford University.

9 Powers, "The Political Folk Song of the Year," *NPR.org*.

10 Badiou and Tarby, *Philosophy and the Event*, 14.

11 Ibid., 74.

Epilogue

1 North, *Novelty*, 206. (Emphasis mine.)

2 Brook, *The Empty Space*, 9.

Bibliography and Select Discography

Note: For the sake of space, only the most pertinent albums and songs are included here. For a full discography, visit www.nothinghasbeendonebefore.com.

Adorno, Theodor. *Aesthetic Theory*. Translated by Robert Hullot-Kentor. London and New York: Bloomsbury Academic, 1997. (First published in German by Suhrkamp Verlag, 1970.)

Adorno, Theodor. *Negative Dialectics*. Translated by E.B. Ashton. London: Routledge, 1973. (First published in German by Suhrkamp Verlag, 1966.)

Adorno, Theodor. "On the Social Situation of Music." In *Essays on Music*. Edited by Richard Leppert. Translated by Susan H. Gillespie and others, 391–436. Berkeley: University of California Press, 2002.

Advocate editors. "These Are the Trans People Killed in 2016." *Advocate.com*, n.d., http://www.advocate.com/transgender/2016/10/14/these-are-trans-people-killed-2016 (accessed February 5, 2017).

Against Me! *New Wave*. Sire 101304–2, 2007.

Alden, Grant. "Quicksilver Girl: Gillian Welch Leaves Much Unspoken, Trusting Her Music." *No Depression* 35 (September/October 2001): 84–95.

Anderson, Chris. "Free! Why $0.00 Is the Future of Business." *Wired*, February 25, 2008. https://www.wired.com/2008/02/ff-free/ (accessed February 4, 2017).

Angelakos, Michael. "Passion Pit Address Controversy." *Fresh 1027.CBSlocal.com*. September 18, 2012. http://fresh1027.cbslocal.com/2012/09/18/passion-pit-address-taco-bell-take-a-walk-controversy-its-an-amazing-opportunity/ (accessed January 28, 2017).

Anti-Flag. *The Terror State*. Fat Wreck Chords FAT643-2, 2003.

Archers of Loaf. *Curse of the Loaf: Live at Cat's Cradle*. ARRA Records ARRA 002–1, 2015.

Archers of Loaf. *What Did You Expect?* Directed by Gorman Bechard. Connecticut: What Were We Thinking, 2012.

Aswad, Jem. "Why Missy Elliott? Super Bowl Halftime EP Explains Her Surprise Appearance." *Billboard*, February 4, 2015. http://www.billboard.com/articles/events/super-bowl-2015/6458479/missy-elliott-super-bowl-halftime-explained (accessed February 5, 2017).

Auslander, Philip. *Liveness: Performance in a Mediatized Culture*. Second edition. New York: Routledge, 2008.

Azerrad, Michael. *Our Band Could Be Your Life: Scenes from the American Indie Underground 1981–1991*. New York: Back Bay Books/Little, Brown and Company, 2001.

Badiou, Alain. *Being and Event*. Translated by Oliver Feltham. London and New York: Bloomsbury Academic, 2013. (First published in French by Editions du Seuil, 1988. First published in English by Continuum, 2005.)

Badiou, Alain. "Fifteen Theses of Contemporary Art." *Lacanian Ink*, 23, n.d. http://www.lacan.com/frameXXIII7.htm (accessed May 23, 2017)

Badiou, Alain. *Philosophy and the Event*. With Fabien Tarby. Translated by Louise Burchill. Cambridge: Polity, 2013. (First published in French by Éditions Germina, 2010.)

Bakhtin, M.M. *Speech Genres and Other Late Essays*. Edited by Caryl Emerson and Michael Holquist. Translated by Vern W. McGee. Austin: University of Texas Press, 1986.

Banhart, Devendra. *Oh Me Oh My ... The Way the Day Goes By the Sun Is Setting Dogs Are Dreaming Lovesongs of the Christmas Spirit*. Young God Records YG20, 2002.

Bernstein, Charles et al. "Being Contemporary." *Performing Arts Journal* 100 (2012): 93–110.

Bill Carney's Jug Addicts. Facebook: https://www.facebook.com/Bill-Carneys-Jug-Addicts-295204180509222/ (accessed January 25, 2017).

Billboard. "Hot 100 Week of February 7, 2015." *Billboard*. http://www.billboard.com/charts/hot-100/2015-02-07 (accessed February 3, 2017)

Billboard. "Missy Elliott-Charts." *Billboard*. http://www.billboard.com/artist/311508/missy-elliott/chart (accessed February 2, 2017).

The Black Angels. *Passover*. Light in the Attic LITA 018, 2006.

Bloom, Harold. *The Anxiety of Influence*. New York: Oxford University Press, 1973.

Blow Up Hollywood. *Diaries of Private Henry Hill*. Self-released, 2006.

Boyd, Todd and Yusuf Nuruddin. "Intergenerational Culture Wars: Civil Rights vs. Hip-Hop." In *That's the Joint! The Hip-Hop Studies Reader*. Edited by Murray Forman and Mark Anthony Neal, 438–450. Second edition. New York: Routledge, 2012.

Bright Eyes (Conor Oberst). "When the President Talks to God." Download. *Saddle Creek*, 2005. (*Motion Sickness: Live Recordings*. Team Love Records TL-06, 2005.)

Brook, Peter. *The Empty Space*. New York: Atheneum, 1968.

Butler, Judith. *Bodies That Matter: On the Discursive Limits of "Sex."* New York: Routledge, 1993.

Butler, Judith. "The Body You Want." Interview by Liz Kotz. *Artforum*, November 1992, 82–89.

Butler, Judith. *Gender Trouble: Feminism and the Subversion of Identity*. New York: Routledge, 1991.

Butler, Judith. *Undoing Gender*. New York: Routledge, 2004.

Byrne, David. *How Music Works*. San Francisco: McSweeney's, 2012.

Calvert, John. "Janelle Monáe: A New Pioneer of Afrofuturism." *The Quietus*, September 2, 2010. http://thequietus.com/articles/04889-janelle-mon-e-the-archandroid-afrofuturism (accessed February 2, 2017).

Cantwell, Robert. *When We Were Good: The Folk Revival*. Cambridge, MA: Harvard University Press, 1996.

Carolina Chocolate Drops. *Genuine Negro Jig*. Nonesuch 516995–2, 2010.

Caulfield, Keith. "US Album Sales Volume Falls to New Low." *Billboard*, January 15, 2015. http://www.billboard.com/articles/news/5869761/us-album-sales-volume-falls-to-new-low (accessed February 1, 2017).

Chang, Jeff. *Can't Stop Won't Stop: A History of the Hip-Hop Generation*. New York: Picador, 2005.

Chase, Chris. "Katy Perry Blew Away the Super Bowl Halftime Show." *USA Today*, February 1, 2015. http://ftw.usatoday.com/2015/02/katy-perry-halftime-show-review-super-bowl (accessed February 4, 2017).

Christgau, Robert. "GGGB." *Village Voice*, April 18, 1995. Reposted at http://www.robertchristgau.com/xg/rock/archers-95.php (accessed May 25, 2017).

Christgau, Robert. "Green Day: American Idiot." *Consumer Guide*, n.d. https://www.robertchristgau.com/get_album.php?id=12713 (accessed May 25, 2017).

Christman, Ed. "Music in 2014: Taylor Takes the Year, Republic Records on Top, Streaming to the Rescue." *Billboard*, January 9, 2015. http://www.billboard.com/articles/business/6436399/nielsen-music-soundscan-2014-taylor-swift-republic-records-streaming?page=0%2C2 (accessed February 1, 2017).

Christman. "U.S. Album Sales Fall 12.8% in 2010," *Billboard*, January 5, 2011. http://www.billboard.com/articles/news/473772/us-album-sales-fall-128-in-2010-digital-tracks-eke-out-1-gain (accessed February 1, 2017).

Coyle, Michael and Jon Dolan. "Modeling Authenticity, Authenticating Commercial Models." In *Reading Rock and Roll: Authenticity, Appropriation, Aesthetics*. Edited by Kevin J. Dettmar and William Richey, 17–35. New York: Columbia University Press, 1999.

Dale, Peter. *Popular Music and the Politics of Novelty*. New York: Bloomsbury Academic, 2016.

Danto, Arthur. *After the End of Art: Contemporary Art and the Pale of History*. Princeton: Princeton University Press, 1997.

Davies, Stephen. *Musical Works and Performance: A Philosophical Exploration*. Oxford: Oxford University Press, 2001.

Debord, Guy. *Commentary on the Society of the Spectacle*. London: Verso, 1998.

Debord, Guy. *The Society of the Spectacle*. Originally translated by Donald Nicholson-Smith. Detroit: Black and Red, 1977. (Revised English translation (1977). Reprinted in 2016.)

Debord, Guy. *The Society of the Spectacle*. New York: Zone Books, 1994. (Third French Edition, with new preface by author.)

DeGusta, Michael. "The Real Death of the Music Industry." *Business Insider*, February 18, 2011. http://www.businessinsider.com/these-charts-explain-the-real-death-of-the-music-industry-2011-2 (accessed February 3, 2017).

Deley, Alexander T. "Bob Dylan and Plagiarism: To Catch a Master Thief." *Dissident Voice*, December 12, 2013. http://dissidentvoice.org/2013/12/bob-dylan-and-plagiarism/ (accessed January 30, 2017).

Dery, Mark. "Black to the Future: Interviews with Samuel R. Delany, Greg Tate, and Tricia Rose." In *Flame Wars: The Discourse of Cyberculture*. Edited by Mark Dery. Durham: Duke University Press, 1994.

Dixie Chicks. *The Dixie Chicks: Shut Up and Sing*. Directed by Barbara Kopple and Cecilia Peck. Streaming. Cabin Creek Films: 2006.

Dixie Chicks. *Home*. Open Wide/Monument/Columbia CK 86840, 2002.

Dixie Chicks. *Taking the Long Way*. Open Wide/Columbia 82876 80739 2, 2006. Vendetta. Interview with R.L. October 12, 2016.

Dockterman, Eliana. "Watch Taylor Swift Shut Down 'Sexist' Music Critics." *Time*, October 20, 2014. http://time.com/3524641/taylor-swift-feminism-critics-sexist/ (accessed February 2, 2017).

Drive-By Truckers. *Southern Rock Opera*. Lost Highway D 244542, 2002.

Du Bois, W.E.B. *The Souls of Black Folk*. Chicago: A.C. McClurg and Co., 1909. (Google Books.)

Dylan, Bob. "Bob Dylan, at 60, Unearths New Revelations." Interview with Mikal Gilmore. *Rolling Stone*, November 22, 2001.

Dylan, Bob. "Bob Dylan Unleashed." Interview with Mikal Gilmore. *Rolling Stone*, September 27, 2012.

Dylan, Bob. *Chronicles: Volume One*. New York: Simon and Shuster, 2004.

Dylan, Bob. *"Love and Theft"*. Columbia CK 85975, 2001.

Dylan, Bob. *No Direction Home*. DVD. Directed by Martin Scorsese. Hollywood: Paramount, 2005.

Dylan, Bob. *The Other Side of the Mirror: Bob Dylan at the Newport Folk Festival*. DVD. Directed by Murray Lerner. New York: Sony Legacy, 2007.

Dylan, Bob. Press Conference, KQED. San Francisco, December 3, 1965. *YouTube*. https://www.youtube.com/watch?v=wPIS257tvoA (accessed May 26, 2017).

Earle, Steve. *Jerusalem*. Artemis 751147-2, 2002.

Eagleton, Terry. *The Ideology of the Aesthetic*. Malden, MA: Blackwell Publishing, 1990.

Edwards, Gavin. "Kendrick Lamar on Ferguson, Leaving Iggy Azalea Alone and Why 'We're in the Last Days.'" *Billboard*, January 9, 2015. http://www.billboard.com/articles/news/6436268/kendrick-lamar-billboard-cover-story-on-new-album-iggy-azalea-police-violence-the-rapture (accessed February 5, 2017).

Eells, Josh. "Taylor Swift Reveals Five Things to Expect on *1989*." *Rolling Stone*, September 16, 2014. http://www.rollingstone.com/music/news/taylor-swift-reveals-five-things-to-expect-on-1989-20140916 (accessed February 2, 2017).

Eig, Jonathan and Sebastian Moffett. "Did Bob Dylan Lift Lines from Dr. Saga?" *Wall Street Journal* (subscription required), July 8, 2003. https://www.wsj.com/articles/SB10576176194220600 (accessed February 2, 2017).

Eng, David L., Judith Halberstam, and José Esteban Muñoz. "What's Queer about Queer Studies Now?" *Social Text* 23, no. 3–4 (Fall-Winter 2005): 1–17.

English, Daylanne K. and Alvin Kim. "Now We Want Our Funk Cut: Janelle Monáe's Neo-Afrofuturism." *American Studies* 52, no. 4 (2013): 217–230.

Filene, Benjamin. *Romancing the Folk: Public Memory and American Roots Music*. Chapel Hill: The University of North Carolina Press, 2000.

Flippo, Chet. "Nashville Skyline: Willie and the War." *CMT.com*. January 8, 2004. http://www.cmt.com/news/1484226/nashville-skyline-willie-and-the-war/ (accessed February 5, 2017).

Francescani, Chris. "Bob Dylan's 'Da Vinci Code' Revealed." *The Daily Beast*, May 18, 2014. http://www.thedailybeast.com/articles/2014/05/18/bob-dylan-s-da-vinci-code-revealed.html (accessed January 30, 2017).

Frere-Jones, Sasha. "Black Noise." *The New Yorker*, June 24, 2013. http://www.newyorker.com/magazine/2013/06/24/black-noise (accessed February 2, 2017).

Frith, Simon and Simon Zagorski-Thomas. *The Art of Record Production: An Introductory Reader for a New Academic Field*. Edited by Simon Frith and Simon Zagorski-Thomas. New edition. Ashgate Popular and Folk Music Series. New York: Routledge, 2012.

Frith, Simon. *Performing Rites: On the Value of Popular Music*. Cambridge, MA: Harvard University Press, 1996.

Future Punx. *This Is Post-Wave*. Dull Tools ADAGIO830#136, DT013, 2015.

Gallo, Phil. "Katy Perry's Halftime Show the Most Watched in Super Bowl History." *Billboard*, February 2, 2015. http://www.billboard.com/articles/news/6458264/katy-perry-super-bowl-halftime-record (accessed February 2, 2017).

Garst, John. *Delia*. N.p.: Loomis House Press, 2012.

Genius. Annotation of "The Blacker the Berry." *Genius.com*, n.d. https://genius.com/Kendrick-lamar-the-blacker-the-berry-lyrics (accessed February 5, 2017).

Gibbons, Fiachra. "Bruce Springsteen: 'What Was Done to My Country Was Un-American.'" *The Guardian*, February 17, 2012. https://www.theguardian.com/music/2012/feb/17/bruce-springsteen-wrecking-ball (accessed February 4, 2017).

Giddens, Rhiannon. "Cry No More." *YouTube.com*. https://www.youtube.com/watch?v=PU3cGLtULeI (accessed May 20, 2017).

Giddens, Rhiannon. Interview with R.L. February 13, 2012.

Gipson, Grace. "Afrofuturism's Musical Princess Janelle Monáe: Psychedelic Soul Message Music Infused with a Sci-Fi Twist." In *Afrofuturism 2.0: The Rise of Astro-Blackness*. Edited by Reynaldo Anderson and Charles E. Jones, 91–107. Lanham, MD: Lexington Books, 2016.

Goodbye Tomorrow. *100K*. Rostrum Records, 2015.

Goodbye Tomorrow. Interview by "Hip Hop Nonstop." University of Illinois-Chicago Radio, November 11, 2015. https://www.youtube.com/watch?v=ByJVEPp_ZrI (accessed May 26, 2017).

Goodbye Tomorrow. *Journey Through the Mind of a Non-Believer*. Rostrum Records, 2015.

Google Books. Ngram Viewer for "innovate." February 7, 2017. https://books.google.com/ngrams

Gordimer, Nadine. "Lust and Death." Review of *Everyman* by Philip Roth. *New York Times*, May 7, 2006, Sunday Book Review. http://www.nytimes.com/2006/05/07/books/review/07gord.html (accessed January 30, 2017).

Gordon, Jeremy. "Kendrick Lamar's 'Alright' Chanted by Protesters during Cleveland Police Altercation." *Pitchfork*, July 29, 2015. http://pitchfork.com/news/60568-kendrick-lamars-alright-chanted-by-protesters-during-cleveland-police-altercation/ (accessed February 4, 2017).

Gracyk, Theodore. *Rhythm and Noise: An Aesthetics of Rock*. Durham: Duke University Press, 1996.

Green Day. *American Idiot*. Reprise Records 9362-48777-2, 2004.

Greenberg, Clement. "Modernist Painting." In *The New Art*. Edited by Gregory Battcock, 100–110. New York: E.P. Dutton and Co., 1966.

Greenblatt, Stephen. *The Swerve: How the World Became Modern*. New York: W.W. Norton and Co., 2011.

Groys, Boris. *Art Power*. Cambridge, MA: MIT Press, 2013.

Groys, Boris. Interview with the author and Matt Mitchem. New York City, October 12, 2016.

Groys, Boris. *On the New*. Translated by G.M. Goshgarian. London: Verso, 2014. (First published as *Über das Neue* in 1992.)

The Guardian. "The Counted." Database. https://www.theguardian.com/us-news/series/counted-us-police-killings (accessed February 5, 2017).

Guided By Voices. *Alien Lanes*. Matador OLE 123-2, 1995.

Hajdu, David. "Where Has 'Where Have All the Flowers Gone?' Gone?" *The New Republic* 230, no. 24 (2004): 33–36.

Hager, Steven. "Afrika Bambaataa's Hip-Hop." *The Village Voice*, September 21, 1982. Reprinted in *And It Don't Stop: The Best American Hip-Hop Journalism of the Past 25 Years*, edited by Raquel Cepeda, 12–26. New York: Faber and Faber, 2004.

Halperin, David. "The Normalization of Queer Theory." *Journal of Homosexuality* 45, no. 2/3/4 (2003): 339–343.

Henke, James. "Neil Young: The Rolling Stone Interview." In *Neil Young: The Rolling Stone Files: The Ultimate Compendium of Interviews, Articles, Facts and Opinions*. Edited by the editors of *Rolling Stone*, 238–250. New York: Hyperion, 1994.

Heylin, Clinton. *Behind the Shades: The 20th Anniversary Edition*. London: Faber and Faber, 2011.

Heylin, Clinton. *Bootleg: The Rise and Fall of the Secret Recording Industry*. New York: St. Martin's, 1994.

Hilburn, Robert. "Judging Songs by Their Titles." *Los Angeles Times*, September 19, 2001. http://articles.latimes.com/2001/sep/19/entertainment/ca-47192 (accessed February 2, 2017).

Hilderbrand, Lucas. "'Luring Disco Dollies to a Life of Vice': Queer Pop Music's Moment." *Journal of Popular Music Studies* 25, no. 4 (2013): 415–438.

Himes, Geoffrey. *Born in the USA*. 33 1/3. New York: Continuum, 2007.

Hood, Patterson. "The South's Heritage Is So Much More Than a Flag." *The New York Times Magazine*, July 9, 2015. https://www.nytimes.com/2015/07/09/magazine/the-souths-heritage-is-so-much-more-than-a-flag.html?_r=0 (accessed February 1, 2017).

Hope, Clover. "The Overwhelming Blackness of Kendrick Lamar's *To Pimp a Butterfly*." *Jezebel*, March 17, 2015. http://themuse.jezebel.com/the-overwhelming-blackness-of-kendrick-lamars-butterfly-1691770606 (accessed February 4, 2017).

Hurray for the Riff-Raff. *Small Town Heroes*. ATO Records ATO0212, 2014.

Iron & Wine. *The Creek Drank the Cradle*. Sub Pop SPCD 600, 2002.

Iron & Wine. *Our Endless Numbered Days*. Sub Pop SPCD 630, 2004.

Jagose, Annamarie. *Queer Theory: An Introduction*. New York: New York University Press, 1996.

James, Robin. "'Robo-Diva R&B': Aesthetics, Politics, and Black Female Robots in Contemporary Popular Music." *Journal of Popular Music Studies* 20, no. 4 (2008): 402–423.

Jennings, John and Clint Fluker. "Forms of Future/Past: Black Kirby, Afrofuturism and the Visual Technologies of Resistance." In *Afrofuturism 2.0: The Black Speculative Arts Movement*. Edited by Reynaldo Anderson and Charles E. Jones. Lanham, MD: Lexington Books, forthcoming.

Jones, Frank. "'The Only Good Pig Is a Dead Pig': A Black Panther Paper Editor Explains a Political Cartoon." *History Matters*, George Mason University. Original Source: 1970. Congress, House, Committee on Internal Security, Black Panther Party, Part 4, 91st Congress, 1970 (Washington, DC: Government Printing Office, 1971). http://historymatters.gmu.edu/d/6460/ (accessed February 5, 2017).

Judt, Tony. *Thinking the Twentieth Century*. With Timothy Snyder. New York: Penguin, 2012.

Juzwiak, Rich and Aleksander Chan. "Unarmed People of Color Killed by Police, 1999–2014." *Gawker* (archive), December 8, 2014. http://gawker.com/unarmed-people-of-color-killed-by-police-1999-2014-1666672349 (accessed February 5, 2017).

Kaufman, Gil. "Kanye West's 'Blood on the Leaves' and the History of 'Strange Fruit.'" *MTV.com*, June 19, 2013. http://www.mtv.com/news/1709304/kanye-west-blood-on-leaves-strange-fruit/ (accessed February 3, 2017).

Katz, Mark. *Capturing Sound: How Technology Has Changed Music*. Revised edition. Berkeley: University of California Press, 2010.

Kinney, David. *The Dylanologists: Adventures in the Land of Bob*. New York: Simon and Schuster, 2014.

Kitwana, Bakari. "The Challenge of Rap Music from Cultural Movement to Political Power." In *That's the Joint! The Hip-Hop Studies Reader*. Edited by Murray Forman and Mark Anthony Neal. 451–461. Second edition. New York: Routledge, 2012

Kot, Greg. *Ripped: How the Wired Generation Revolutionized Music*. New York: Scribner, 2009.

Kweli, Talib. *Eardrum*. Blacksmith/Warner Bros. 277244-2, 2007.

Kweli, Talib. *Quality*. Rawkus 088 113 048-2, 2002.

Lamar, Kendrick. *To Pimp a Butterfly*. Top Dawg/Aftermath/Interscope AFTMB002295802CD, 2015.

Lamere, Paul. "Exploring Age-Specific Preferences in Listening." *Music Machinery*, February 13, 2014. https://musicmachinery.com/2014/02/13/age-specific-listening/ (accessed February 1, 2017).

Lazerhawk. *Redline*. Rosso Corsa RCR001, 2010.

LCD Soundsystem. *LCD Soundsystem*. Capitol CDP 0946 3 32307 2 9, 2005.

Leggett, Steve. "Genuine Negro Jig." *AllMusic.com*. http://www.allmusic.com/album/genuine-negro-jig-mw0001956326 (accessed January 29, 2017).

Lipsitz, George. *Time Passages: Collective Memory and American Popular Culture*. Minneapolis: Minnesota University Press, 1990.

Lott, Eric. *Love & Theft: Blackface Minstrelsy and the American Working Class*. Oxford: Oxford University Press, 1993.

Lynskey, Dorian. *33 Revolutions Per Minute: A History of Protest Songs from Billie Holiday to Green Day*. London: Ecco, 2011.

Marcus, Greil. *Bob Dylan by Greil Marcus: Writings 1968–2010*. New York: Public Affairs, 2010.

Marcus, Greil. Email to R.L., July 1, 2015.

Marcus, Greil. *The History of Rock 'n' Roll in Ten Songs*. New Haven: Yale University Press, 2014.

Marcus, Greil. *Lipstick Traces: A Secret History of the Twentieth Century*. Cambridge, MA: The Belknap Press of Harvard University Press, 1989.

Marcus, Greil. *Mystery Train: Images of America in Rock 'n' Roll Music*. Fifth Revised Edition. New York: Plume/Penguin, 2008. Originally published in 1975.

Marinetti, F.T. *The Founding and Manifesto of Futurism*. Originally published in *Le Figaro*, February 20, 1909. Reprinted at http://www.unknown.nu/futurism/manifesto.html (accessed May 26, 2017).

Markman, Rob. "Kendrick Lamar Has Strong Words for His 'Blacker The Berry' Critics." *MTV.com*, April 3, 2015. http://www.mtv.com/news/2123601/kendrick-lamar-billboard-blacker-the-berry-critics/ (accessed February 5, 2017).

Marsh, Dave. *Glory Days: Bruce Springsteen in the 1980s*. New York: Pantheon, 1987.

Meltzer, Mitchell. "A Literature of Secular Revelations." In *A New Literary History of America*. Edited by Greil Marcus and Werner Sollors, 108–112. Cambridge, MA: The Belknap Press of Harvard University Press, 2009.

Meyer, Leonard. "Innovation, Choice, and the History of Music." *Critical Inquiry* 9, no. 3 (March 1983): 517–544.

Miers, Jeff. "A Good Thing." *Buffalo News*, August 9, 2002. https://www.highbeam.com/doc/1P2-22473496.html (subscription required) (accessed January 30, 2017).

Milner, Greg. *Perfecting Sound Forever: An Aural History of Recorded Music*. New York: Faber and Faber, 2009.

Mitchem, Matthew. *True Life: Democratic-Materialism and The Philosophical Exception*. PhD diss., European Graduate School, 2012. (Unpublished manuscript, revised 2016.) Word document.

Monáe, Janelle. *The ArchAndroid*. Bad Boy Entertainment/Wondaland 512256-2, 2010.

Monáe, Janelle. *The Electric Lady*. Bad Boy Entertainment/Wondaland 536210-2, 2013.

Monáe, Janelle. "Gimme Some Monáe!" Interviewed by Eliza C. Thompson. *Bust*, August/September, 2013: 40–45.

Monáe, Janelle and Wondaland. "Hell You Talmbout." *Soundcloud*, 2015. https://soundcloud.com/wondalandarts/hell-you-talmbout (accessed May 27, 2017).

Moody's. "Music Industry Consolidation Should Help Major Labels Grow Their Digital Revenue." *Moodys.com*, May 21, 2013. https://www.moodys.com/research/Moodys-Music-industry-consolidation-should-help-major-labels-grow-their–PR_273725 (accessed February 2, 2017).

Morley, Paul. *Ask: The Chatter of Pop*. London: Faber and Faber, 1986.

Muñoz, José Esteban. *Cruising Utopia: The Then and There of Queer Utopia*. New York: New York University Press, 2009.

Namikas, Michael. "(Im)mortal Men: Kendrick Lamar, Tupac Shakur, and the Pimping of Butterflies." *HipHopDX.com*, March 16, 2015. http://hiphopdx.com/editorials/id.2790/title.immortal-men-kendrick-lamar-tupac-shakur-and-the-pimping-of-butterflies (accessed February 5, 2017).

Nas. *Stillmatic*. Columbia CK 85736, 2001.

Nelson, Maggie. *The Argonauts*. Minneapolis: Graywolf Press, 2015.

Neuman, Julia. "The Nostalgic Allure of 'Synthwave.'" *Observer*, July 30, 2015. http://observer.com/2015/07/the-nostalgic-allure-of-synthwave/ (accessed February 1, 2017).

Newsom, Joanna. *The Milk-Eyed Mender*. Drag City DC263CD, 2004.

Nielsen/Billboard, "2012 Music Industry Report." *BusinessWire*, January 4, 2013. http://www.businesswire.com/news/home/20130104005149/en/Nielsen-Company-Billboard%E2%80%99s-2012-Music-Industry-Report (accessed February 3, 2017).

NOFX. *The War on Errorism*. Enhanced CD. Fat Wreck Chords FAT657-2, 2003.

North, Michael. *Novelty: A History of the New*. Chicago: University of Chicago Press, 2013.

O Brother, Where Art Thou? Directed by Ethan and Joel Coen. Hollywood: Buena Vista, 2000.

O'Connor, Flannery. *Mystery and Manners: Occasional Prose*. Selected and edited by Sally and Robert Fitzgerald. New York: Farrar, Straus, and Giroux, 1969.

Oppelaar, Justin. "Roots Still Strong." *Daily Variety* 275, no. 4 (March 7, 2002): 6.

Pareles, Jon. "Critics Notebook: Plagiarism in Dylan, or a Cultural Collage?" *The New York Times*, July 12, 2003. http://www.nytimes.com/2003/07/12/books/critic-s-notebook-plagiarism-in-dylan-or-a-cultural-collage.html (accessed January 30, 2017).

Passion Pit. *Gossamer*. Columbia 88725 41651 1, 2012.

Pearis, Bill. "LCD Soundsystem Played Pepsi's Kola House Opening." *Brooklyn Vegan*, September 21, 2016. http://www.brooklynvegan.com/lcd-soundsystem-played-pepsis-nyc-kola-house-opening-picsvideo/ (accessed February 3, 2017).

Perry, Katy. *Prism*. Capitol B001921502, 2013.

Perry, Katy. *The Prismatic World Tour*. Directed by Katy Perry. Streaming. Eagle Rock Entertainment, 2015.

Perry, Katy. "Super Bowl XLIX Halftime Show." (February 1, 2015.) *NFL/YouTube*, September 13, 2016.

Perry, Katy. *Teenage Dream*. Capitol 509996 84601 2 9, 2010.

Petrusich, Amanda. *It Still Moves: Lost Songs, Lost Highways, and the Search for the Next American Music*. New York: Faber and Faber, 2008.

Pollstar. "2015 Year End Business Analysis." *Pollstarpro.com*, 2015. http://www.pollstarpro.com/files/charts2015/2015YearEndBusinessAnalysis.pdf (accessed February 3, 2017).

Powers, Ann. "The Political Folk Song of the Year." *NPR.org*, December 11, 2014. http://www.npr.org/sections/therecord/2014/12/11/370125443/the-political-folk-song-of-the-year (accessed February 5, 2017).

Prince. *Art Official Age*. NPG Records/Warner Bros. 545612-2, 2014.

Prince. *Black Sweat* (video). Directed by Sanaa Hamri. 2006.

Prince. Interview with Chris Rock. *VH1*, 1997. https://www.youtube.com/watch?v=nd97mAsvR0g (accessed May 26, 2017).

Pruitt, Lesley. "Real Men Kill and a Lady Never Talks Back: Gender Goes to War in Country Music." *International Journal on World Peace* 24, no. 4 (December 2007): 85–106.

Reynolds, Simon. *Retromania: Pop Culture's Addiction to Its Own Past*. New York: Faber and Faber, 2011.

Rolling Stone. "10 New Artists You Need to Know: March 2015." *RollingStone*, March 26, 2015. http://www.rollingstone.com/music/lists/10-new-artists-you-need-to-know-march-2015-20150326/goodbye-tomorrow-20150325 (accessed February 4, 2017).

Rose, Tricia. *Black Noise: Rap Music and Black Culture in Contemporary America*. Middletown, CT: Wesleyan University Press, 1994.

Rushkoff, Douglas. *Present Shock: When Everything Happens Now*. New York: Current, 2013.

Sacks, Howard L. and Judith Rose Sacks. *Way Up North in Dixie: A Black Family's Claim to the Confederate Anthem*. Urbana: University of Illinois Press, 2003.

Schneider, Jason. "Gillian Welch Is No Longer an Orphan Girl." *Exclaim!* January 1, 2006. Originally published December 2001. http://exclaim.ca/music/article/gillian_welch_is_no_longer_orphan_girl (accessed January 29, 2017).

Scott-Heron, Gil. *Small Talk at 125th and Lenox*. Flying Dutchman/RCA 07863, 66611–2, 1993. (Originally released in 1970.)

Segarra, Alynda Lee. "Hurray for the Riff Raff's New Political Folk." Interview with Ann Powers. *NPR*, January 23, 2014. http://www.npr.org/sections/therecord/2014/01/22/265039131/hurray-for-the-riff-raffs-new-political-folk (accessed February 5, 2017).

Small, Christopher. *Musicking: The Meanings of Performing and Listening*. Middletown: Wesleyan, 1998.

Smith, Grady. "Why Country Music Was Awful in 2013." *YouTube*, December 20, 2013. https://www.youtube.com/watch?v=WySgNm8qH-I (accessed May 26, 2017)

Smith, Nathan. "The Queer Legacy of Prince." *Out*, June 7, 2016. http://www.out.com/music/2016/4/22/queer-legacy-prince (accessed February 2, 2017).

Sony Legacy, "*10 Facts about Springsteen's Seeger Sessions*." WeareSonyLegacy.com, April 25, 2016. http://www.wearesonylegacy.com/news/10-facts-springsteens-seeger-sessions

Sounds Like a Revolution. Directed by Summer Love and Jane Michener. Download. Deltatime Productions and Guerilla Funk Film Works, 2010. http://doc.soundslikearevolution.com/ (accessed February 3, 2017).

Springsteen, Bruce. *Born to Run* (memoir). New York: Simon and Schuster, 2016.

Springsteen, Bruce. Interview with Stephen Colbert. *The Late Show with Stephen Colbert*, CBS, September 23, 2016.

Springsteen, Bruce. *Nebraska*. Columbia CK 38358, 1990. (Originally released in 1982.)

Springsteen, Bruce. *The Promise: The Darkness on the Edge of Town Story*. (Box set liner notes.) Columbia 88697 76525 2, 2010.

Springsteen, Bruce. "Rock and Read." Interview with Will Percy. *DoubleTake* 12: 1995. http://www.doubletakemagazine.org/mag/html/backissues/12/steen/ (accessed February 3, 2017).

Springsteen, Bruce. *Wrecking Ball*. Columbia 88691 94254 2, 2012.

Stanford Encyclopedia of Philosophy. "Heraclitus." Stanford University, February 1, 2017. https://plato.stanford.edu/entries/heraclitus/

Stevens, Sufjan. *Seven Swans*. Sounds Familyre SF 013, 2004.

Surico, John. "Spotify Shoots Down Band's Silent Album Fundraising Hack." *Spin*, April 25, 2014. http://www.spin.com/2014/04/spotify-sleepify-vulfpeck-silent-album-hack-response/ (accessed February 2, 2017).

Strauss, Neil. "After the Horror, Radio Stations Pull Some Songs." *The New York Times*, September 19, 2001. http://www.nytimes.com/2001/09/19/arts/the-pop-life-after-the-horror-radio-stations-pull-some-songs.html (accessed February 3, 2017).

Swartley, Ariel. "This Prince Is No Pretender." In *Rock She Wrote: Women Who Write about Rock, Pop, and Rap*. Edited by Evelyn McDonnell and Ann Powers, 233–237. New York: Cooper Square Press, 1999.

Swift, Taylor. *1989*. Big Machine BMRBD0550A, 2014.

Tan, Monika. "Eminem Rape Lyrics: Iggy Azalea Bored by Trend of Threatening Women." *TheGuardian.com*, November 21, 2014. https://www.theguardian.com/music/2014/nov/21/eminem-lyrics-iggy-azalea-bored-by-trend-of-threatening-women (accessed February 1, 2017).

Tillich, Paul. *The Courage to Be*. Binghamton: Vail-Ballou Press, 1953.

Tillich, Paul. *The New Being*. New York: Charles Scribner's Sons, 1955.

Tosches, Nick. *Unsung Heroes of Rock 'n' Roll: The Birth of Rock in the Wild Years before Elvis*. New York: Da Capo, 1999.

Various artists. *O Brother, Where Art Thou?* (soundtrack). Lost Highway 088 170-069-2, 2000.

Various artists. *Drive* (soundtrack). Lakeshore Records LKS342322, 2011.

Vega, Suzanne. "The Ballad of Henry Timrod." *New York Times*, September 17, 2006. http://www.nytimes.com/2006/09/17/opinion/17vega.html (accessed January 30, 2017).

Vulfpeck. *Thrill of the Arts*. Vulf Records VULF1202-CD, 2015.

VJ Vendetta. Interview with R.L. October 12, 2016.

Waits, Tom. *Real Gone*. Anti- 86678–2, 2004.

Wald, Elijah. *Dylan Goes Electric! Newport, Seeger, Dylan, and the Night That Split the Sixties*. New York: Dey St., 2015.

Walt, Stephen. "Where Have All the Political Songs Gone? (With Apologies to Pete Seeger)." *Foreign Policy*, March 6, 2009. http://foreignpolicy.com/2009/03/06/where-have-all-the-political-songs-gone-with-apologies-to-pete-seeger/ (accessed February 1, 2017).

The Washington Post. "Police Shootings." Database, February 5, 2017. https://www.washingtonpost.com/graphics/national/police-shootings/

Weisbard, Eric. *Top 40 Democracy: The Rival Mainstreams of American Music*. Chicago: The University of Chicago Press, 2014.

Welch, George Patrick. *Britannia: The Roman Conquest & Occupation of Britain*. Middletown, CT: Wesleyan University Press, 1963.

Welch, Gillian. *Time (the Revelator)*. Acony ACNY-0103, 2001.

West, Cornel. *The Cornel West Reader*. New York: Basic Civitas Books, 1999.

West, Kanye. *My Beautiful Dark Twisted Fantasy*. Roc-A-Fella Records B0014695-02, 2010.

West, Kanye. *Yeezus*. Def Jam B0018653-02, 2013.

Wilentz, Sean. *Bob Dylan in America*. New York: Doubleday, 2010.

Wilentz, Sean. "The Sad Song of Delia Green and Cooney Houston." In *The Rose and the Briar: Death, Love and Liberty in the American Ballad*. Edited by Sean Wilentz and Greil Marcus, 147–158. New York: W.W. Norton and Co., 2005.

Wilkinson, Alec. "The Ghostly Ones." *New Yorker* 80, no. 27 (September 20, 2004): 78.

Williams, Stereo. "Who Exactly Is Kendrick Lamar Raging against in 'The Blacker the Berry?'" *The Daily Beast*, February 11, 2015. http://www.thedailybeast.com/articles/2015/02/11/who-exactly-is-kendrick-lamar-raging-against-in-the-blacker-the-berry.html (accessed February 5, 2017).

Willis, Ellen. *Out of the Vinyl Deeps: Ellen Willis on Rock Music*. Minneapolis: University of Minnesota Press, 2011.

Witt, Stephen. *How Music Got Free: The End of an Industry, The Turn of the Century, and the Patient Zero of Piracy*. New York: Viking, 2015.

Womack, Ytasha L. *Afrofuturism: The World of Black Sci-Fi and Fantasy Culture*. Chicago: Lawrence Hill Books, 2013.

The Wrens. *The Meadowlands*. Absolutely Kosher AK009, 2003.

Zabel, Gary. "Adorno on Music: A Reconsideration." *The Musical Times* 130, 1754 (April 1989): 198–201.

Acknowledgments

My thanks to Bloomsbury Academic and my editor Leah Babb-Rosenfeld and editorial assistant Susan Krogulski, both of whom have provided great encouragement and guidance. I'm grateful to the Alternate Takes series editors Simon Frith and Matthew Brennan for their feedback, to the peer reviewers who submitted helpful takes of their own, and to former editor Ally-Jane Grossan for her initial interest in my proposal.

Portions of this book originally appeared online and have been significantly revised. I deeply appreciate the editorial assistance from Stephen Twilley and Ed Winstead at *Public Books*, which published the book review that kicked off this whole thing. I also thank Michael Goetzman at the *Los Angeles Review of Books*. I'd especially like to thank *PopMatters* and its managing editor Karen Zarker, who has always given me free rein and smart criticism.

As I've written this book, I've been reminded time and again how lucky I am to be surrounded by kind and smart people. My deepest thanks to my colleagues at Columbus College of Art and Design, especially Joshua Butts, Charlene Fix, Sonya Fix, Lesley Jenike, Sophia Kartsonis, Joey Pigg, Mike Laughead, Stew McKissick, Jeannine Kraft, and Julie Taggart. Special thanks go to Matthew Mitchem, whose conversation has been invaluable to the development of my thinking in this book. I also thank CCAD students Heather Miller and Gretchen Yerian for their assistance, and Okell Lee and the CCAD Black Student Leadership Association for the discussion. I want to thank the college itself for the faculty development grant in the fall of 2016, which allowed for travel and research. My gratitude goes out to Boris Groys for his warm reception, Greil Marcus for his generous advice, J.P. Olsen for taking me to Barbès, and to David Beal, Corey Creekmur, Donna Dragotta, Edward Forman, Jared Gardner, Goodbye Tomorrow, Jason Gray, John Jennings, Talib Kweli, Kirby Lee, David Newgarden, Mona Okada, Jeff Rosen, Alynda Lee Segarra, and Kyle Siegrist.

For their love and support, I'm grateful to my parents, extended family, and friends. I'm deeply indebted to Andrew Gard, Bill Heingartner, and Eric Nassau for their thoughtful manuscript comments, late-night conversations, music-making, and friendship over many years. And to my wife Jamie, my first reader but above all the love of my life, thank you for making every day new.

Permissions

The author gratefully acknowledges the permissions granted by the following rights holders:

Excerpts from "Tweedle Dum and Tweedle Dee" by Bob Dylan. Copyright © 2001 by Special Rider Music. Used by permission. All rights reserved.

Excerpts from "High Water (for Charley Patton)" by Bob Dylan. Copyright © 2001 by Special Rider Music. Used by permission. All rights reserved.

Excerpts from "Atlantic City" by Bruce Springsteen. Copyright © 1982 Bruce Springsteen (Global Music Rights). Reprinted by permission. International copyright secured. All rights reserved.

Excerpt from "Where Do We Go?" by Talib Kweli, Shareese Ballard, and James Yancey. Copyright © 2002 Rawkus Entertainment LLC. Used by permission. All rights reserved.

Excerpts from "The Body Electric" by Alynda Lee Segarra. Copyright © 2014 Hurray for the Riff Raff under exclusive license to ATO Records, LLC. Used by permission. All rights reserved.

Index

Note: The letter 'n' following locators refers to notes

Abbey Road (Beatles), 172
Accidents and Accusations tour (Dixie Chicks), 179
AC/DC, 70
Adorno, Theodor, 91, 156–8, 178–9, 229
Aesthetic Theory (Adorno), 156
"Affirmation III" (Prince), 130
Afghanistan War, 163, 173
The Afghan Whigs, 60
Afrofuturism, 148–51, 157
After the End of Art (Danto), 4, 5, 38, 99, 131–2
Against Me!, 172
Agalloch, 80
Agamben, Giorgio, 130
The Agent Intellect (Protomartyr), 3
Akron/Family, 175
Alabama Shakes, 3, 70
Aladekoba, Celestina, 125
Alden, Grant, 22
All the Nation's Airports (Archers of Loaf), 57–8
"Alright" (Lamar), 198, 208–9, 214
Alvin, Dave, 24
"American Band" (Grand Funk Railroad), 54
American Idiot (Green Day), 173, 192
American Idol, 86, 146
American Recordings (Cash), 224–5
"American Skin (41 Shots)" (Springsteen), 190, 200
American Wow, 85–104, 114, 121, 122, 138, 143, 144, 158, 163, 209–10, 214, 234
    consumerism, 106, 113, 116

definition, 86
identity, 93–4, 127–8, 134, 139, 150, 154, 155
nostalgia, 96–7, 98
persona, 146–8, 152
public authenticity, 127–8, 150
"Amerika V 6.0 (The Best We Can Do)" (Earle), 168
Anderson, Chris, 114
Angelakos, Michael, 114–15
Anti-Flag, 168, 169
anxiety of influence, 55–7, 58–60, 65, 70, 75
The Anxiety of Influence (Bloom), 55–6
"April the 14th Part I", 20
The ArchAndroid (Monáe), 146.
Archers of Loaf, 54, 57–8, 60–2, 69
Archers of Loaf vs. The Greatest of All Time (Archers of Loaf), 57
The Argonauts (Nelson), 133
Armstrong, Billie Joe, 173
Art Official Age (Prince), 129–31, 191
"Art Official Cage" (Prince), 129
Art Power (Groys), 143–4
The Ash and Clay (Milk Carton Kids), 24
Ashes Against the Grain (Agalloch), 80
Ashley, Clarence, 32
Assassin, 142, 206, 208
"Atlantic City", 186, 188–91, 193
authenticity, 19, 28, 38, 39, 50, 74, 125, 127–9, 134, 150, 207–8, 218. See also public authenticity
"Automatic" (Prince), 1, 121

"Avalanche" (Prince), 233
Azalea, Iggy, 222
Azerrad, Michael, 58

"Baby I'm a Star" (Prince), 1
Bachmann, Eric, 57, 62
"Back to the Lake" (Guided By Voices), 63
Badiou, Alain, 11–13, 154, 167, 169, 240 n.8. *See also* event
  "Fifteen Theses of Contemporary Art", 154
  popular music, 103, 246 n.6
Badu, Erykah, 146
Baker, Jordan, 220
Bakhtin, Mikhail, 24, 65, 71
Bambaataa, Afrika, 199, 201, 204
Banhart, Devendra, 163, 174, 175–6, 178
Beach House, 3
Beam, Sam, 176, 177, 178
The Beastie Boys, 170, 210
"Beat Connection" (LCD Soundsystem), 59
The Beatles, 6, 8, 56, 60, 198
Beckett, Samuel, 11
Beenie, 142
Being and Event (Badiou), 13
Bell, Sean, 197, 215, 220
Bernstein, Charles, 164, 167
Berry, Chuck, 54
The Better Life (3 Doors Down), 81
Beyoncé, 79, 86, 95, 127
Bieber, Justin, 94
"Big Chief Chinese Restaurant" (Guided By Voices), 63
Big Daddy Kane, 201
Biggie Smalls, 204
Bikini Kill, 58
Bill Carney's Jug Addicts, 76
"Birthday" (Perry), 101, 102
Birth of Venus (Botticelli), 229
Bissell, Charles, 54
The Black Album (Jay Z), 6
The Black Album (Prince), 2, 129
The Black Angels, 172–3, 179, 192

The Black Babies (Banhart), 175
"The Blacker the Berry" (Lamar), 205–7, 208, 213, 218
Blackjack David (Alvin), 24
Black Noise (Rose), 208
The Black Panthers, 203, 204, 215
Black, Rebecca, 80
"Black Skinhead" (West), 142
"Black Steel in the Hour of Chaos" (Public Enemy), 201
Black string bands, 25, 27–8, 29, 50
The Black Swans, 152
"Black Sweat" (Prince), 123, 124–5, 126, 127, 129
Bland, Sandra, 197, 215, 220
"Blank Space" (Swift), 78
Blige, Mary J., 200
Blind Blake, 224
"Blood on the Leaves" (West), 143
Bloom, Harold, 55–6, 58–60, 63, 65, 67, 70, 169. *See* anxiety of influence
"Blowin' in the Wind" (Dylan), 46
Blow, Kurtis, 204
Blow Up Hollywood, 172
Blue Öyster Cult, 70
The Blueprint (Jay-Z), 140
"Blurred Lines" (Thicke), 222
"Bob George" (Prince), 129
Boccioni, Umberto, 137
Bodies That Matter (Butler), 127
"The Body Electric" (Hurray for the Riff Raff), 221–31
Boggs, Dock, 32
The Bomb Squad, 201
"Bomb the World" (Franti), 168
Boogie Down Productions, 201
Bookmobile, 65
"Boom!" (System of a Down), 167
Borges, Jorge Luis, 108
Born in the U.S.A. (Springsteen), 188, 189
"Born in the U.S.A." (Springsteen), 181, 182
Born to Run (memoir) (Springsteen), 190, 194, 195 n.245
"Born to Run" (Springsteen), 183

Botticelli, Sandro, 229
Boudica, 36
"Bound" (Ponderosa Twins), 142
"Bound 2" (West), 142
Bowman, James, 172
Box and Cox: In One Act, 32
Boyd, Todd, 210
Bracciolini, Poggio, 71
Brandenburg, Karlheinz, 113
"The Breakdown" (Prince), 129
Brecht, Bertolt, 161
Bright Eyes. *See* Conor Oberst
Brillo Box (Warhol), 4, 131, 132
Bringing It All Back Home (Dylan), 36, 132
"Bring the Noise" (Public Enemy), 201
Broadway Boogie-Boogie (Mondrian), 138
Brook, Peter, 235
Brother D and the Collective Effort, 200
The Brothers Karamazov (Dosteovsky), 100
Brown, James, 145, 147
Brown, Michael, 197, 206, 216, 220
"Bulls on Parade" (Rage Against the Machine), 168
Burden, Chris, 152
Bush, George W., 171
Bush v. Gore, 22
Butler, Judith, 126–7, 128–9, 131–4, 150, 151, 227
Butler, Octavia, 148
Byrne, David, 108

Cabaret Voltaire, 72
"California Gurls" (Perry), 96–7
"Call Me Maybe" (Jepsen), 87
Campbell, Isobel, 80
Campbell, Larry, 50
Camper Van Beethoven, 25
Cantrell, Blu, 27
Can't Stop Won't Stop (Chang), 210
Cantwell, Robert, 175, 177
Capturing Sound (Katz), 109
Carey, Miriam, 197, 220
Carolina Chocolate Drops, 27–30

Carpenter, John, 72
Carter, Calvin, 49
Carter, James and the Prisoners, 25
"A Case of You" (Mitchell), 1, 10
Cash, Johnny, 224–5
"A Cast of Dice" (Mallarmé), 26
Chance the Rapper, 155
"Chandelier" (Sia), 152
Chang, Jeff, 209–10
Chekhov, Anton, 185
"Chelsea Rodgers" (Prince), 123
Chief Keef, 142, 153
Childish, Billy, 5
"Ching-a-Ling" (Elliott), 98
"Chocolate Box" (Prince), 123
The Chocolate Invasion (Prince), 122
Christgau, Robert, 58, 61, 173
The Chronic (Dr. Dre), 210
Chronicles (Dylan), 35, 39–40, 48
Chuck D, 201
The City Rises (Boccioni), 137
Claytor, Timberly, 222
Clear Channel, 111, 169, 180
Clemons, Clarence, 194
clinamen, 55, 70. *See also* anxiety of influence
Clinton, George, 133
Clinton, Hillary, 200
"Clouds" (Prince), 129, 130
C-Murder, 143
C-Note (Prince), 122
Cobain, Kurt, 57, 61
Coco Rosie, 174
Cocteau Twins, 3
Coen Brothers, 18, 23
"Cold Irons Bound" (Dylan), 41
"Cold War" (Monáe), 145, 146, 157–8
College (band), 72
The College Dropout (West), 140
Collins, Bootsy, 203
"Colonized Mind" (Prince), 123
Columbia Records, 44, 50, 112
Columbus, Ohio, 62, 65, 74, 216

"Come On Over (Turn Me On)" (Campbell and Lanegan), 80
"Comment #1" (Scott-Heron), 141, 215
Comments on the Society of the Spectacle (Debord), 110
"Complexion (A Zulu Love)" (Lamar), 217–18
composition, 7, 74. *See also* ontology of music
"Computer Blue", 1, 2
Confessions of a Yakuza (Saga), 33, 46
"Controversy" (Prince), 121
Cook, Edward, 48
Cooley, Mike, 68, 69
The Coup, 192
The Courage to Be (Tillich), 64
"Courtesy of the Red, White, and Blue (The Angry American)" (Keith), 162, 174
"Cracklin' Rosie" (Diamond), 95
Crawford III, John, 197, 213, 220
"Crazy Frog", 80, 92
Crazy Horse (band), 191
"Crazy in Love" (Beyoncé), 95
The Creek Drank the Cradle (Iron & Wine), 176
Crooked Rain, Crooked Rain (Pavement), 55
Crosby, Bing, 47
crowdfunding, 114
Cruising Utopia (Muñoz), 130, 134
"Cry No More" (Giddens), 226–7, 230
"Crystal Ball" (Prince), 129
"Cry a While" (Dylan), 32, 44
cultural archive. *See* cultural economy of exchange
cultural economy of exchange (Groys), 35, 39, 234
   boundary, 42
   cultural archive, 34–6, 39, 42, 43–4, 46, 60, 65, 71, 77–8, 91, 233
   and the event, 39
   internet, 108
   negative, 45, 69, 77, 150, 223
   and newness, 35, 39, 80, 81

   politics, 171
   profane realm, 35–6, 42, 50, 91
Curse of the Loaf (Archers of Loaf), 61
"Cut Your Hair" (Pavement), 55

Daft Punk, 59, 140, 152
"Daft Punk Is Playing at My House" (LCD Soundsystem), 59
Dahl, Roald, 140
Dale, Peter, 169, 170, 171, 172
"Dancing in the Street" (Martha and the Vandellas), 95
D'Angelo, 70
Danger Mouse, 6, 8
Danto, Arthur, 4, 5, 38, 39, 68, 99–100, 131–2
"Dark Fantasy" (West), 140
"Dark Horse" (Perry), 90–1, 92, 94
Darkness on the Edge of Town (Springsteen), 183, 185, 187
Das Kapital (Marx), 89
Davies, Stephen, 6
Davis, Miles, 217
"Day After Tomorrow" (Waits), 165, 179
"A Day in the Life" (Beatles), 60
"Days of Graduation" (Drive-By Truckers), 69
Dayton, Ohio, 65
"Dear Someone" (Welch), 21
"Death to My Hometown" (Springsteen), 182, 193, 194
Debord, Guy, 88–90, 100, 120, 127, 128, 138, 141, 156. *See also* spectacle
Debussy, Claude, 133
Decoration Day (Drive-By Truckers), 68
definitive recording, 7, 9–10
Delaney, Samuel L., 151
Deleuze, Gilles, 133
Deley, Alexander T., 47, 48
"Delia" (Dylan), 224–5
"Delia" (trad.) 222, 224–5
"Delia's Gone" (Cash) 224–5
"Delirious" (Prince), 1
Depeche Mode, 72

Deren, Maya, 146
Dery, Mark, 148–9
"Desolation Row" (Dylan), 55
"Detroit Has a Skyline" (Superchunk), 106–7
Devils and Dust (Springsteen), 192
Diallo, Amadou, 190, 197, 200, 220
dialogism (Bakhtin), 24–5, 27, 65, 71
Diamond, Neil, 95
Diamonds and Pearls (Prince), 129
"Diamonds and Pearls" (Prince), 233
The Diaries of Private Henry Hill (Blow Up Hollywood), 172
"Didn't Leave Nobody But the Baby" (Welch), 19
Dinosaur Jr., 58
Dirty Mind (Prince), 1, 2
The Dirty South (Drive-By Truckers), 68
"Disco Infiltrator" (LCD Soundsystem), 59
"Distress Signal" (Lazerhawk), 73
Dixie Chicks, 161–2, 164, 166, 169, 179–80, 214
DJ Kool Herc, 199, 200
"D.M.S.R." (Prince), 1
Dodge, Harry, 133
"Do Me Baby" (Prince), 126
Donnie Trumpet and the Social Experiment, 155
"Don't Stop Now" (Guided By Voices), 64
The Doobie Brothers, 184
The Doors, 172
Dostoevsky, Fyodor, 100
Douglas, Michael, 182
"Down for My Niggaz" (C-Murder), 143
Down from the Mountain tour, 19
Drake, Nick, 116
Dr. Dre, 204, 210
drill, 90, 141, 152
Drive (soundtrack), 72
Drive-By Truckers, 67–70, 71, 75, 191
Du Bois, W. E. B., 203, 213
Duchamp, Marcel, 4, 5
"Dust Storm Disaster" (Guthrie), 20

Dylan, Bob, 31–51, 55, 56, 80, 94, 108, 170, 191, 224–5, 233
and cultural archive, 34–5, 60, 141
as an event, 35–8, 131–2
persona, 33, 42–6, 106
transgression, 33–4, 46–51
Dylan Goes Electric! (Wald), 37

Eagleton, Terry, 157
Eardrum (Kweli), 209
Earle, Steve, 163–4, 165, 168
"Easy Money" (Springsteen), 181, 193
EDM, 8, 59, 141
808s and Heartbreak (West), 140, 141, 142
"Eileen Aroon" (Dylan), 40–1
Eldred v Ashcroft, 108
"Electric Intercourse" (Prince), 1
The Electric Lady (Monáe), 146
Electric Youth, 72
Elliott, Missy, 97–8
"Elvis Presley Blues", 21
Emerson, Ralph Waldo, 64
Eminem, 168, 210, 222
Emmett, Dan, 28–9, 48
"Empty Room" (Prince), 233
"The Entertainer" (Joplin), 123
The Epic (Washington), 80
Epicurus, 70
Eric B. and Rakim, 201
E Street Band, 182, 183, 188, 189, 193
event (Badiou), 11–13, 38–9, 81, 100–1, 110, 111, 124, 176, 200–2, 235. See also Dylan, Bob, and Prince
and electronic music, 74
evental site, 12, 236 n.13
evental sphere, 13
fidelity, 202, 207, 217
forcing the count, 201–2, 230
Idea, 230
interpretative intervention, 25–6, 39, 74, 201, 230
interval, 202, 208, 219, 226, 230
and jazz, 13
politics, 166, 167, 179

rap, 199, 200
situation, 11–12, 13, 26, 36, 81, 103, 120, 199, 200–1, 237 n.19
　and the spectacle, 91, 103
　and synthwave, 74–5
　truth-procedure, 166, 172, 208, 209, 218
Evers, Medgar, 207
"Everybody Wants to Rule the World" (Tears for Fears), 173
"Every Nigger Is a Star" (Gardner), 203
"Everything Is Free" (Welch), 20
"Everyone Chooses Sides" (The Wrens), 53–4, 55

The Fairfield Four, 25
Falling Down, 182
Fall Out Boy, 59–60, 81
Farley, Nate, 62
"Faster" (Monáe), 148
Fat Mike, 171
Federal Communications Commission, 111
Feltham, Oliver, 13
"Fight the Power" (Public Enemy), 201
"Fighting in Iraq" (Black Angels), 172
Filene, Benjamin, 38
"Firework" (Perry), 91, 100, 101–2
First Avenue, 1, 12, 120
"The First Vietnamese Dead" (Black Angels), 172
Flavor Flav, 201
Flemons, Dom, 27, 28
Flippo, Chet, 180
"Floater (Too Much to Ask)" (Dylan), 32, 44, 47
Flo Rida, 87
Fluker, Clint, 149
folk music, 21, 22, 24, 48, 132, 147, 190, 191
　freak-folk, 70, 174–8, 230
　new millennial revival, 23, 27, 230
　1960s folk revival, 36–9, 49, 170, 175
"For Free?-Interlude" (Lamar), 214

"For Sale?-Interlude" (Lamar), 214
The Founding and Manifesto of Futurism (Marinetti), 73
"Frankie and Albert"/"Frankie and Johnny" (trad.), 224
Franti, Michael, 168
Franz Ferdinand, 70
freak-folk. *See* folk music
Freedom (Young), 191
Frenchkiss Records, 112
French Revolution, 13, 93, 167
Frith, Simon, 8, 164
From Under the Cork Tree (Fall Out Boy), 59
"Funky Duck" (Vulfpeck), 77
"Fury" (Prince), 123
Future Punx, 76, 77
"Future Soul Song" (Prince), 123
futurism, 18
Futurism, 74–5, 137–8
　synthwave and, 74–5

Gardner, Boris, 203
Garner, Eric, 197, 206, 216, 220
Garst, John, 225
Garvey, Marcus, 203
Gender Trouble (Butler), 126
Gentling, Matt, 61
Genuine Negro Jig, 27, 29
"Genuine Negro Jig" (Snowdens, Emmett), 27–9
"Get By" (Kweli), 211
"Get Ur Freak On" (Elliott), 97–8
The Ghost of Tom Joad (Springsteen), 192
Giddens, Rhiannon, 27–8, 29, 226, 229
Gilmore, Mikal, 49
"Gimme Indie Rock" (Sebadoh), 54, 56
Gimme Shelter (documentary), 19
"Girl You Know It's True" (Milli Vanilli), 78
"God Moves on the Water" (Johnson), 20
Goldberg, Barry, 37
Golden Vanity (Dylan), 40
The Gold Experience (Prince), 122

"Goldheart Mountaintop Queen Directory" (Guided By Voices), 63
"The Gold Standard" (Prince), 129
Good As I Been to You (Dylan), 41
Goodbye Tomorrow, 152–6
"Good Feeling" (Flo Rida), 87
good kid, m.A.A.d. city (Lamar), 202, 219
"A Good Man Is Hard to Find" (O'Connor), 187
"A Good Man Is Hard to Find (Pittsburgh)" (Springsteen), 186
"Goodnight Sweetheart, Goodnight" (Spaniels), 49
"Good Times Blues (An Outlaw's Lament)" (Hurray for the Riff Raff), 228
Gordimer, Nadine, 43
"The Gosport Tragedy" (trad.), 225
Gossamer (Passion Pit), 105, 111, 112, 115
Grace, Laura Jane, 172
Gracyk, Theodore, 6
Graduation (West), 140
Grammy Awards, 34, 40, 145, 147, 152, 179–80
Grandmaster Flash, 199, 200
Gray, Freddie, 197, 216, 220
Gray, Kimani, 197, 220
"Greatest of All Time" (Archers of Loaf), 61–2
The Great Gatsby, 46, 50
Great White Wonder (Dylan), 108
Greenberg, Clement, 68, 70, 79
Greenblatt, Steven, 71, 95
Green Day, 34, 86, 173, 192
Green, Delia, 222, 225, 229
The Grey Album (Danger Mouse), 6, 8
Groys, Boris, 4, 34–5, 45, 51, 71, 79, 91, 93–4, 141, 234. *See also* cultural economy of exchange and iconoclasm, 143–4
Guattari, Félix, 133
"Guerilla Monsoon Rap" (Kweli), 211
"Guerrilla Radio" (Rage Against the Machine), 168

Guided By Voices, 60, 62–5
"Guitar" (Prince), 123
Guthrie, Woody, 20, 170

Haggard, Merle, 162
Hajdu, David, 168, 169
Haley, Alex, 212
Hall, John, 184
Hamilton, Dontre, 216
Hamri, Sanaa, 125
"Hard Time Killing Floor Blues" (King), 25
"Harnessed in Slums" (Archers of Loaf), 61
Harris, Eric, 202
Harrison, George, 172
Hartford, John, 24, 29
Hays, Garrett, 72, 74, 75
"Hell You Talmbout" (Monáe), 215–17, 224, 226, 230
Hendrix, Jimi, 2, 120, 123
Heraclitus, 133
"Here It Goes Again" (OK Go), 87
Here's Where the Strings Come In (Superchunk), 107
"Highlands" (Dylan), 41
"High Water (for Charley Patton)" (Dylan), 32, 43
"Highway Patrolman" (Springsteen), 187
Highway 61 Revisited (Dylan), 36, 43, 132
Hill, Lauryn, 70
Himelrick, Shasta, 222
Himes, Geoffrey, 187
hip-hop. *See* rap
The History of Rock 'n' Roll in Ten Songs (Marcus), 5
"Hit 'Em Up Style (Oops!)" (Cantrell), 27
Hobbes, Thomas, 194
"Hold My Liquor" (West), 142
"Hold On" (Alabama Shakes), 3, 70
"Holiday" (Green Day), 173
Holiday, Billie, 143
Holly, Buddy, 62
Home (Dixie Chicks), 161, 163

"Honest With Me" (Dylan), 43
Hood, Patterson, 67, 68, 69
"Hood Politics" (Lamar), 212
Hope, Clover, 203
"Hopeless" (Wrens), 54
Houston, Moses "Cooney", 225
"How Much a Dollar Cost" (Lamar), 212
"How Much Is That Doggie in the Window" (Prince), 120
How Music Works (Byrne), 108
"How We Gonna Make the Black Nation Rise?" (Brother D), 200
Hudson, James "Pookie", 49
The Hunger Games (film), 85, 90, 92, 98
Hurray for the Riff Raff, 222–3, 226, 230

"i" (Lamar), 218
"I Am a God" (West), 142
"I Am a Man of Constant Sorrow" (Hartford), 24, 29
Icky Mettle (Archers of Loaf), 57
iconoclasm, 138, 139, 143–4
"Idiot Son of an Asshole" (NOFX), 171
"I Dream a Highway" (Welch), 20, 21
"If I Was Your Girlfriend" (Prince), 121
"I Kissed a Girl" (Perry), 92, 94, 95
"I Know It's Wrong (But That's Alright)" (Hurray for the Riff Raff), 228
"I'll Be Alright" (Passion Pit), 115
"I'll Fly Away" (trad.), 19, 140
Illinois (Stevens), 177
"I Love U But I Don't Trust U Anymore" (Prince), 123
"Imagine" (Lennon), 169
"I'm In It" (West), 142
The Impressions, 193
"Incense and Candles" (Prince), 123, 125
Indigo Nights (Prince), 123
Infidels (Dylan), 35
innovation, 39, 45, 79, 108–9, 117, 164, 167, 170
    versus newness, 80, 107
"Institutionalized" (Lamar), 212, 214
Interpol, 70

Iraq War, 161, 163, 164, 172–3, 176, 180
Iron & Wine, 24, 163, 174, 176–7, 187
"I Sing the Body Electric" (Whitman), 228, 229
"I Slept with Someone in Fall Out Boy…" (Fall Out Boy), 60
Is This It? (Strokes), 18
"It's All Over Now, Baby Blue" (Dylan), 37
"It's Not My Fault, I'm Happy" (Passion Pit), 115
"It Takes a Lot to Laugh (It Takes a Train to Cry)" (Dylan), 37
"It Was Always You" (Maroon 5), 81
It Won't Be Soon Before Long (Maroon 5), 81
"I've Been Wrong Before" (Future Punx), 76
"I Wanna Be With You" (Raspberries), 95
"I Wanna Be Your Lover" (Prince), 121
"I Wish I Was in the Land of Dixie" (Snowdens, Emmett), 28–9, 48
"I Would Die 4 U" (Prince), 1, 121

"Jack of All Trades" (Springsteen), 181
"Jailhouse Rock" (Presley), 54
James, Robin, 157
Jay-Z, 6, 8, 140, 141, 152, 153–4, 204, 210
"Jay Z" (Goodbye Tomorrow), 152, 153–4
jazz, 13, 27, 40, 80, 148, 150, 157, 190, 198, 217
J. Cole, 217
Jennings, John, 149
Jepsen, Carly Rae, 87
Joel, Billy, 81
"John Henry" (trad.), 20, 190
Johnny and Jack, 49
"Johnny B. Goode" (Berry), 54
"Johnny 99" (Springsteen), 187
Johns, Jasper, 137
Johnson, Blind Willie, 20
Johnson, Eric, 57, 61
Johnson, Robert, 32
"John Walker's Blues" (Earle), 164, 165, 179

Jones, Aiyana, 197, 211, 220
Jones, Frank, 204–5
Jones, Mertilla, 211
Joplin, Scott, 123
Jordan, Michael, 153, 154
Joseph, Miranda, 134
A Journey Through the Mind of a Non-Believer (Goodbye Tomorrow), 152
Judt, Tony, 194
Juicy J, 90

Katz, Mark, 109
Kavinsky, 72, 74
Keith, Toby, 162
Ken and "Dub", 108, 109
Kickstarter, 114
"Killing in the Name" (Rage Against the Machine), 168
King, Chris Thomas, 25
"King Kunta" (Lamar), 212, 213
King Louie, 142
King, Martin Luther, Jr., 143, 203, 205
King, Tyre, 216, 220
The Kingston Trio, 223
"Kiss" (Prince), 233
Kitwana, Bakari, 204
Kool Moe Dee, 204
Kooper, Al, 37
Kot, Greg, 111
Kraftwerk, 2, 72
Kravitz, Lenny, 92, 97, 98, 101
KRS-One and Boogie Down Productions, 201
"Kryptonite" (3 Doors Down), 81
Kweli, Talib, 209, 211, 217

Labelle, Patti, 148
"The Ladder" (Prince), 121
Ladner, Gerhart, 176
Lady Gaga, 79, 86
La Havas, Lianne, 130
Lamar, Kendrick, 198, 202–3, 205–9, 211, 212–15, 217–19, 229
Landau, Jon, 189

"Land of Hope and Dreams" (Springsteen), 193–4
Lanegan, Mark, 80
Lang, Fritz, 150
"Last Friday Night (T.G.I.F.)" (Perry), 98
The Last Poets, 204
Lauper, Cyndi, 78
Lazerhawk, 72–6, 78, 79, 80
LCD Soundsystem, 106
Leaves of Grass (Whitman), 228
Lee, Brenda, 142
Lennon, John, 169, 198
Lerner, Murray, 37
"Let's Go Crazy" (Prince), 9, 10
"Let There Be Rock" (Drive-By Truckers), 67–8, 69, 70
Leviathan (Hobbes), 194
Levine, Adam, 81
"Library of Babel" (Borges), 108
"Light One, Pour One" (Goodbye Tomorrow), 153
"Like a Rolling Stone" (Dylan), 36, 37
Lipsitz, George, 24, 25
Lipstick Traces (Marcus), 90, 128
"Listen!!!" (Kweli), 209
"Little Red Corvette" (Prince), 1, 123, 233
Live 1975–85 (Springsteen), 182
LiveR Than You'll Ever Be (Rolling Stones), 108
Living with War (Young), 191, 192
L.L. Cool J, 20, 21
Lomax, John, 177, 224
Lomax, Ruby, 224
"The Lonesome Road", 47
"Lonesome Valley" (Fairfield Four), 25
Lorde, 87
"Lose Control" (Elliott), 97, 98, 101
"Losing My Edge" (LCD Soundsystem), 59
"Lost in the World" (West), 141
Lott, Eric, 48
Lotusflower/MPLSound (Prince), 123
"Love and Theft" (Dylan), 31–4, 40, 42–6, 47–9, 80, 191
Love and Theft (Lott), 48

"Love in Vain" (Johnson, R), 32
"Love Sick" (Dylan), 41, 106
Lovesexy (Prince), 2, 129
Lowell, Robert, 176
The Lowest Pair, 80
"Lowest Part Is Free" (Archers of Loaf), 61
Lucretius, 55, 70–1
Lupe Fiasco, 210, 217
Lynch, David, 80
Lynch, Tameka, 222
Lynskey, Dorian, 173
Lynyrd Skynyrd, 62, 67, 69

McGraw, Tim, 86
McTell, Blind Willie, 224
Madison Square Garden, 184, 189
Madonna, 78, 112, 121
"Maggie's Farm" (Dylan), 37
Magic (Springsteen), 192
Maguire, Martie, 161
Mahal, Taj, 20
Maines, Natalie, 161–2, 163, 179, 180
Malcolm X, 203
Malefactors of Great Wealth, 152
Malevich, Kazimir, 138, 141
Mallarmé, Stéphane, 26
The Man Machine (Kraftwerk), 2
Mann, Kate, 25
"Mansion on the Hill" (Springsteen), 187
"Many Moons" (Monáe), 146
Marcus, Greil, 5, 36, 40, 90, 119, 122, 128, 134
Marinetti, F.T., 73, 137
Maroon 5, 81, 86
Mars, Bruno, 94, 96
Martha and the Vandellas, 95
Martin, Trayvon, 205, 206, 220
Marx, Karl, 89
"Masters of War" (Dylan), 34, 40, 170
The Matrix, 102
The Meadowlands, 53–5, 59
mediocrity, 81
Meeropol, Abel, 143
Mega Drive, 75

Meltzer, Mitchell, 64
Melvoin, Wendy, 2
Meshes of the Afternoon (Deren), 146
"The Message" (Grandmaster Flash and the Furious Five), 200
meta-rock, 53–5, 56–7, 59–65, 69–70, 80, 91
Metropolis (Lang), 150
Metropolis (The Chase Suite) (Monáe), 146, 150
Meyer, Leonard B., 79
Meyers, Augie, 32
MF Doom, 152
Miami Nights 1984, 74
Michigan (Stevens), 177
The Milk Carton Kids, 24
Milli Vanilli, 78
Minaj, Nikki, 140
Minima Moralia (Adorno), 156
Minnie, Memphis, 47
"Mississippi" (Dylan), 32
"Mississippi Goddam" (Simone), 207
Miss Molly, 63
Mitchell, Jamycheal, 198
Mitchell, Joni, 1
Mitchem, Matthew, 93, 124
Modern Times, 47, 48
Molly Hatchet, 67
"Momma" (Lamar), 212
Monáe, Janelle, 145–51, 155, 156–8, 215, 220, 224, 226, 229
Mondrian, Piet, 138
"Monster" (West), 140
Montreux Jazz Festival, 123
Morley, Paul, 87
Morris, Doug, 114
"Mortal Man" (Lamar), 218–19
Mos Def and Talib Kweli Are Black Star (Def and Kweli), 211
"Mosh" (Eminem), 168, 179
"Motor Away" (Guided by Voices), 64
Motown, 3, 70, 217
Mount Vernon, Ohio, 28
"Movin' Out" (Joel), 81

MP3, 106–7, 108, 109, 113
"Mr. Tambourine Man" (Dylan), 37
Muldar, Maria, 37
Mumford and Sons, 86
Muñoz, José Esteban, 130, 131, 134
Murphy, James, 59
Musicology (Prince), 120, 123
My Beautiful Dark Twisted Fantasy (West), 137, 140, 141, 215
"My Country" (Nas), 173, 210
"My Father's House" (Springsteen), 187
Mystery and Manners (O'Connor), 186
Mystery Train (Marcus), 119, 122, 134

Namikas, Michael, 219
Napster, 113
Nas, 173–4, 179, 192, 210, 216
Nash, Graham, 184
Nassau, Eric, 62
Nassau String Band, 224
Nathaniel Rateliff and the Night Sweats, 70, 78
Nation of Islam, 204
Nebraska (Springsteen), 185, 186–8, 189, 190, 191, 192
"Nebraska" (Springsteen), 187, 188
Negative Dialectics (Adorno), 157
negative persona, 152
Nelson, Maggie, 133
Nelson, Paul, 37
Neoteric, 80, 81
"Nettie Moore" (Dylan), 48
The New Being (Tillich), 176
New Lost City Ramblers, 49
"new man", 176, 187
newness in music
  contemporary dilemma of, 4, 86–7
  the event and, 11–13
  vs. the old, 77, 79–80
  technology and, 107
  tradition, 30, 34–5, 45, 49
  transgression, 33–4, 51
Newport Folk Festival (1965), 36, 131, 168
N.E.W.S. (Prince), 122

"New Slaves" (West), 143
Newsom, Joanna, 174, 175, 178
New Testament, 176, 187
New Wave (Against Me!), 172
"Nice People" (Banhart), 175
Nicholson, Jack, 34, 40
Nietzsche, Friedrich, 99
9/11, 175, 178
1989 (Swift), 77, 78–80, 86, 171, 191
1999 (Prince), 1
Nirvana, 57
No Depression (magazine), 22
No Direction Home (documentary) 41
NOFX, 171, 179
"No More Auction Block" (trad.), 46
No Nukes (concert), 184
North, Michael, 20, 21, 22, 23, 70, 167, 176, 234
"Not Ready to Make Nice" (Dixie Chicks), 179, 180
"Nottamun Town" (trad.), 170
novelty, 80
Novelty: A History of the New (North), 20, 23, 167, 176, 234
novelty song, 80
N.W.A., 204, 210

Obama, Barack, 234
Oberst, Conor, 163, 170–1
O Brother, Where Art Thou?, 23–5, 26, 29, 30, 70, 174
O'Connor, Flannery, 185–7, 188, 189, 190–1, 193
"O Death" (Stanley et al.), 24, 25
Oh Me Oh My... (Banhart), 175–6
Oh Mercy (Dylan), 33
OK Go, 87
"Ol' Dan Tucker" (trad.), 190
"Old Thunderbird" (Banhart), 175
"Old Time Rock 'n' Roll" (Seger), 54
"O Mary Don't You Weep" (trad.), 190
"Omie Wise" (trad.), 224
"The One" (Prince), 123
"100K" (Goodbye Tomorrow), 152, 153

One of the Boys (Perry), 95
1000 Forms of Fear (Sia), 152
On Nature (Parmenides), 3
"On Sight" (West), 142
On the Nature of Things (Lucretius), 70–1
On the New (Groys), 4, 34, 45, 51, 141
ontology of music, 6–11
　composition, 7, 74
　definitive recording, 7, 9–10
　instance, 8–9, 133
　performance, 6–11, 12, 13 (*see also* performance)
　sound recording, 6–8
　unfinishing, 10, 40, 188, 190, 233
　variability, 9–10, 115, 121, 132, 188
"Oops! … I Did It Again" (Spears), 87
Osbourne, Ozzy, 70
The Other Side of the Mirror (Lerner), 37
Our Endless Numbered Days (Iron & Wine), 24, 174, 176, 187
Outkast, 81, 148
"Out of the Woods" (Swift), 78
Overexposed (Maroon 5), 81
"Over the Neptune/Mesh-Gear Fox" (Guided By Voices), 64

Painterly Realism of a Boy with a Knapsack—Color Masses in the 4th Dimension (Malevich), 138
Panic at the Disco, 59–60, 81
Pareles, Jon, 47
Paris (rapper), 170, 210
Parliament-Funkadelic, 133, 148
Parmenides, 3, 70
Passion Pit, 105, 106, 111, 114–15
Passover (Black Angels), 172–3, 179, 192
PATRIOT Act, 169, 180
Paul the Apostle, 176, 187
The Paul Butterfield Band, 37
Pavement, 54, 55, 57, 58, 60
"Payphone" (Maroon 5), 81
Pearl Jam, 57, 170
"Pedal to the Metal" (Lazerhawk), 73
"People Get Ready" (Impressions), 193

performance
　and the body, 227
　commodity, 115–17
　event, 12–13, 81, 101
　gender and sexuality, 93–4, 126–7, 128, 227, 228
　identity, 89, 93–4, 126–29, 130–1, 132–4, 208
　live performance, 42, 87, 109–10, 124, 125 (*see also* ontology of music)
　politics, 164, 165–6
　queerness, 126–9, 130–1, 132–4, 227, 228
　technology, 106, 108, 109–10, 115, 149
Performing Rites (Frith), 8, 164
Perkins, Pinetop, 138
Perlstein, Yosi, 227
Perry, Katy, 85–7, 88, 90–2, 95, 95–7, 98, 101–2
persona, 91, 94, 124, 145–58, 162, 164, 208, 229
"Peter Gunn", 72
Peterson, Laci, 222
Petrusich, Amanda, 176
Philosophy and the Event (Badiou), 201
Pick a Bigger Weapon (The Coup), 192
Pinckney, Clementa, 197, 215
"Pinetop's Boogie-Woogie", 138
"Pink Moon" (Drake), 116
Pixies, 58, 60
Planet Earth (Prince), 123
"Plastic Flowers on the Highway" (Drive-By Truckers), 69
"Play in the Sunshine" (Prince), 121
"Plumbline" (Archers of Loaf), 57
"Po' Lazarus" (James Carter and the Prisoners), 25
The Political Force of Musical Beauty (Shank), 171
Pollard, Bob, 62–4, 65
Pollard, Jim, 63
Ponderosa Twins Plus One, 142
"Pop Life" (Prince), 95
Porno for Pyros, 57
"Post Wave" (Future Punx), 76

"Power" (West), 140
Powers, Ann, 227, 230
Present Shock (Rushkoff), 18, 99, 178
Presley, Elvis, 20, 21, 54
Pretty. Odd. (Panic at the Disco), 60
"Pretty Polly" (trad.), 224, 225
Preyer, L. Richardson, 204
Price, Mark, 61
Prince, 9–10, 11, 13, 95, 112, 119–35, 141, 146, 191, 233
  debut of *Purple Rain*, 1–2, 12
  event of, 120–2
  queerness, 121, 124–7, 130
  and the Revolution, 2, 12
Prismatic tour (Perry), 87, 98, 101
profane realm. *See* cultural economy of exchange
protest songs, 165, 166–74, 179–80, 211, 216
  vs. topical songs, 166–7
Protomartyr, 3
"The Proud" (Kweli), 211
Pryor, Richard, 203
Psyche, 72
public authenticity, 127–9, 134, 150, 207–8
Public Domain (Alvin), 24
Public Enemy, 167, 169, 201, 204
Purple Rain (Prince), 2, 12
"Purple Rain" (Prince), 1, 9–10, 120, 121, 233
Pussy Galore, 56

Quality (Kweli), 211
Queen, 60
"Q.U.E.E.N." (Monáe), 146
queerness, 121–2, 124–7, 128, 146, 148, 150, 227–8, 233
  and transfiguration, 133–4
  and utopia, 130–1
race and ethnicity
  appropriation, 48–9, 138, 141, 146–7
  commodification, 146, 153–4
  consumerism, 214
  folk music, 27–30

identity, 121, 127, 141, 149–51, 153–4
police brutality, 197, 198, 206, 215–16

Rage Against the Machine, 168, 169, 179
The Rainbow Children (Prince), 120, 122, 129
"Range Life" (Pavement), 55
rap and hip-hop, 3
  commodification of, 209–10
  event of, 26, 199
  history of, 199–200, 201
  revolutionary politics, 201, 204, 208, 209–11, 217
"Rapper's Delight" (Sugarhill Gang), 209
The Raspberries, 95
Rattlesnake on the Road (Mann), 25
Rave Un2 the Joy Fantastic (Prince), 123
Rawlings, David, 19–20, 22, 191
"A Real Hero" (College/Electric Youth), 72
recombination, 20–2, 25–6, 27, 32, 47, 50, 70, 91, 108, 149, 199
record labels and corporations, 111–14
recurrence, 23, 25–6, 70, 91
Red, Katey, 229
Redline (Lazerhawk), 72–3, 74, 78, 80
"Reflection" (Prince), 123
reformation, 205, 206, 223
Reid, Jermaine, 197, 220
Rejoicing in the Hands (Banhart), 175
R.E.M., 58
restoration, 176–7, 178
Retromania (Reynolds), 3, 5, 58–9, 68, 70, 71, 178
"Revelator" (Welch), 19, 20
revivals, 18–19, 23, 24–5, 175, 234. *See also* folk music
  as interpretative intervention, 26, 29, 230
  as recurrence, 23, 26
Revolting Rhymes (Dahl), 140
revolution, 141, 149, 163, 167, 226, 228, 230, 234
  in political hip-hop, 198–200, 201, 203–5, 206, 207, 210, 214–15, 217–19
  vs. reformation, 204–5, 206, 223

"Revolution" (Beatles), 198
Reynolds, Simon, 3, 5, 58–9, 68, 70, 71, 178
Rhythm and Noise: An Aesthetics of Rock (Gracyk), 6
Rice, Tamir, 197, 220
Richman, Jonathan, 59
Rihanna, 87, 96
The Rising (Springsteen), 191
"The River" (O'Connor), 186, 187
The River (Springsteen), 184, 185, 186, 187, 188
"The River" (Springsteen), 182, 184
"Roar" (Perry), 85–6, 87
Robinson, Justin, 27
Robison, Emily, 161
Rock and Roll Hall of Fame and Museum, 34, 39
"Rock and Roll Is Here to Stay" (Danny and the Juniors), 54
"Rock and Roll Music" (Berry), 54
Rock, Chris, 124
"Rocky Ground" (Springsteen), 194
The Rolling Stones, 19, 108
Rooney, Jim, 37
Roots (Haley), 212
"Roots (If the Sky Were a Stone)" (Banhart), 175
The Rose and the Briar (various), 225
Rose, Tricia, 208
Rosso Corsa Records, 75
"Roulette" (Springsteen), 183–4, 245 n.1
"Royals" (Lorde), 87
"Ruination Day" (Welch), 20
"Rule" (Nas), 173–4, 192, 210, 216
Run D.M.C., 201
Run the Jewels, 217
"Rush" (Kweli), 211
Rushkoff, Douglas, 18, 74, 87, 89, 93, 99, 112, 178

Sacks, Howard L. and Judith Rose, 28–9
The Sacred Heart Sessions (Lowest Pair), 80

Saga, Junichi, 34, 46
Sam and Dave, 70
Sandler, Adam, 143
Santos, Al, 44
Sayre, Tiffany, 222
The Scarlet Letter (Hawthorne), 162
Schwarzenegger, Arnold, 173
Scott-Heron, Gil, 141, 215, 216, 230
Scott, Walter, 197, 209, 220
Sebadoh, 56
Secaucus (The Wrens), 53
"Seeds" (Springsteen), 182
Seeger, Pete, 36–7, 170, 190, 191
"See Saw" (Banhart), 175
Seeger Sessions Tour (Springsteen), 190–1, 193, 195
Segarra, Alynda Lee, 222, 223–4, 225, 226, 227, 228–9, 230
Seger, Bob, 54
Seven Swans (Stevens), 177
The Sex Pistols, 56
Sexton, Charlie, 50
"Sexuality" (Prince), 121
"Sexy Back" (Timberlake), 87
"Shackled and Drawn" (Springsteen), 181, 193
Shadowrun, 73
"Shake It Off" (Swift), 78
Shakespeare, William, 56
"Shake Your Pom Pom" (Elliott), 98
Shakur, Tupac, 198, 204, 219
Shank, Barry, 171
Sharon Jones and the Dap Kings, 70
"She Caught the Katy (And Left Me a Mule to Ride)" (Mahal), 20
Sheeran, Ed, 94
Sheila E., 2
Shepherd's Bush Empire Theatre, 161, 179
Shut Up and Sing, 162
Sia, 152
Simon, Carly, 184
Simone, Nina, 142, 207
Simon and Garfunkel, 24
Singleton, Sharonda, 197, 220

Skull and Shark (Lazerhawk), 72, 74
Sleater-Kinney, 60
Sleepify (Vulfpeck), 77
Slowdive, 3
"Slow Worm" (Archers of Loaf), 57
Small Talk at 125th and Lenox (Scott-Heron), 215
Small Town Heroes (Hurray for the Riff Raff), 222, 228
"Smells Like Teen Spirit" (Nirvana), 57
Smith, G.E., 40
Smith, Grady, 3
Smith, Nathan, 125
Smith, Patti, 56
Snipes, Wesley, 214
Snowden, Ben and Lew, 28–9
Snowden, Ellen, 28–9
Snowden Family Band, 28
"Snowden's Jig (Genuine Negro Jig)" (Carolina Chocolate Drops), 27, 28–9
"Snuggled on Your Shoulder", 47
The Society of the Spectacle (Debord), 88–90, 91–2, 102–3, 127–8, 138
"Something" (Beatles), 172
"Son of a Bush" (Public Enemy), 167
Songs About Jane (Maroon 5), 81
Sonic Jihad (Paris), 170
Sonic Youth, 58
Southern rock, 2, 67, 68–9
Southern Rock Opera (Drive-By Truckers), 67–70, 80, 191
The Spaniels, 49
"Spanish Castle Magic" (Hendrix), 123
Spd Gvnr, 65
Spearhead. *See* Franti, Michael
Spears, Britney, 87
spectacle (Debord), 120, 141, 144, 156, 162, 210
  and the American Wow, 88–90, 91–2, 95, 96, 102–3, 138, 139
  and the body, 156
  identity, 90–1, 93–4, 127–9, 139, 142, 150

  newness in, 91–2, 102–3, 121
  types of, 110–11
"Spin the Black Circle" (Pearl Jam), 57
"Spirit in the Night" (Springsteen), 183
Springsteen, Bruce, 12, 181–95, 200, 229, 235
  and Flannery O'Connor, 185–7
  politics of, 182–5, 192–5
Spy Hunter, 72
Stankonia (Outkast), 148
The Stanley Brothers, 47
Stanley, Ralph, 24, 25
"Stardust" (Bill Carney's Jug Addicts), 76, 77
Starr, Edwin, 182
"Steal Away" (trad.), 21
Steely Dan, 76
Stevens, Sufjan, 163, 174, 177, 178
Stillmatic (Nas), 173
"Stolen Car" (Springsteen), 185
"Stop the Violence" (KRS-One), 201
"Strange Fruit" (Meeropol), 142, 143
"Strange Things Happening Every Day" (Tharpe), 32
streaming music, 76–7, 89, 96, 107, 113, 114
A Streetcar Named Desire (Williams), 32
The Strokes, 18, 70
"Stronger" (West), 140
Students for a Democratic Society (SDS), 215
"Style" (Swift), 78, 79
"Sugar Baby" (Dylan), 32, 47
Suicide, 59
"Suite IV Electric Overture" (Monáe), 146
"Summer Days" (Dylan), 32, 43, 44, 47, 50
Sunday at Devil Dirt (Campbell and Lanegan), 80
Sun Ra, 148, 149
Super Bowl, 85–6, 88, 91, 119–20, 161
Superchunk, 57, 106
"Supercute" (Prince), 122
Suprematism, 138, 142

Suprematism: Airplane Flying (Malevich), 138
Surf (Chance/Donnie Trumpet), 155
Swartley, Ariel, 125
"Sweet Nothings" (Lee), 142
The Swerve (Greenblatt), 71, 95
Swift, Taylor, 77–9, 86, 94, 139, 191
synthwave, 72–6, 79, 81, 142
System of a Down, 167, 169

Taco Bell, 105, 106, 114, 115, 117
"Take a Walk" (Passion Pit), 105, 112, 114, 115, 116, 117
Taking the Long Way (Dixie Chicks), 179
Talking Heads, 108
Target with Four Faces (Johns), 137
Tears for Fears, 72, 173
"Tear Shit Up" (Paris), 170, 210
Telecommunications Act of 1996, 111
terminals, 42. *See also* cultural economy of exchange
"Testarossa Autodrive" (Kavinsky), 74
Tharpe, Sister Rosetta, 32
"These Walls" (Lamar), 212
They Live (Carpenter), 72
Thicke, Robin, 222
Thinking the Twentieth Century (Judt), 194
.38 Special, 67
3121 (Prince), 123
33 1/3 Revolutions (Lynskey), 173
"This Boy Is Exhausted" (Wrens), 54
"This Depression" (Springsteen), 194
This Is Post-Wave (Future Punx), 76
"This Love" (Maroon 5), 81
"This Note's for You" (Young), 105
3 Doors Down, 81
Three Mile Island, 183, 184
"Thunder Road" (Springsteen), 193
"Tightrope" (Monáe), 146, 148
Till, Emmett, 220
Tillich, Paul, 64, 176
Timberlake, Justin, 87, 96
Time Out of Mind (Dylan), 32, 33, 41, 43, 50

"The Times They Are A-Changin'" (Dylan), 184
Time (The Revelator), 18, 19–23, 24, 26, 30, 32, 49, 191
Timrod, Henry, 47
Tocqueville, Alexis de, 134
To the 5 Boroughs (Beastie Boys), 170
"Tom Dooley" (trad.), 223
topical songs. *See* protest songs
To Pimp a Butterfly, 198, 202–3, 204–9, 212–15, 217–219
Top of the World Tour (Dixie Chicks), 161
Tosches, Nick, 3
"Trail of the Buffalo" (Dylan), 41
transfiguration, 131–5
transgression, 33, 39, 44, 46–51, 144, 155
trap, 153
"Travelin' Soldier" (Dixie Chicks), 161, 163, 164, 169
tribute shows, 62–5
TRON, 74
Trump, Donald J., 233, 234
Turbulence (Miami Nights 1984), 74
"Turn Down for What", 4
Turner, Big Joe, 32
Turner, Nat, 219
"Tweedle Dum and Tweedle Dee" (Dylan), 31
2014 Forest Hills Drive (Cole), 217
21 Nights (Prince), 123
20Ten (Prince), 123

"u" (Lamar), 212
ultra-fusion, 2, 13, 120, 121, 129, 132, 146, 147, 217
"Umbrella" (Rihanna), 87
"Uncle John's Bongos" (Johnny and Jack), 49, 50
unfinishing, 10, 40, 188, 190, 233
Universal Zulu Nation, 199
"Unleashed! The Large-Hearted Boy" (Guided by Voices), 63
Unplugged (Dylan), 41
"Uptown Funk" (Mars), 86

"Upward Over the Mountain" (Iron & Wine), 176
"Used Cars" (Springsteen), 187

variability, 9–10, 115, 121, 132, 188
Vee Vee (Archers of Loaf), 57, 61
Vega, Suzanne, 47
"Vegas" (Eminem), 222
Velvet Underground, 56, 172
Vernon, Justin, 142
Vetiver, 174
Vevo, 114
"Victory" (Monáe), 146
Vietnam War, 163, 172
Visitors (Lazerhawk), 72, 74
VJ Vendetta, 74–5
Vulfpeck, 76–7, 80

"Waitin' for the DJ" (Kweli), 211
Waits, Tom, 165, 169
Wald, Elijah, 37
"Walkies" (Vulfpeck), 77
Walt, Stephen, 170
"War" (Starr), 182
Warhol, Andy, 4, 5, 38, 68, 131
Warmuth, Scott, 47, 48, 49
Washington, Booker T., 203
Washington, Kamasi, 80
"Watch Me Jumpstart" (Guided By Voices), 63
The Waterboy, 143
"Way Back Home" (Prince), 129, 130
Way Up North in Dixie (Sacks), 28
"We Are Alive" (Springsteen), 194
Weinberg, Max, 184, 189
Welch, Gillian, 19–24, 32, 49, 56, 191, 230
"Welcome to the Terrordome" (Public Enemy), 201
"We're So Starving" (Panic at the Disco), 60
We Shall Overcome: The Seeger Sessions (Springsteen), 190, 192
"We Shall Overcome" (Tindley), 185
"Wesley's Theory" (Lamar), 203, 214

West, Cornel, 200, 208, 210
West, Kanye, 137–44, 153, 191, 211, 215
"We Take Care of Our Own" (Springsteen), 181
What Did You Expect? (documentary), 61
"When Eye Lay My Hands on U" (Prince), 122
"When the President Talks to God" (Oberst), 170, 171, 192
When We Were Good (Cantwell), 175
"When You Were Mine" (Prince), 1
White Album, 6
White Blood Cells, 18
"White People for Peace" (Against Me!), 172
White, Philip, 197, 220
The White Stripes, 5, 18, 70
Whitman, Walt, 228, 229, 230
The Who, 57
"Who Will Survive in America?" (West), 141, 216
"Why Is That?" (KRS-One), 201
Wiig, Kristen, 152
Wilentz, Sean, 48, 225
Williams, Hank, 43
Williams, Stereo, 206–7
Williams, Tennessee, 32
Willis, Ellen, 47, 86, 95, 147
The Wizard of Oz, 24
"W.M.D." (Blow Up Hollywood), 172
Wondaland Records, 215, 220, 224, 226
Woodstock (1969), 57
Woodstock (1994), 57
The Woosley Band, 65
"The Word" (Prince), 123
"Work It" (Elliott), 97, 98
World Gone Wrong (Dylan), 41, 225
"World Wide Suicide" (Pearl Jam), 170
Wrecking Ball (Springsteen), 181–3, 188, 192, 193–5, 230
"Wrecking Ball" (Springsteen), 193
Wrens, The, 53–4, 56, 58, 59, 65, 69
Wurster, Jon, 106

Xpectation (Prince), 122

Yancy, Tommy, 197, 208, 220
Yarrow, Peter, 37
Yeezus (West), 141–4, 191
Yo! MTV Raps, 210
"You Ain't Gotta Lie (Momma Said)" (Lamar), 218
"You Can Kill the Protestor, But You Can't Kill the Protest" (Anti-Flag), 168, 174

"You'll Never See My Face in Kansas City" (Malefactors/Black Swans), 152
The Young Lords, 215
"Young Men Dead" (Black Angels), 172
Young, Neil, 69, 105, 191

Zevon, Warren, 34
Ziegler, Maddie, 152

www.ingramcontent.com/pod-product-compliance
Lightning Source LLC
Chambersburg PA
CBHW051805230426
43672CB00012B/2640